P9-DDV-583

BATTLESHIPS AND BATTLECRUISERS

BATTLESHIPS AND BATTLECRUISERS

Richard Humble

Connoisseur

Printed in Belgium by Henri Proost & CIE PBVA

Produced by Winchmore Publishing Services Limited
40 Triton Square, London NW1 3HG

Edited by Sue Butterworth
Designed by Bob Burroughs
Picture Research by Jonathan Moore
Maps by Richard Natkiel
Typeset by SX Composing

CONTENTS

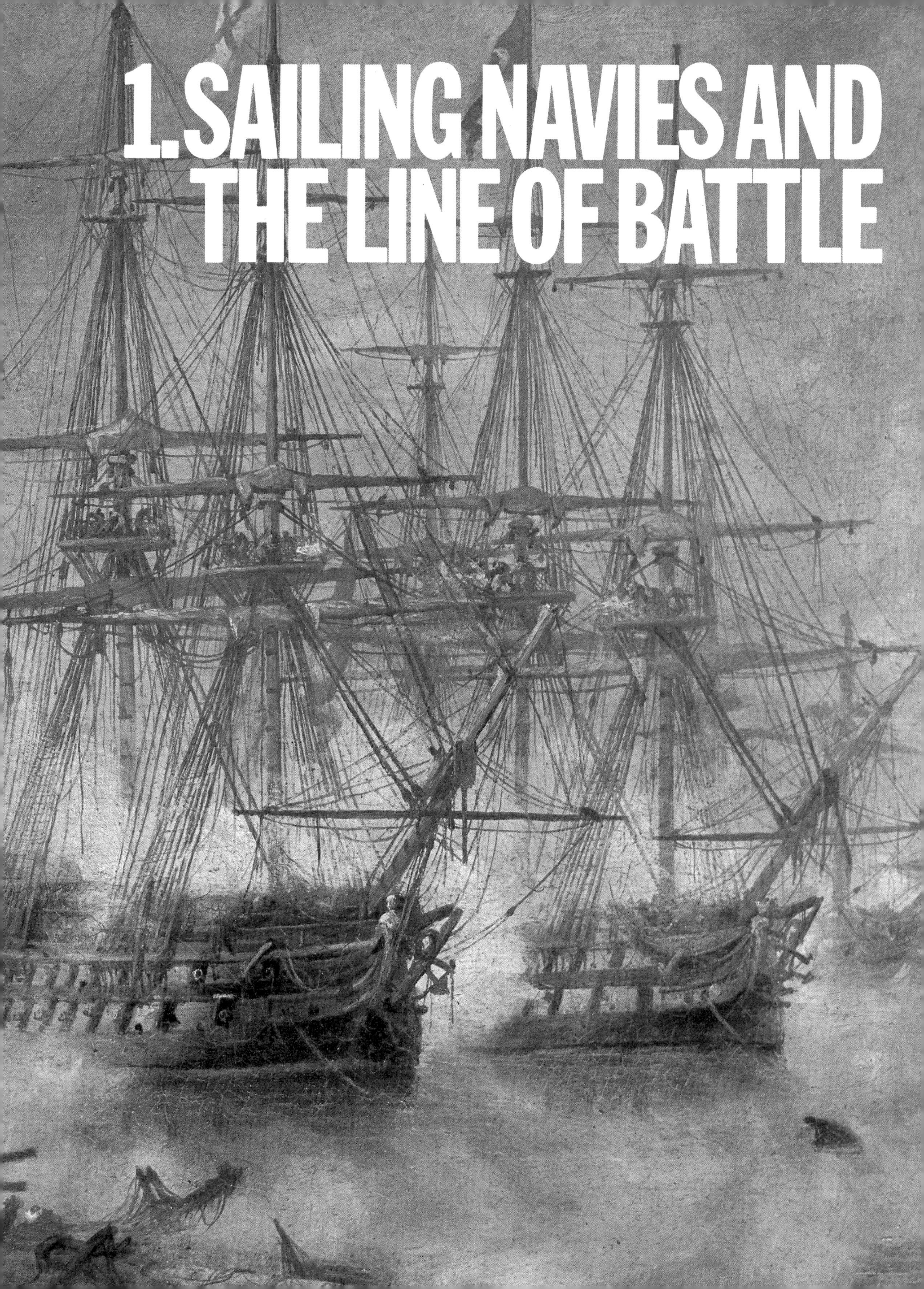

1. SAILING NAVIES AND THE LINE OF BATTLE

As THE MOST POWERFUL fighting ship which the wit of man could devise, the battleship remained the ultimate weapon of naval warfare for a longer period than any other type of fighting ship. After a startling but premature debut in the early sixteenth century, the multi-decked wooden 'line of battle' ship had become the mainstay of the world's leading fleets by the middle seventeenth century. Two hundred years later, still primarily dependent on wind power, wooden battleships had undergone few essential changes other than the installation of auxiliary steam engines. Over the next 30 years the battleship was transformed by the new technology of the Industrial Revolution, with steam power, explosive shell, armour plate and rifled breech-loading guns replacing the wind power, solid battering shot, wooden hulls and smooth-bore muzzle-loaders of the stately past. In this grim new incarnation the battleship's reign continued for another 60-odd years, to be cut short in the Second World War by the superior range and weaponry of naval aviation.

Even after its transformation in the later nineteenth century, the battleship retained two enduring features from its long past. First, the battleship remained the heaviest concentration of fire-power which could be built into a sea-going warship. Second, the battleship remained the biggest floating structure contrived by man until its last four decades of supremacy, surpassed only in sheer bulk by the giant passenger liner, and by the post-1945 heavy aircraft-carrier and mercantile 'super-tanker' of the last 25 years. Throughout its long career, the battleship's prime function was to serve both as delivery vehicle and firing platform for its batteries of heavy guns. It was a floating, self-propelled fortress, with the massive construction needed both to carry its own guns into action and endure the fire of the enemy.

Reduced to its bare essentials, medieval sea fighting under sail had come to rely on two main tactics by the time of the advent of shipboard cannon in the later fifteenth century. The first tactic was the attrition of enemy crews by missile fire and incapacitating substances like powdered quicklime (the latter unpleasantness being released downwind to sear the enemy's eyeballs). Incendiary missiles – fireballs hurled by catapults – were rarely used as often at sea as ashore, for the risk of fire aboard the attacking ship was always as great as that aboard the intended victim.

After this preliminary bombardment, the second and decisive tactic was invariably that of closing the enemy ship and boarding it, the engagement being decided by hand-to-hand fighting on the enemy's deck. With particular reference to the English naval victory of the French at Sluys in June 1340, the chronicler Jean Froissart bleakly noted that 'Sea fights are always fiercer than fights on land, because retreat and flight are impossible.' The main objective was the capture rather than the destruction of the enemy ship. And in precisely the same way as with the garrison of a castle under attack on land, a defending ship's company of fighting men which failed to eject a superior force of boarders had little prospect of survival, unless a formal surrender was made and accepted in good time.

Froissart also makes it clear that well-equipped ships also carried special missiles calculated to disable enemy ships as well as assisting the decimation of their crews. In a particularly hard-fought action off Winchelsea in 1350 a Spanish fleet had come down Channel well stocked with piles of stones and heavy iron bars for the discomfiture of the English. 'The Spanish ships being bigger and higher than [the English], they were able to shoot down at them and hurl the great iron bars which did considerable damage.' Such disabling tactics were common and could be improvised on the spur of the moment. In the Winchelsea fight one Spanish ship, seeking to tow away the lighter English vessel to which it was grappled, was captured:

> when one of Sir Robert's men called Hanekin performed a notable feat of daring. With his drawn sword in his hand, he braced himself and sprang on board the enemy ship, forced his way to the mast, and cut the sail cable so that the sail sagged and no longer drew. Then he skilfully severed the four main ropes which stayed the mast and the sail, so that this collapsed and the ship came to a stop. Seeing this, Sir Robert of Namur and his men leapt eagerly on board the Spaniard, with their swords drawn. They attacked its crew so heartily that they killed them all and threw them overboard, and captured the ship.

The characteristic silhouette of the medieval warship was dominated by the two fighting towers or 'castles' built fore and aft of the single mast with its square sail. Castles could be easily added to merchant ships commandeered for fighting service and as easily removed when the vessel was released. Their function was to provide a good field of fire for archers, cross-bowmen and,

Previous pages: The cannonade of Navarino (20 October 1827), last fleet action of the age of fighting sail. Though the position and crescent-shaped formation of the Turkish fleet were well judged, the superiority of the allied fleet in ships of the line (12 to seven) proved the decisive factor. After a four-hour pounding match, over half the Turkish fleet had been sunk. The allies did not lose a single ship.

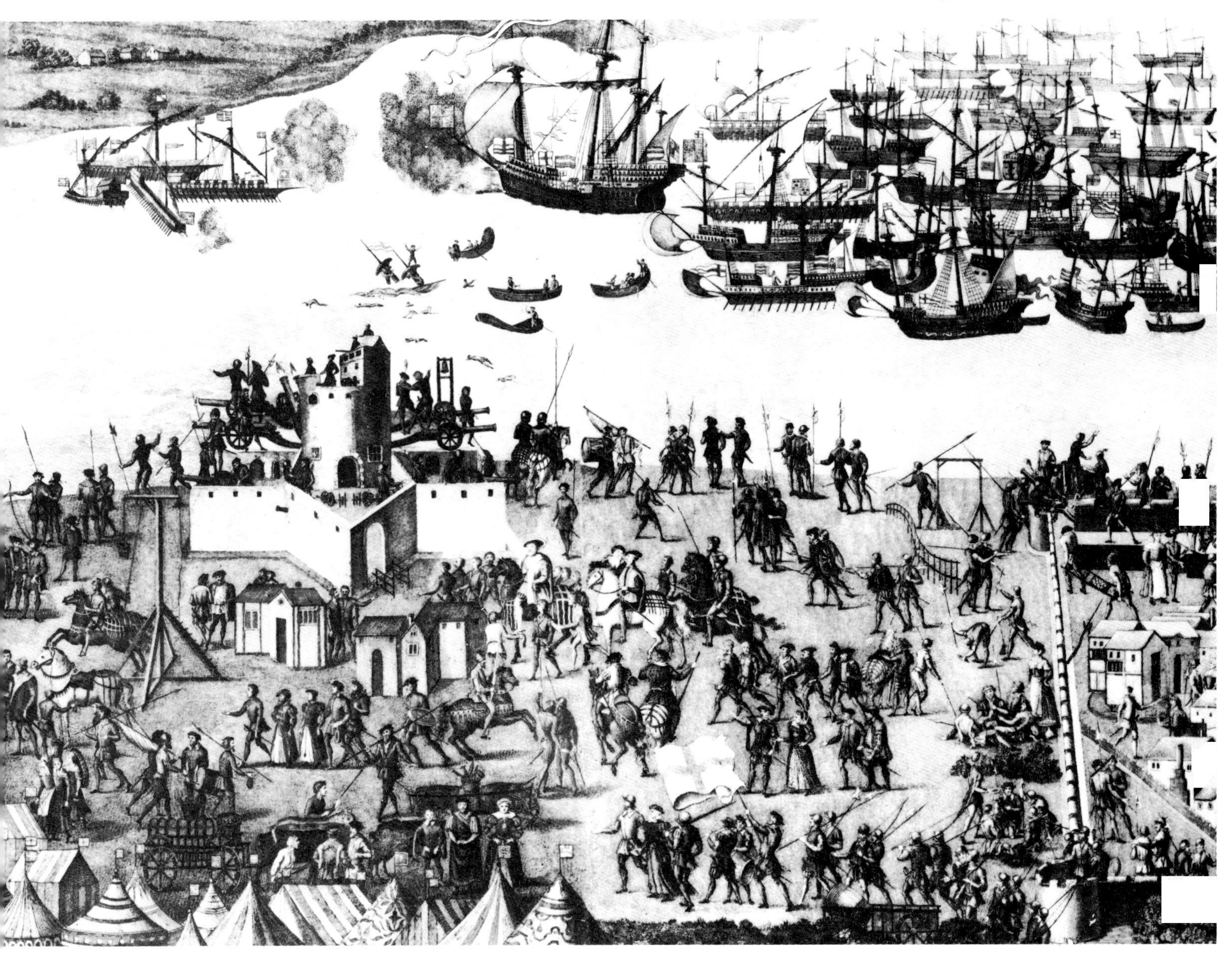

from the later fifteenth century, hand-gunners – not merely for the long-range attrition of enemy crews, but just as importantly to provide a cross-fire against enemy boarders. The defensive function of these castles was so important that it survived the shipbuilding revolution of the middle fifteenth century, when the ability to sail close to the wind was conferred by the addition of fore and mizzen masts and sails, and the medieval cog gave place to the multi-masted, ocean-going carrack. Castle structures with the same, traditional function were also regarded as vital features of the new warships, built to carry heavy guns mounted in tiered broadsides, which began to appear in the early sixteenth century.

King Henry VIII (1509–47) set out to build the best fleet of regularly maintained warships which England had ever had, and he amply succeeded. The two most splendid ornaments of his fleet, *Great Harry* and *Mary Rose*, may fairly be called the earliest recognisable sailing battleships, each with multi-decked broadside gun armaments of bronze muzzle-loading cannon and iron breech-loaders firing through gunports. Specimens recovered from the sunken *Mary Rose* in the Solent show that the guns of these remarkable ships were decades (and, in the case of the iron breech-loaders with their screw-on powder chambers, centuries) ahead of their time. But Henry VIII always looked as much to the past as he did to the future, hoping to surpass the exploits of England in the 'Hundred Years War' with France. The startling innovations in naval artillery made on his orders were seen as auxiliaries to the tested weaponry and tactics of the Middle Ages, not as an entirely new chapter in naval warfare. In the contemporary depictions of *Great Harry* and *Mary Rose* (in each case made *after* the ships' extensive reconstruction in the 1530s) there is no ignoring the massive, even grotesque castle structures sweeping upwards at stern and bow, each with guns emplaced fore and aft to sweep enemy boarders off the deck. The castles built into these unwieldy giants with such deliberation were manned not only by hand-gunners but by archers, armed with the good old

Above: Panorama of the battle off Southsea, Isle of Wight (19 July 1545) in which Henry VIII's experimental battleship *Mary Rose* sank as she sailed out to engage the French Fleet. Two of her masts are shown above the surface, with a lone survivor waving for help from the mizzen top. Inept ship-handling seems to have caused *Mary Rose* to heel too far, rolling her lower gunports below the surface. She was certainly not sunk by the light guns in the French galleys (*centre*), shown trading shots with the giant *Great Harry*. Though the perspective in this picture is inaccurate, *Great Harry* seems to be yawing to starboard to bring her forward portside guns to bear on the galleys. One of the most revealing details is the hotch-potch nature of the English fleet at upper right: galleys, converted merchant carracks, even single-masted cogs of the type which had fought at Sluys 200 years before.

Above right: Clash of the Dutch (*top*) and English battle lines in the 'St James' Day Battle' off the North Foreland (25 July 1666). Having won the advantage of the wind – the weather gauge – the English fleet under Albemarle is preparing to concentrate its fire on the centre and van of the Dutch line. The English fleet is shown deployed as ordered by the 'Fighting Instructions' of the Duke of York (afterwards King James II): line-ahead in three squadrons, van (white), centre (red), and rear (blue). De Ruyter, who commanded in the Dutch centre, was badly supported by his rear squadron under Cornelis van Tromp. At one stage the English brought 22 ships to bear against the stubborn resistance of de Ruyter's eight. The Dutch lost 20 ships out of 88 ships of the line and frigates, and de Ruyter did well to keep his fleet from total disintegration. The English lost only one ship in the battle.
Below right: Surrender of *Ville de Paris*, flagship of the French Admiral de Grasse, after the battle of the Saints (12 April 1782). Rodney's deliberate breach of the French line at two points in the battle set a precedent for the classic victories of Jervis, Duncan and Nelson.

longbow which had helped win Edward III's sea fights at Sluys and Winchelsea 200 years before.

A telling extract from an English manual of naval tactics dating from the 1530s shows that the old sequence of enemy crew attrition followed by closing and boarding still ruled the roost:

> In case you board, enter not till you see all the smoke gone, and then shoot off all your pieces, your port-pieces, the pieces of hail-shot and cross-bar shot to beat his cage-deck; and if you see his deck well rid, then enter with your best men, but first win his top in any wise if it be possible.

The 'cage-deck' (clearly shown in the Antony Roll depictions of *Great Harry* and *Mary Rose*) was the upper deck protected with netting to foil boarders. 'Hail-shot', as the name implies, was anti-personnel scattering shot, the ancestor of grapeshot and canister (musket balls packed in a thin metal cylinder). 'Cross-bar shot' seems to refer to a disabling missile, known in later years as 'dismantling shot', made of two bars of semi-circular cross-section, clapped face to face and rivetted together in the middle to fit snugly into the gun. It was clearly the direct descendant of the 'great iron bars' mentioned by Froissart; on being fired the two halves of the shot would skew open to form a hideous whirling missile, equally potent for slicing rigging aloft or mowing down enemy crewmen massed on deck. Nowhere is any stress laid on the effect of the heavy guns' solid shot smashing into the timbers of the enemy ship, each impact causing a deadly spray of jagged wood splinters as effective as any 'hail-shot'.

Thus 200 years after Sluys, in ships fitted with the most advanced naval guns in the world, we find the old medieval formula

still prevailing: close the enemy, disable his rigging if you can, certainly concentrate all available fire-power on the soldiers defending his upper deck, then settle the matter by boarding. To this end, sea-worthiness had been ruthlessly sacrificed in the rebuilding of Henry VIII's 'great ships'; and this is confirmed by all contemporary accounts and archaeological evidence of the dramatic sinking of *Mary Rose* (19 July 1545) as she wallowed out to engage the French fleet in the Solent. She came out with all guns loaded and their ports opened, but with her upperworks crammed with armoured soldiers, archers and hand-gunners – it has been suggested maybe 200–300 more than her normal complement of 415 sailors and soldiers. This was to be a sea fight in the good old style, with gunnery supplementing archery in the softening-up opening phases. But when the ungainly hull heeled to the wind and its lower gunports dipped under, *Mary Rose* sank like a stone and effectively took the old style of sea fighting with her.

Forty years later, with the supreme showdown with the Spanish Armada approaching, it was a very different story. As Sir Walter Raleigh eloquently stated, seaworthiness, manoeuvrability and balanced gun armament were now the paramount virtues in the English fleet:

> We find by experience that the greatest ships are the least serviceable, go very deep to water, and of marvellous charge and cumber . . . they are less nimble, less mainable, and very seldom employed. *Grande navio grande fatiga*, saith the Spaniard. A ship of 600 tons will carry as good ordnance as a ship of 1,200 tons; and though the greater have double her number, the lesser will turn her broadsides twice before the greater can wind once. The high charging of ships it is that brings them ill qualities, make them extreme leeward, makes them sink deep in the water, makes them labour and makes them overset.

Raleigh ended his dissertation with a particularly vivid phrase: a plea for 'more steadiness and less tottering cage-work'. That a ship should be seaworthy and a good gun platform; these were not only the best qualities of the low-slung Elizabethan galleons which fought the Armada, but the prerequisites of the battleship which Grand-Admiral Tirpitz would still be stressing during the building of the Imperial German High Seas Fleet, over 300 years later. But Raleigh's contemporary Sir William Monson argued that there was still much to be said for the traditional 'great ship', listing its virtues as 'Majesty and terror to the enemy; more commodious for the harbouring of men; carry more artillery; of greater strength inboard and make the better defence; will over-top a lower and snug ship; the men cannot be so well discerned'. To thinking Tudor seamen like Raleigh and Monson, it was clear that the ideal warship would marry the towering strength of the 'great ship' to the speed, handiness and balanced fire-power of the galleon; for the present, however, they would have to make do with what they had.

The new galleons built from the 1570s onward were the best warships in the English fleet, but they were no more the numerical mainstay of the fleet in July 1588 than Spitfires were the mainstay of RAF Fighter Command in 1940. The bulk of the English fleet consisted of converted merchantmen and 'great ships', with their forecastles and stern superstructures cut down to improve sea-worthiness. In numbers of actual fighting ships the Spanish Armada had only a slight advantage over the English – with the vital difference that the English did not have a lumbering convoy of transports and troop carriers to protect at all costs. English tactics were as simple as they were entirely novel: to harrass the Armada, as it moved up-Channel, with superior manoeuvrability and the stand-off hitting power of gunnery. Nothing would have suited the Spaniards better than an old-style closing and boarding engagement, but the English refused to oblige and fought on their own terms instead.

What neither side had anticipated – this being the first naval confrontation of its kind in the history of the world – was the prodigious expenditure of ammunition in a running sea fight arbitrated by gunnery. When the Armada reached the Dover Straits virtually intact, after six days of harrassment since passing Plymouth, the English captains were screaming for more powder and shot; the Armada was well stocked with powder but had never expected to fire off so much shot, which was in equally short supply in the Spanish ships. It took the famous fireship attack on the Armada as it lay off Calais (on the night of 28–29 July) to succeed where English gunnery had so far failed and panic the Armada out of its defensive 'crescent moon' formation. Once scattered the ships of the Armada immediately fell victim off Dunkirk, as this single Spanish account shows, to English attacks which swarmed in and 'balled' individual Spanish ships as bees combine against intruders into their hive:

Battle of Porto Novo (20 June 1783), fought in Indian waters between the British fleet of Admiral Hughes and the French under Admiral the Bailli de Suffren. Here the British line, at left, is trying to overtake the head of Suffren's line and 'cross his T'. Suffren, however, declined to accept a full-blooded fleet action. He stuck to his main objective and lured the British fleet out to sea, raising the siege of the French garrison in Cuddalore.

> The *San Felipe* was surrounded by seventeen of the enemy's ships. They directed against her a heavy fire on both sides and on her stern. They approached so close that the muskets and harquebusses of the galleon were brought into service, killing a large number of men on the enemy's ships. They did not dare, however, to come to close quarters but kept up a hot artillery fire from a distance, disabling the rudder, breaking the foremast, and killing over 200 men on the galleon.

At least most of *San Felipe*'s survivors had the luck to be taken off by one of the Armada's transport ships; after the dog-fight off Dunkirk her crippled hulk was towed by the Dutch into Vlissingen, where it sank. By this time *San Felipe*'s surviving consorts had fled north on their ruinous voyage back to Spain around the British Isles, with mortality soaring from wounds and disease. But in the exultant English fleet, whose *battle* casualties had been far less than in the crammed ships of the Armada (estimated at around 100 English lives, against maybe 4,000 Spanish) conditions were little better. On 10 August the victorious English admiral, Lord Howard, wrote in fury to Lord Burghley that:

> Sickness and mortality begins wonderfully to grow amongst us; and it is a most pitiful sight to see, here at Margate, how the men, having no place to receive them into here, die in the streets. I am driven myself, of force, to come a-land, to see them bestowed in some lodging; and the best I can get is barns and such outhouses; and the relief is small that I can provide for them here. It would grieve any man's heart to see them that have served so valiantly to die so miserably.

Apart from the lack of medical facilities, these needless losses were mostly caused by the failure to anticipate how long the fleet would have to remain at sea, and embark sufficient stores. Though the Armada fighting of July 1588 conclusively proved the virtues of the tiered broadside, both in long-range bombardment and close ship-to-ship action, the galleon's stowage capacity for ammunition, replacement gear and provisions was only moderate at best. Though the English stuck to the galleon for the remaining 16 inconclusive years of the Spanish war (ended by King James I in 1604), it was not long before shipbuilders of all the leading sea powers began to experiment with heavier warships, which would have better habitability and greater storage capacity as well as more powerful armament.

Despite the otherwise appalling neglect of the English fleet under James I (1603–25) the reign nevertheless produced the *Prince Royal* of 1610: a design by master shipbuilder Phineas Pett, unmistakably based on the galleon type but expanded to incorporate three gun decks. Originally of 56 guns, *Prince Royal* underwent two reconstructions which finally raised her armament to the startling total of 90 guns. The 1620s saw the establishment of a French fleet on the orders of Cardinal Richelieu, when five French two-deckers of 60 guns were built. But the most famous warship of these experimental years remains the 64-gun *Vasa* of Sweden, which like Henry VIII's *Mary Rose* sank on her maiden voyage (10 August 1628) and lay preserved by marine silt until her rediscovery after the Second World War. *Vasa*'s loss occurred because she was built far too narrow in the beam and carried insufficient ballast, causing her to roll her lower gunports under as soon as she heeled to the wind.

Apart from the fact that they could have blown any Armada galleon of barely 30 years before clean out of the water, all these new ships had one very obvious feature in common. They flaunted gorgeous decorative schemes from stem to stern – elaborate figureheads, carved friezes and scrolls along the sides, ports highlighted with wreaths, massive sculptures adorning the stern, blazing with gold leaf. All this splendour was by no means mere vanity or extravagance: on the contrary, it underlined the ship's importance as a deliberate investment in seaborne hitting-power, and the wealth and resources of the state which had built the ship. The baroque splendours of these new seventeenth-century warships echoed Monson's comment in praise of the otherwise obsolescent 'great ship': 'majesty and terror to the enemy'. In short, they marked the true beginning of the battleship's *moral effect* as the ultimate ocean-going deterrent – a phenomenon destined to endure without a break from the 1620s to the Second World War, long after the gorgeous ornamentation and dashing paint schemes had given place to the sombre menace of battleship grey.

By the 50th anniversary of the Armada a total revolution had been achieved in warship design by that remarkable English shipbuilding dynasty, the Petts. Phineas Pett, who had built the *Prince Royal*, and his son Peter had launched the *Sovereign of the Seas*: a three-decked, 100-gun giant which set the pattern of capital ship construction for the next 200 years. Built to the orders of King Charles I (1625–49) and launched in 1637, the *Sovereign* was not only the biggest warship in the world but also the most beautiful, glittering with gilded decoration from one end of her elegant hull to the other. From the Dutchmen whom she fought in three successive Anglo-Dutch wars over the

Nicholas Pocock's fine watercolour of *Victory* breaking through the Franco-Spanish line at Trafalgar, raking the stern of the French flagship, *Bucentaure* with a devastating broadside.

ensuing 40 years, the *Sovereign* earned the thoroughly respectful nickname of *de gouden duivel* – 'the golden devil' – because of her deadly blend of beauty and crushing fire-power.

If Charles I had devoted as much care to his sailors' pay and welfare as he did to building mirrors to his glory like *Sovereign of the Seas*, he would have kept the fleet from defecting *en masse* to the Parliamentarian cause, and probably would have won the English Civil War. Instead his great battleship (renamed *Sovereign* by the Republican 'Commonwealth', and *Royal Sovereign* after the Restoration of King Charles II in 1660) fought with high distinction in the fleets of his killers and of his sons. *Sovereign* underwent two major reconstructions and was still very much in service, with the navy of William of Orange, when she was accidentally destroyed by fire in January 1696. Without this untimely end *Sovereign* would certainly have exceeded the active career of Nelson's *Victory* (57 years, to *Sovereign*'s 54).

The impressive longevity of *Sovereign*'s career established another enduring feature of the big battleship: excellent value for taxpayers' money. The bigger and tougher a ship's hull is built, the slower it is to degenerate when laid up or 'mothballed' between wars. It is also more suitable for reconstruction and modernisation, both in structure and weaponry. As we shall see, one of the weirdest phenomena of modern naval history is that Britain, after three centuries of experience in prolonging the lives of her warships, should have thrown that experience to the winds after 1945.

Sovereign was no more perfect in all respects than any other trail-blazing warship type; her biggest weakness was her tendency to heel so far in a beam sea that the lower-deck gunports (behind which lay the ship's heaviest guns) had to be kept closed on the lee side. In certain conditions this could enable a two-decker, with lower-deck ports further above the waterline, to fight her on momentarily equal terms. It was a weakness retained to a greater or lesser degree by all British three-decked sailing battleships; other navies such as the French and Spanish tended to favour less guns and a wider, more solid hull to provide a steadier gun platform. (Because of their natural predilection for warships of shallower draught, the Dutch also favoured the two-decker).

These qualities made French and Spanish warships coveted prizes for the British, who usually managed to compensate for the structural inferiority of their ships by superior seamanship, aggressive tactics and gun drill. Nevertheless, Spain, not Britain, produced the biggest battleships of the age of sail, in the late eighteenth century – ships like the 112-gun *San Josef, Concepcion, Salvador del Mundo* and *Principe de Asturias*, and the monstrous *Santissima Trinidada* of 136 guns and four decks (the latter captured but sunk as the result of battle damage at Trafalgar in 1805). All these Spanish giants fought at Cape St Vincent on 14 February 1797, against a British fleet containing only two 100-gunners and four of 90 guns or more. But the result was a shattering Spanish defeat in the course of which Nelson's grossly outgunned *Captain* (74) boarded and took in rapid succession the *San Nicolas* (80) and *San Josef* (112). In the age of sail, mere weight of metal was never the ultimate deciding factor.

Once adopted by the English in the 1650s, the basis of fleet tactics remained the line of battle. The line-ahead formation was not only the most efficient exploitation of broadside fire-power: it was the best way of exercising coherent command over the fleet, normally divided between the junior admirals commanding the van, centre and rear of the line. Going 'by the book', the normal ploy on sighting the enemy was to try to get up-wind of him, and thus 'seize the weather gauge'. Having gained this advantage, an attacking fleet could open the battle as it chose. An admiral confident in his fleet's proficiency in gunnery would not, however, be unduly downhearted if he were forced to accept the downwind or 'lee gauge'; in such a position disabled victims of his ships' fire were bound to drift downwind to total ruin.

Once the rival lines of battle had been formed and manoeuvred to the optimum gunnery range (100 yards or less) the slaughter would begin, the aim of each ship being to mark down an opponent and batter it until it was incapable of fighting on. A badly handled ship which presented bow or stern to an enemy broadside could expect to be promptly 'raked', the enemy's fire smashing from one end of the victim's hull to the other with devastating effect. An unusually resolute commander and disciplined crew were required for a ship to fight on after being raked more than once – ideally from both bow and stern.

Ships were very rarely sunk in battle during the age of sail; most shot holes in the

hull were taken above the waterline. Sinkings of battle-damaged ships *after* the battle, as with both sides after Trafalgar, were common. Beaten ships were expected to strike their colours when so many men had been killed or wounded, and so many guns knocked out, that further resistance was impossible. Flagships usually tried to close with their opposite numbers in hopes of killing or capturing the enemy admiral and leaving his fleet leaderless. It was never any part of an admiral's function to lie back, like a general in a land battle, and direct the action from the rear; his was to lead, if not from the front, at least from the thick of the action.

Even when more fluid tactics began to creep in at the end of the eighteenth century, and 'breaking the enemy's line' in more than one place became a new ideal, the basic importance of the line of battle survived unchanged. Ships were 'rated' by their nominal ability to stand up to the enemy's fire in the line of battle. Thus a 'first-rate' ship of the line carried 100 guns or more, 'second-rate' 84–100, 'third-rate' 70–84 and 'fourth-rate' 50–70. Fifth-rate (32–50) and sixth-rate (any number up to 32) ships were classed as frigates, unfit to 'take their place in the line'. By the end of the Napoleonic Wars in 1815 the fourth-rate ship had become almost totally obsolete and only ships of the first three rates were considered fit for the line of battle. As we shall see, these distinctions by rate outlived the matériel changes wrought by the Industrial Revolution and were still very much alive – especially in the debate over the battlecruiser's true status – by the end of the First World War.

One of the stupidest blunders committed in the French Revolution was the disbandment of the excellent divisions of seaman gunners maintained by the French Navy of the *ancien régime*. These specialists were denounced as an 'aristocracy' (nowadays we would doubtless say élite) 'of artillerymen' by the Republican Convention of 1792. As a result French naval gunnery deteriorated overnight and the fleets of the Republic relied heavily on the old medieval ploy of closing and boarding, while the reactionary British continued to rely on drilled gunnery.

The sailing battleship's be-all and end-all was the power and regularity of its broadsides of solid, battering shot. A broadside did not mean that every gun fired as one; this would have placed an intolerable strain on the ship's timbers. It was, rather, a rapid

At Trafalgar, Nelson was counting on the inability of the enemy admirals to handle their fleet in any formation other than the traditional line-ahead. Once the Franco-Spanish line had been sliced in three by Nelson's two-pronged attack, the battle became a welter of ship-to-ship dog-fights in which superior British gunnery won the day.

Below: The bombardment of Algiers, chief lair of the notorious Barbary Pirates, by Lord Exmouth's battle squadron (27 August 1816). This was a well-prepared exploitation of battleship fire-power at almost point-blank range. It was seldom that battleships ever had the chance of engaging shore batteries virtually at surface level, as Exmouth knew was the case at Algiers. As the British and French would discover at the Dardanelles, 100 years later, shore batteries emplaced on higher ground were a very different proposition.

drumming sequence of fire from stem to stern as each gun came to bear on a recognisable target: an unscathed section of hull, say, or a notably active gun crew in the enemy ship. Though the captain of the gun supervised the frantic ballet of sponging out the gun after each shot, reloading, running the gun out, and the actual firing, the most important man in the crew was the gunlayer who supervised the aim. And the gunlayer's importance was destined to prevail until the advent of centralised fire control, with director guidance rather than individual gunlayers' firing, on the eve of the First World War.

The establishment of the battleship as the ultimate ship of war, together with the line of battle and the start of the rating system, all date from the middle seventeenth century. The same applies to the battleship's other role, which proved far more enduring than its predominance in fleet actions, and is still relevant even in the missile era of the 1980s. This was the role of bombarding shore targets and silencing enemy batteries as a preliminary to raids from the sea or landings in force. One of the earliest instances was the feat of Cromwell's Admiral Robert Blake on 20 April 1657, when he took a fleet of 25 ships amid the bristling shore defences of Santa Cruz, Teneriffe, to liquidate a sheltering Spanish treasure fleet. Blake entered the harbour in line-ahead, silencing the fire of the encircling forts while battering 16 Spanish ships into surrender; these were then boarded and burned, while Blake withdrew on the ebb tide without the loss of a single English ship. It was while attempting to repeat this feat at Santa Cruz with insufficient force (only four ships of the line) that Nelson was beaten off with heavy loss in July 1797, losing his right arm in the process.

At Copenhagen (2 April 1801) Nelson took the immense gamble of sailing close inshore to trade broadsides with a Danish line of battle protected by shore forts and floating batteries. Despite a particularly

gory ordeal of fire the weight of shot thrown by the British line proved adequate to overcome the combined fire of the Danish ships and batteries, though only just. The same held true of the bombardment of the Barbary Corsairs' fortified lair at Algiers (27 August 1816), undertaken by Lord Exmouth with five ships of the line and ten frigates. In an intense cannonade Exmouth's ships shattered the town, silenced the harbour forts at virtually point-blank range and destroyed the Corsair fleet. Well aware of the narrow margin between defeat and victory in such a venture, Exmouth had prudently reinforced his ships' hulls, strengthened their armament and exhaustively drilled his gun crews in marksmanship and rate of fire.

The potential of the sailing battleship was again displayed at Navarino (20 October 1827), the last fleet action of the age of sail, when an allied Anglo-Russian-French fleet destroyed the greatly superior Turkish fleet in Navarino Bay (southern Greece). The allied fleet consisted of 12 ships of the line, eight frigates and about half a dozen smaller warships; the Turkish fleet was 65 ships strong, but only seven of them ships of the line. It was drawn up at anchor in a massive horseshoe formation and protected by two forts commanding the entrance to the bay. The resultant converging field of fire thus presented to the allied fleet was not, however, strong enough to silence the allied ships of the line which deliberately anchored at its heart. After a four-hour bombardment the Turks had lost 35 ships, most of them burned by their own crews in lieu of formal surrender. Though the allied ships suffered severe damage, not one of them was lost.

Navarino brought to a close two centuries of naval warfare in which the wooden, sail-driven battleship had ruled supreme by virtue of intense broadside fire at the closest possible range. There was, in 1827, little or no indication of the revolutionary changes in battleship design which the ensuing 50 years held in store.

Below: The British flagship *Asia* in the thick of the action at Navarino. 'As each ship of our opponents became disabled,' wrote Admiral Codrington, 'such of her crew as could escape from her endeavoured to set her on fire; and it is wonderful how we avoided the effect of their successive and awful explosions.'

2. FROM WOODEN WALL TO STEAM IRONCLAD, 1827-1866

Previous pages : The famous tug-of-war between the British steam frigates *Rattler* and *Alecto* in 1845, which proved conclusively that screw propulsion was superior to paddlewheel propulsion. In warships the paddlewheel's greatest drawbacks were the drag it exerted when the ship was under sail, and its inevitable reduction of broadside gun armament.
Below : The 'wooden walls' of Navarino had one great advantage over the first steam-powered warships. A sailing ship's hull capacity could be used to the full, instead of being devoured by as much as a third by engine-room space.

THE 40 YEARS BETWEEN the Battle of Navarino in 1827 and the Battle of Lissa in 1866 saw the essential ingredients of the modern battleship – steam power, explosive shell, armoured protection and turret-mounted main armament – go into the melting-pot. The development of each of these ingredients required a technological revolution in its own right, and the overall process was complicated by the temporary addition of a feature hitherto reserved for oared galleys: the exploitation of steam power to enable warships to sink the enemy outright by ramming him below the waterline.

With hindsight it is all too easy to sneer at the crusty conservatism in naval circles which clung to wood and sail and opposed the new gifts of science at every turn. This conservatism certainly existed, but there was a lot more to it than blind tradition-worship. There were far more practical objections to the new ideas than emotional ones, and the most telling practical objection (still alive and well in the 1980s, technology-mania notwithstanding) was that the existing systems worked as well as could be desired. The immediate effect of the new systems (if they could ever be made to work anything like as well, which seemed unlikely) would be to render the existing systems worthless at a stroke. It was precisely in this spirit that Earl St Vincent had opposed Robert Fulton's experimental submarine when this was offered to the British Admiralty in 1803, refusing point-blank 'to encourage a mode of warfare which those who commanded the seas did not want and which, if successful, would at once deprive them of it.'

The idea of steam propulsion for warships extended St Vincent's line of thinking by another 50 years. By the time of Navarino steam-powered ships were an undeniable reality and their virtues were obvious to all. Steam tugs and transports for river and coastal work, always ready for service independent of currents, tides and winds, were a marvellous innovation. There were few if any objections to the building of

The allies steam to war in the Crimea. This is the French steam-powered 3-decker *Charlemagne* passing the Bosphorus on her way to the Black Sea, 23 October 1854.

steam-powered light warships designed specifically for coastal and inshore work. But the prospect of *ocean-going* ships ever relying wholly on steam seemed as remote, in the 1830s, 40s and 50s, as that of men flying to the moon (or, for that matter, anywhere, in craft other than balloons). The first steam vessels were driven by huge paddlewheels; and their boiler furnaces devoured prodigious quantities of fuel. When fitted to ocean-going sailing ships, paddlewheels were a monstrous drag on the ship's speed and sea-worthiness. Quite apart from the bunker space required to store enough fuel even for short bursts of auxiliary power, the bulky engines also ate heavily into the ship's available internal space. And fitting paddlewheels to warships intended to lie in the line of battle was an obvious non-starter, because paddlewheel mountings reduced broadside armament by over half.

The development of screw propulsion – a propeller at the stern instead of paddles at the side – solved the broadside problem; the screw had an added advantage in that it could be hoisted inboard for unimpeded progress under sail. The question of whether paddlewheels or screws were the more efficient was answered in March and April 1845 by a series of contests between two 880-ton British frigates, each fitted with a 200 horsepower engine. HMS *Rattler* was driven by screw, HMS *Alecto* by twin paddlewheels, and the tests were carried out in the calmest conditions available. The speed test was a race of 100 miles, easily won by *Rattler*. The power test was the clincher: a stern-to-stern tug of war between the two ships which ended with *Alecto*, paddles frantically thrashing at full power, being towed helplessly astern at a speed of almost 3 knots. Though paddlewheel propulsion survived into the twentieth century because of the matchless manoeuvrability it gave small craft, the *Alecto*/*Rattler* trials conclusively proved the superior speed and fuel-to-power economy of screw propulsion. By the 1850s, with the reliability and compactness of marine steam engines improving yearly, the installation of auxiliary steam propulsion was at last spreading from flotilla craft and frigates to the multi-decked wooden giants of the line of battle.

As far as the development of the battleship was concerned, it was a happy fluke of history that the first war in which steam-powered battleships were put to the test was the Crimean War of 1854–56. The leading European navies, those of Britain and France, found themselves required to operate in uneasy alliance against the Russian Empire. The two major theatres of the naval war against Russia were the land-locked Baltic and Black Seas – ideal waters for experimental fleet evolutions with what were still experimental ships. It was not a demanding war for the Anglo-French battle squadrons, none of which were of sufficient force to guarantee decisive results in ineffective bombardments of Russian coastal defences. The battleships' main contribution in the Black Sea, once the troops were ashore in the Crimea, was landing heavy guns to bombard Sevastopol's landward defences, and contributing boats for inshore raiding. But in the rocky, confined waters of the Gulf of Finland auxiliary steam power proved itself a real blessing. It freed the most valuable warships in the allied fleet from the centuries-old nightmare of being caught by an untimely wind on a hostile lee shore. If steam-powered battleships had had to make their operational debut in a conventional naval war, enforcing distant blockade from the safety of the open sea, steam would have been hardly if ever used and the virtues of sail would have been re-stated instead.

Yet the Crimean War achieved far more than ensuring that new battleships would be designed and built with steam engines as well as sail. (There was only one such ship in the allied armada in 1854: the newly-completed HMS *Agamemnon*.) With its dramatic revelations of the power of explosive shell and the strength of armour plate, the Crimean War also served notice on the traditional 'wooden wall' battleship and its short-range, solid shot.

Solid shot crushes the target or (if the target is thin enough) smashes clean through, with disastrous effects on anyone or anything in its path, but with a destructive effect notably limited to its line of flight. An explosive shell, with its bursting charge detonated by a fuse set either at the instant of firing or seconds before, is a much more destructive projectile. It not only hurls lethal splinters over a much wider area than a solid shot: the flash and heat of an exploding shell starts fires. Until the first half of the nineteenth century, however, shells were only used in *indirect fire*: lobbed out of mortars on a high, slow-travelling trajectory which came down on the target from above. Because their shells could be dropped on the far side of high ground or the upperworks of fortifications, heavy mortars were an indispensable element of siege artillery. Because of their size and bulk and the weight of their projectiles, mortars were unsuitable for rapid deployment with the field artillery. A mortar shell or 'bomb' could weigh 200 pounds while the heaviest field artillery pieces were usually 9 or at most 12-pounders. These pieces used *direct fire*, with the projectile following a low trajectory or, at short ranges, a direct flight-path from the gun's muzzle to the target. Field artillery began to use explosive shrapnel shells, packed with bullets, in the last decade of the Napoleonic Wars; but shrapnel shells also used indirect fire, their purpose being to riddle concentrations of enemy troops by bursting in the air.

For 150-odd years the only explosive shells used in naval warfare were mortar bombs fired by specially-built 'bomb ketches'. These, the sea-going equivalent of siege artillery, lacked foremasts and carried their mortars well up in the bows. They were ideal for bombarding harbour defences or ships protected by fortified anchorages. It was in the latter role that the bomb ketch made its debut in 1682 in a French attack on the Barbary Corsairs of Algiers (an international pest which was not removed, even after the dramatic Anglo-Dutch bombardment of 1816, until the conquest of Algiers by the French in 1829). But it was not until after the Napoleonic Wars that serious attempts were made to adapt the new explosive shells, as used in land warfare, to the main armament of warships.

In 1821 a French Army artilleryman, General Henri Paixhans, began to experiment with the idea of marrying the greatly superior range of the long-barrelled gun to the superior destructive power of the explosive shell and producing a naval gun capable of firing shells in direct, low-trajectory fire. His researches prospered, and in 1824 an old 80-gun ship of the line, *Le Pacificateur*, became the first warship to be sunk by naval shellfire, though only as an immobile target ship. Thus encouraged, the French Ministry of Marine approved the adoption of naval 'shell-guns' in the 1820s and 1830s: the first genuine improvement of naval artillery (other than mere increases in weight of shot over the years) in three centuries. The new 'shell-guns' were first fired in anger on 27 November 1838, by a French squadron sent out to put pressure on the Mexican government. When negotiations got nowhere, Rear-Admiral Baudin, commanding the squadron, decided on a show of force: a bombardment of the offshore fort of San Juan d'Ulloa at Vera Cruz. Two and a half hours' bombardment by a force consisting only of four frigates sufficed to blow up the fort's powder magazines, silence its guns and leave the wretched Mexican commandant

British battleships *Sanspareil* and *Agamemnon* bombarding the Sevastopol forts (23 October 1854). Even if the fleet had not landed so many guns for the army to use as siege artillery from the landward (also without avail), the Sevastopol defences were still too tough for wooden warships. The Russian gunners hit back stoutly and inflicted considerable damage on the bombarding force, with about 300 British seamen killed and wounded in the action.

with no option but to order the formal surrender of the fort.

When news of the incident reached Britain it drew a respectful mention in the House of Lords from no less an authority than the Duke of Wellington – 'the only instance I know', he admitted, 'of a land fortress being reduced purely by naval force'. Naval conservatives were however less impressed, pointing out that this victory had only been won over a second-rate fort (a Mexican one at that) and that a ship-to-ship action would have been a very different story. It took another 15 years before this confidence was shaken, in which time the 'shell-gun' became sufficiently well established for it to be adopted by the Russian Navy (1852). And it was the latter service which carried out the first shellfire bombardment by battleships: the so-called 'Massacre of Sinope' (30 November 1853).

It happened during the Russo-Turkish conflict which, in the following year, was to escalate into the Crimean War. Seven Turkish frigates and two corvettes under Vice-Admiral Osman Pasha had taken shelter behind coastal batteries in the southern Black Sea port of Sinope, where they were blockaded by Admiral Paul Nakhimov with three Russian ships of the line. Having been joined by the rest of his battle fleet from Sevastopol – three wooden first-rates armed with shell-firing 68-pounders – Nakhimov attacked out of a timely morning mist, silenced the coastal batteries and sank every Turkish ship in the harbour. There has seldom been a more shattering vindication of a new weapon; though the victims were grossly outmatched (frigates against first-rates) they were destroyed in a position which, according to orthodox naval thinking, was considered secure from seaward attack.

The savage competence of Nakhimov's attack on Sinope was completely lacking on the allied side when the British and French landed in the Crimea (14 September 1854) and marched politely on Sevastopol without any siege guns. These had to be provided by the warships: over 50 guns, half the fleet's ammunition and about a third of its men. As a result the allied bombardment of Sevastopol's defences by land and sea (17 October) was too feeble to do any serious damage. The Sevastopol forts were assisted by Nakhimov's warships, which shot back to such good effect that five British battleships were heavily damaged and 300 of their men killed.

Despite a year of allied misery and futility outside Sevastopol, the Russians failed to relieve the city from the landward and it fell on 9 September 1855. By this time both sides knew that this was a pointless war with no possibility of a traditional solution; but as the peace feelers went out the allies decided on a final operation to put pressure on the Russians. This took the form of an amphibious attack on the Russian forts at Kinburn at the mouth of the River Bug, which if successful would leave the Russian naval arsenal of Nikolayev (only 25 miles away) open to direct attack. And the bombardment force included three weird objects built on the orders of the French Emperor Napoleon III: floating batteries armoured against counter-bombardment with 4-inch sides of iron plate. For good measure these batteries were feebly powered by steam engines, though by no means could they be described as ships; they were towed to the scene of action and only used their engines to move into their firing positions without endangering their tugs.

After a westward feint towards Odessa,

Herald of a new era: the French ironclad frigate *Gloire* of 1859, with an oak hull protected by an iron belt. Hardly less novel was her broadside of breech-loading rifled guns, firing explosive shell. Though fully ship-rigged, *Gloire* had a top speed of 13½ knots under steam.

10,000 allied troops were safely landed on Kinburn spit on 15 October 1855, safely out of reach of the Russian guns. Eleven warships moved into firing positions at about 1,000 yards range and opened fire on the forts while the French ironclad batteries cast off their tows and lumbered into close range before joining in. The results were shattering. After only three hours' bombardment at 800 yards range which blasted great chunks of masonry from the walls at each hit, the Russian forts surrendered. Presented with immobile targets at point-blank range, the Russian batteries had scored 132 hits on the nearest two French ironclad batteries, of which only five had managed to dent the armour. The British naval C-in-C, Admiral Lyons, was in no doubt that a new era was being ushered in by these ironclad batteries, reporting to the

Top : Britain's *Warrior* was far more advanced than her rival *Gloire* – the first warship built entirely of iron, with her armoured belt backed by 18 inches of teak.
Above : Defence, only three years after *Warrior*, was completed with a 'cleaver' bow for ramming instead of the conventional frigate stem.

British Admiralty that 'the only effect upon them was the appearance of a few rust-like marks where the shot struck and bounded off'.

Having thus established the value of armoured floating structures under fire, the French swiftly took the process to its logical conclusion and produced the first true armour-plated steam warship. This was the *Gloire*, designed by Stanislas Dupuy de Lôme and launched in 1859. Originally ordered as a wooden 90-gun ship of the line, *Gloire* was completed as a steam frigate with a single deck of 36 66-pounder guns. The hull was sheathed at the waterline with a belt of iron plate armour 4·7 inches thick. And it was the latter feature, rendering the ship able to survive while bombarding and sinking unprotected enemy ships, which drove the British to building ironclad ships of their own.

Once this happened the sensation caused by *Gloire*'s appearance was bound to be brief, because in the late 1850s Britain's superiority in high-grade iron and steel production was still second to none. The British had already blazed the trail with iron-hulled passenger and freight-carrying ships. Isambard Kingdom Brunel's *Great Britain*, launched in 1843, was the first iron-hulled screw-driven ship to cross the Atlantic. The soundness of her construction was involuntarily demonstrated on her fifth voyage when she ran aground in Ireland and lay stranded for 11 months (1846–47) before being salvaged in excellent condition – an ordeal which few if any wooden ships of her size could have survived. Hence the confidence with which the British designed, built, and launched HMS *Warrior* (1859–60) as an answer to *Gloire*.

Warrior was the first warship built entirely of iron and her armoured protection – $4\frac{1}{2}$ inches of armour plate backed by 18 inches of teak – was greatly superior to that of *Gloire*. *Warrior*'s 40 guns (26 68-pounders, ten 110-pounders and four 70-pounders) were, like those of *Gloire*, mounted in conventional broadside on a single deck. But *Warrior* displaced 9,210 tons to *Gloire*'s 5,600 tons; she could steam at $14\frac{1}{2}$ knots to *Gloire*'s 13 knots; and she was, at 380 feet, no less than $127\frac{1}{2}$ feet longer than the French ironclad.

Though *Gloire* and *Warrior* both retained the full ship-rig of three masts and a conventional press of canvas, both could easily have sunk the mightiest wooden first-rates in service with any navy. Given this undoubted fact, their nominal classification as 'steam frigates' (from their common single-decked broadside) was an obvious anomaly, though 27 years were to pass before *Warrior* was officially re-classified as a 3rd class armoured screw *battleship*. Though rivals in design, *Gloire* and *Warrior* together represented the addition of armour plate and iron construction to the existing combination of steam power and shell-firing guns. An entirely new era in the balance of world sea power was thus opened: that of challenge and counter-challenge, with each new warship type threatening to make obsolete the most modern ships not only of rival fleets but of its own fleet as well. Though completed to the same basic formula, each of *Warrior*'s immediate successors (*Black Prince, Resistance*, and *Defence*, 1860–63) showed a conscious effort to improve on the standards set by its predecessor and not merely reproduce them. After *Warrior* the centuries-old reliance on warships of a

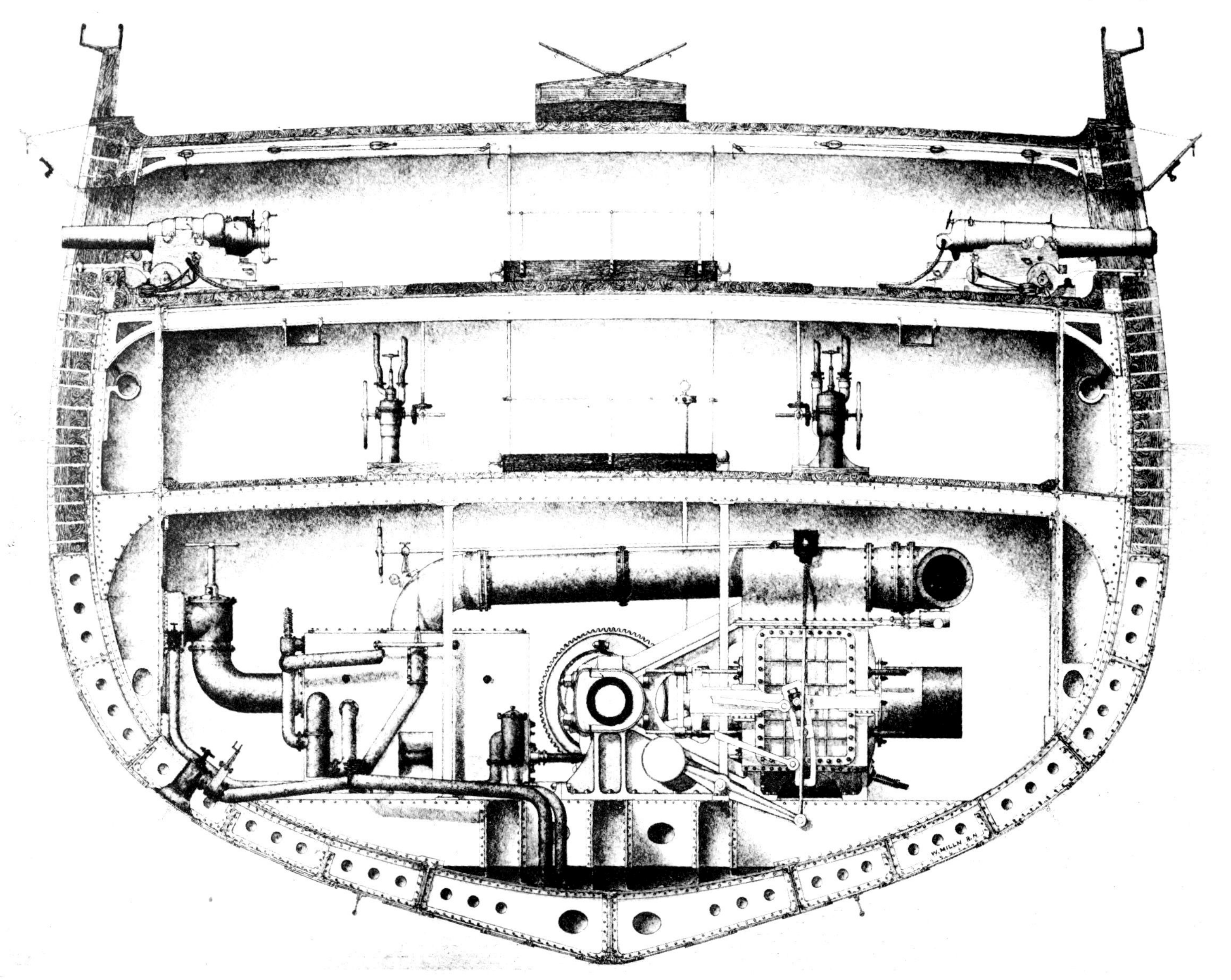

Top : Cross-section of *Warrior*, showing the gun deck and the huge space occupied by her engines.
Right : The old sailing skills remained essential until steam warships could carry enough fuel to dispense with the ship rig. This is *Bellerophon* taking advantage of a following wind by setting studding-sails on foremast and mainmast.

The first ironclad battle: *Monitor* (*left*) and *Merrimack* batter each other at point-blank range in Hampton Roads (9 March 1862). Though heavily outgunned by *Monitor*'s twin 11-inch turret guns, *Merrimack*'s sloping armour stood up well to the Union shells and the fight ended in stalemate.

single, familiar type, built in large numbers from the same pattern, was seen no longer as the formula for naval security, but as a formula for potential disaster.

The next innovation came swiftly, and from a totally unexpected direction: the warring states of the American Republic, split in 1861 by the secession of the Southern slave-owning states to form a new nation, the Confederate States of America. Determined to preserve its precarious identity by military and naval force, undaunted by the fact that all the industrial muscle for the waging of modern warfare was concentrated in the Northern states, the Confederates set to work to build a navy. Like the Elizabethan navy confronted by the massed resources of the Spanish Empire, the fledgling Confederate Navy was forced to improvise from what it had. And under this spur it was the Confederacy, not France or Britain, which produced the first ironclad warship to go into action.

When the State of Virginia joined the Confederacy in April 1861 the wooden steam frigate *Merrimack* was lying in the Navy Yard at Norfolk, undergoing engine repairs. To stop her falling into Confederate hands, *Merrimack* was not only burned but scuttled – a stupid combination which presented the Confederates with an intact if temporarily sunken hull and engines. Having recovered what was left of *Merrimack* the Confederates set to work to make an ironclad of her: armoured protection being called in to challenge overwhelming enemy numbers and combined fire power. Sheer poverty of resources made the rebuilt *Merrimack* (proudly re-christened CSS *Virginia*) the first warship designed to rely solely upon steam. She was stripped to her lowest deck, over which was built a massive wooden penthouse with sloping sides and an outer shell of plates hammered from railway iron (greased with fat to help enemy shell ricochet and make boarding harder). Armoured shutters protected *Virginia*'s guns, a necessarily scratch lot: six 9-inch, two 7-inch and two 6·4-inch. And on her bow was mounted a heavy iron beak with which to ram the wooden-hulled Union warships blockading the James River.

All this made *Virginia* look like nothing on earth, but there was no concealing the menace she radiated as she took shape in her dry dock during the winter of 1861–62. As reports of her progress reached Washington, the uneasy realisation that the Union Navy possessed no armoured ships gave place to panic as *Virginia* slowly but steadily approached apparent completion. The first Union ironclad of European type, USS *Galena*, was hastily ordered in August 1861. Desperate, however, for an 'instant' iron-

clad to set against *Merrimack/Virginia*, the US Navy Department ordered the Swedish-born engineer John Ericsson to build the extraordinary little vessel which he swore could be completed in 100 days: USS *Monitor*.

John Ericsson ranks with Isambard Kingdom Brunel as one of the most exciting innovators of the Industrial Revolution, and his *Monitor* remains unique in warship history. Unlike Britain's *Warrior*, *Monitor* was not an improved version of an existing type of warship; Ericsson had conceived the idea before *Merrimack*'s salvage and reconstruction, and the new ship owed nothing to any existing type. *Monitor* was the test-bed for an entirely novel naval weapon system: the replacement of the traditional broadside by a rotating turret. The great virtue of the turret was that it enabled the guns to be brought to bear without altering the heading of the ship, permitting much greater freedom of manoeuvre. *Monitor* was a purely functional prototype: a small hull supporting an armoured raft, with two 11-inch guns mounted in an armoured, drum-shaped turret amidships. Observers noted that while *Merrimack/Virginia* looked like the roof of a flooded barn drifting downstream, *Monitor* resembled nothing so much as a tin can on a plank.

The completion of both *Virginia* and *Monitor* was beset with design and supply problems, and the drama of their eventual confrontation on 9 March 1862 was heightened by *Virginia* being first into action by a mere 24 hours. She came out into Hampton Roads on the morning of 8 March and made ponderously for the nearest Union warship in the blockade line, the wooden sloop *Cumberland*. *Virginia* approached *Cumberland* from the starboard bow, engaging with her 7-inch bow gun while remaining safe from *Cumberland*'s full broadside; during her approach the ironclad took a broadside from the Union steam frigate *Congress*, every shell of which bounced harmlessly off the armour. Finally, having destroyed *Cumberland*'s bow guns as they vainly tried to stop the oncoming menace, *Virginia* rammed *Cumberland* fair and square below the starboard bow. The iron beak broke off with the impact, but *Cumberland* was doomed. As the stricken ship listed and began to sink, her extremely gallant crew blasted *Virginia* with three broadsides at point-blank range – all to no effect. *Virginia* then took station astern of *Congress* and set her ablaze with shellfire, unharmed by the bombardment of Union field guns from the shore.

As the fires in *Congress* went out of control it seemed that nothing could stop *Virginia* going on to destroy the other Union warships, *Minnesota, Roanoke* and *St Lawrence*; but evening was approaching, the tide was falling and *Virginia*, with her ponderous turning circle and deep draught of 22 feet, withdrew to attack again at high water the next day. As night fell on the 8th, however, *Monitor* came steaming into Hampton Roads, taking station to protect *Minnesota*. Hardly more seaworthy than *Virginia, Monitor* had been towed down from New York, nearly foundering in a gale while on passage.

Nobody who had seen *Virginia* in action on the 8th really believed that the diminutive *Monitor*, outgunned as she was by ten guns to two, could stop her. But that was precisely what happened in the inconclusive 'Battle of Hampton Roads' on the following morning, when *Virginia* came out to finish off *Minnesota*. For nearly three hours the two ironclads hammered unavailingly at each other before disengaging as if by mutual consent, neither having inflicted significant damage on the other. But it might well have been otherwise; there had not been time to prove *Monitor*'s guns at their full powder charge of 30 pounds, and on the 9th her gunners were

Civil War river ironclad with sloping armoured castemate. This war was the first example of a completely outclassed maritime power (the Confederacy) gaining parity by building the newest types of warship. Here we have the Confederate *Atlanta* on the James River, after her capture in 1863.

ordered to load with no more than half-charges. This spared *Virginia*'s makeshift armour from having to take the full shattering impact of 11-inch shells at point-blank range. In the short term it was stalemate: as long as *Monitor* stayed with the Union flotilla off the James River *Virginia* had no hope of breaking the Northern blockade, and as long as *Virginia* remained operational there could be no question of full-scale Union amphibious operations in the James. After an uneasy month throughout which the two ironclads kept each other in check, it became apparent that the Hampton Roads encounter of 9 March had been a long-term strategic defeat for the Confederates. *Monitor*'s presence enabled General McClellan's Union army to land on the Yorktown peninsula, cross the James and oblige the Confederates to evacuate Norfolk. Unable to withdraw up the James because of her deep draught, *Virginia* was blown up by her crew on 11 May 1862 – just over two months after her resounding debut. *Monitor* did not survive her for more than seven months; in December 1862 she foundered off Cape Hatteras in a storm while being towed south to reinforce the blockade of Wilmington, North Carolina. (Her wreck was located, bottom-up on the sea bed, in 1973.)

Though other 'monitors' and ironclad gunboats played a leading role in the river campaigns throughout the rest of the American Civil War, that conflict produced only one fleet action between ironclads. This took place during the forcing of Mobile Bay, Alabama, by Admiral Farragut's Northern fleet (5 August 1864). The Battle of Mobile Bay opened dramatically when the monitor USS *Tecumseh*, leading the Union line, was sunk by an explosive mine (or 'torpedo', as this novel weapon was then called) – the first armoured warship to fall victim to mine warfare. In the ensuing action ramming and close-range gunnery were again the predominating tactics, but this time Northern fire-power proved decisive. Hammered by the twin turrets of the Northern monitor *Chickasaw*, the Confederate ironclad *Tennessee* was obliged to strike her colours after her rudder chains were severed and her armoured shell was cracked and blown open by the torrent of shells. The surrender of *Tennessee*, backbone of the Confederate defence, clinched Farragut's victory.

By the end of the American Civil War in April 1865 the leading European navies were already reacting to the latest lessons from across the Atlantic. The case for steam power, shell-firing main armament of the heaviest calibres, and armoured protection was proven beyond doubt. So, it seemed, was the tactic of ramming, so prevalent in the American conflict – the ultimate method, when all was said and done, of pressing home attacks on the enemy. By 1865 projecting rams, or at least bows reinforced for ramming, were becoming the order of the day in the European navies. The moral advantage enjoyed by a fleet determined to press ramming attacks, even against a superior enemy force, was impressively

Below : Italy's *Re d'Italia*, rammed and sunk at Lissa by the Austrian flagship *Ferdinand Maximilian.*
Bottom : Austrian wooden ironclad *Kaiser*, showing the extensive damage suffered in her ramming attack at Lissa.

demonstrated by the Battle of Lissa in the Adriatic Sea (20 July 1866).

Preparing for action with the Italian Adriatic Fleet in the Austro-Italian war of 1866, the aggressive Admiral Tegetthof chose ramming as his main tactic. The feebly commanded Italian line of armoured and wooden steam frigates at Lissa was repeatedly penetrated by Austrian attempts at ramming, with the Austrian ships pouring in broadsides as they passed through the line. Finally Tegetthof's *Erzherzog Ferdinand Maximilian* rammed the Italian *Re d'Italia* fair and square, sending her to the bottom in under three minutes. The *Kaiser* came off considerably worse than her victim when she rammed the *Re di Portigallo* but was the only Austrian ship to suffer extensive battle damage, the Italians retiring in disorder after the *Palestro* blew up and sank – two ironclads lost for nil return.

By the late 1860s, therefore, the new ironclad ram seemed a well-established type, though any significant improvement in long-range gunnery would clearly make ramming an increasingly hazardous occupation. Far more urgent was the biggest problem obscuring the future of the ocean-going heavy warship. This was the need to retain a full rig of masts and sails for prolonged high seas cruising and the consequent need (due to the obstructions of the upper decks by masts and rigging) to retain the obsolescent broadside armament. The 20 years after Lissa were destined to see that problem solved.

3. FROM BROADSIDE TO TURRET, 1866–1886

Previous pages: HMS *Collingwood* (1886), with main armament mounted fore and aft in open barbettes and secondary broadside armament amidships. The British 'Admirals' of the 1880s were hardly a coherent battleship class, as their armaments differed widely.
Below: The British-built Dutch ironclad ram *Buffel* (1868). The first American ironclads had never dared put out to sea apart from the shortest of inshore voyages; but here, only six years later, was a fully sea-going ironclad with turret-mounted main armament, able to dispense with the full ship-rig.

ONE OF THE BEST WAYS to understand the dilemma facing warship designers in the late 1860s and 1870s is to go to Rotterdam and walk round the superbly restored turret ram *Buffel*. Her name, which means buffalo, immediately suggests the ramming heyday of the 1860s, but despite this clue it is still hard to accept that this trim, modern-looking little warship was built as far back as 1867–68. It is even harder to understand why the British designers of *Buffel* (built for the Dutch Navy by Napier's on the Clyde) were at the same time still turning out successors to *Warrior* with full ship-rig and serried broadside armament. For the silhouette of *Buffel*, designed as she was only eight years after *Warrior*, is dominated by a single squat turret, its twin 9-inch guns now removed to create a circular gallery of displays for the visitor.

What the latter does not at first realise is that this armament was confidently ordered by the Dutch at a time when the Royal Navy was still completing the transition from smooth-bore 100-pounders to rifled, $6\frac{1}{2}$ ton 7-inch guns. Even more embarrassing, only the experimental *Bellerophon* (1864) had been built as a test-bed for the $12\frac{1}{2}$ ton 9-inch gun. As for sail versus steam, the full ship-rig remained an essential feature of every British capital ship throughout the 1860s. *Achilles*, the biggest steam warship in the world when launched only five years before *Buffel*, was also the biggest ship in Royal Naval history to carry the full ship-rig – $29\frac{1}{4}$ miles of cordage and 50,000 square feet of canvas when under full sail, compared with only 32,000 square feet in the clipper *Cutty Sark*. *Buffel* had originally been intended to carry sail on two masts,

HMS *Captain*, the ill-fated British attempt to mount turrets in a fully rigged warship. She capsized and sank with immense loss of life on 7 September 1870.

but this never got past the planning stage; she was a sea-going steamship first and foremost and if she ever hoisted a sail, even as an emergency drill, her log-books and journals failed to record the fact. The little Dutch ironclad may therefore be seen as the turning-point in warship history when sail became auxiliary to steam instead of the other way round.

For the next 40 years, the British repeatedly experienced the embarrassment of being commissioned to build better warships for foreign navies than were built for the Royal Navy. After the preceding centuries which had founded and embellished the Royal Navy's tradition, this was a novel and salutary experience. It was, of course, obvious that small warships like *Buffel* could *afford* to rely wholly upon steam. They were cast in the coastal defence role and would never voyage beyond range of easy replenishment with coal. But the Royal Navy's world-imperial role was far more demanding. To take the case of *Achilles* again, the 750 tons of coal she carried would, in theory, enable her to steam 2,500 miles in ideal conditions – but ideal conditions are rarely found in a voyage round the British Isles, let alone in an Atlantic crossing. For the British there could be no long-term reliance on warships which might some day have to make an ocean crossing and, with coal bunkers exhausted, fight under sail against a modern coastal steam warship with more powerful, turret-mounted guns – a warship which, to add insult to injury, would probably have been designed and built in Britain.

The urgency of the problem by the end

of the 1860s was revealed by the disastrous British attempt to add turret armament to an ironclad steam warship carrying the full ship-rig. This produced the experimental *Captain*, with a turret fore and aft of the mainmast and tripod lower masts in an attempt to give the guns a wider field of fire. Armoured protection 8 inches thick was given to the sides – but the resultant contraption sat ominously low in the water, with barely 9 feet between waterline and upper deck. The inevitable happened on 7 September 1870, while *Captain* was on manoeuvres with the Channel Fleet off Finisterre in a gale. A massive sea heeled her past the 'point of no return' and she capsized, sinking with horrific loss of life – there were only 18 survivors out of a complement of some 500 officers, men and boys. Diehard champions of sail angrily blamed the disaster on plain bad seamanship, the inevitable result of excessive reliance on steam power. As Admiral the Hon. H. J. Rous put it:

> It would be more consonant with common sense to find that [*Captain*] was lost by the officer of the watch not knowing how to shorten sail or to keep his men on deck . . . The fact is, the boiler has emasculated seamanship. No man can serve two masters; he will hold to the tea kettle and despise the canvas. You can no more rear a seaman in a steamer than on the Bridgewater Canal. In ten years' time the British *seaman* will be a rare bird among the sailors in the Royal Navy.

That, of course, was overstating the case; it was quite true that a sailing ship *would* have survived the storm in which *Captain* was lost, but so would a properly designed steamer without so much top-hamper. And it was the latter, no less valid deduction that hastened the completion of a new steam warship which, ten years on, fulfilled the promise of Ericsson's *Monitor*.

With HMS *Devastation* (1871) the modern battleship began to struggle out of the chrysalis and emerge in recognisable form. *Devastation* was the first heavy sea-

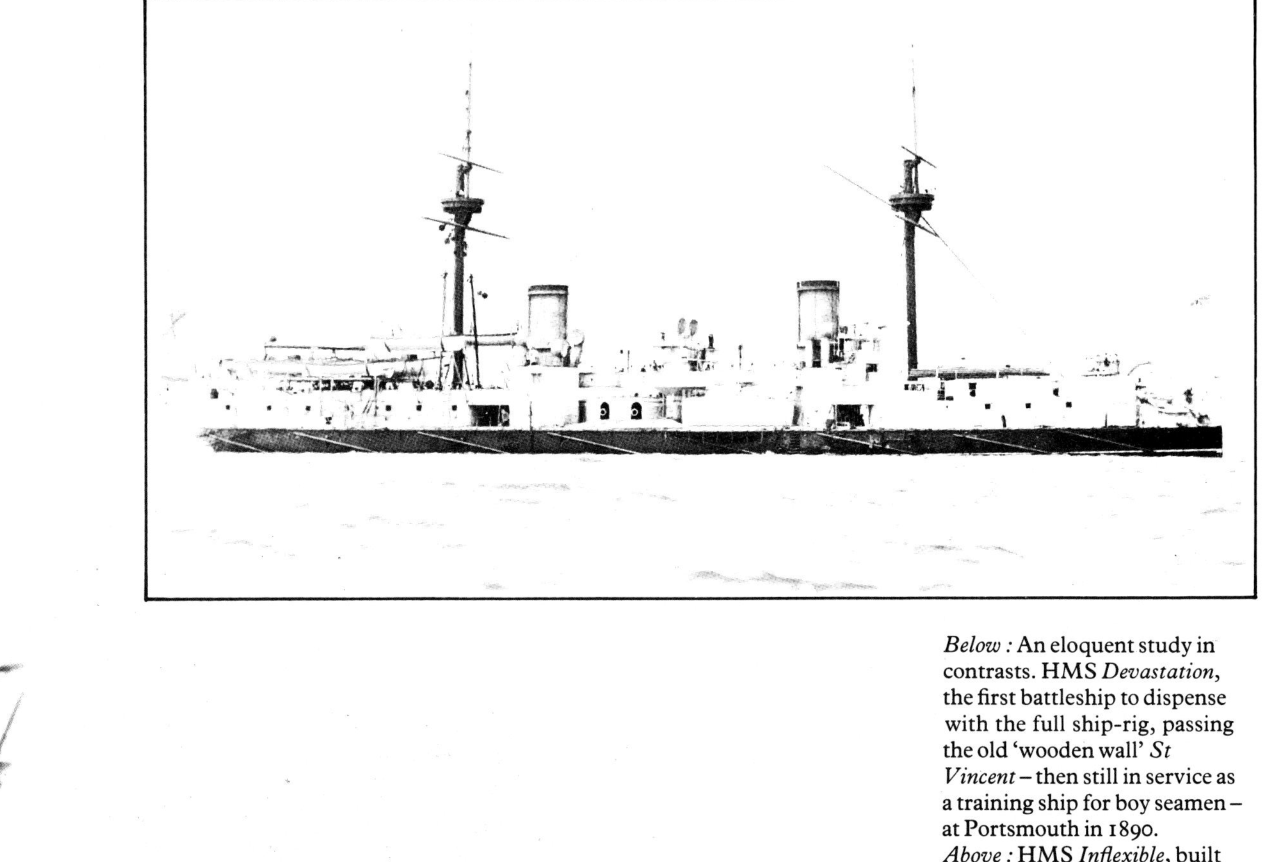

Below : An eloquent study in contrasts. HMS *Devastation*, the first battleship to dispense with the full ship-rig, passing the old 'wooden wall' *St Vincent* – then still in service as a training ship for boy seamen – at Portsmouth in 1890.
Above : HMS *Inflexible*, built for the Royal Navy in imitation of Italy's 'Duilios', with back-to-back midships turrets.

The old guns and the new. *Top:* Muzzle-loaders in HMS *Temeraire*, 1870 (note massive thickness at breech). *Above:* Breech-loading 12-inchers in HMS *Rodney*'s forward barbette only ten years later, showing the limited elevation permitted by this type of mounting.

going warship to dispense entirely with the traditional ship-rig of heavily-shrouded masts and crossed yards. Her derivation from *Buffel*'s design of four years earlier was very noticeable. *Devastation* was really an enlarged version of *Buffel*, 89 feet longer and 22 feet wider in the beam; and she had two turrets to *Buffel*'s one, positioned fore and aft of a central superstructure housing two funnels. Also like *Buffel*, *Devastation* was driven by twin screws and was fitted with a ram bow, though *Devastation*'s was sharply pointed instead of being the elegant rounded 'cleaver' pattern of *Buffel*'s design. But as her name implied, *Devastation*'s most dramatic features were her guns: two 12-inch muzzle-loaders in each turret. Less noticeable to the eye but no less important was an armoured protection of unprecedented strength: $8\frac{1}{2}$–12 inches on the hull sides and 10–14 inches on the turrets. She was the hardest-hitting, best-protected warship yet built – but her supremacy, in a decade of ever quickening experimentation, lasted less than five years.

By the time *Devastation* entered service, warship development had become a race between the gunnery experts pushing the weight and calibre of the muzzle-loading gun to greater and greater limits, and the ship designers required to produce hulls, engines and armoured protection of proportionally increased strength. The British were given little time to assess *Devastation*'s strengths and weaknesses before they were again required to equip a more powerful warship for a foreign navy, this time that of Italy. Designed by Benedetto Brin, the *Duilio* and *Dandolo* were built to carry the monstrous new 15-inch muzzle-loaders (each weighing 50 tons) which the British Admiralty had rejected as impracticable. Brin's design was notable on two counts. The first was the long, fore-and-aft 'flying bridge' connecting the superstructure aft with the two funnels and central mast with its observation top. The second was the attempt to give the turrets wider arcs of fire by moving them outboard from the ship's centreline, the forward turret to starboard and the after turret to port. Battleship design over the next 35 years featured many variations on the latter theme before it was realised that the centreline arrangement pioneered by *Devastation*, back in 1871, was in fact the most efficient one.

The appearance of *Duilio* and *Dandolo* (1876) diverted British designers from the promising beginnings made with *Devastation*. The immediate British reaction to these 15-inch gunned ships with their maximum armoured protection of 22 inches was to raise the ante (as had been done 20 years before on the debut of *Gloire*) and build a more powerful version in reply. The result was *Inflexible*, in which the turret guns were 80-ton 16-inchers and the heaviest armoured protection was 24 inches thick. In virtually every respect other than the long flying bridge connecting the funnels, which was left out of the British design, *Inflexible* was a faithful enlargement of *Duilio*; her two turrets were mounted in the same 'back to back' arrangement amidships. The most powerful British battleship of her brief day, *Inflexible* was soon in action during the British bombardment of Alexandria in July 1882. Though the bombardment was the successful prelude to the British military occupation of Egypt, the colossal amount of black powder smoke belched by *Inflexible*'s guns at each shot required long delays until firing could be resumed. This timely demonstration of the nightmarish conditions which would prevail in a fleet action prompted a reassessment of the outsize black-powder muzzle-loaders, hastening the quest for a smokeless propellant explosive.

The most extraordinary experimental battleships produced in the 1870s have often been objects of derisive mirth: Russia's circular-hulled battleships, the *popoffkas* as they were nicknamed after their begetter, Vice-Admiral Popov. The *popoffkas* (the first of which, *Admiral Popov*, appeared in 1875) looked like floating manhole covers, each with twin 12-inch guns nestling between two side-by-side funnels. Though the circular hull soon proved to be the reddest of red herrings, it nevertheless showed the total freedom from traditional design limitations which warship design had reached by the 1870s. The *popoffkas* were also examples of the remarkable breadth of imagination and inventiveness of which Tsarist Russia, despite its lack of industrial development, repeatedly showed itself capable. Popov hit on the idea of the circular hull in his search for the ideal gun platform – the battleship's essential role – which would remain steady regardless of wind and weather. But the *popoffkas*, powered by eight engines driving six screws, were only able to steer a straight course when heading upstream against a strong current. They spun like tops when coming downstream and their decks were flooded by the slightest seaway.

Though ludicrous failures as sea-going warships, the *popoffkas* nevertheless pioneered the new gun mounting, rendered essential by fundamental improvements to the heavy naval gun, which was adopted by all battleship navies over the next 20 years (1875–95). This was the 'barbette', a rotating platform inside an open-topped, armoured cylindrical shield over which the guns projected. The barbette was one answer to the problem imposed by turreted muzzle-loaders, which had to recoil inside the turret to be reloaded. As guns grew bigger and longer, reloading inside the turret became more and more difficult, and keeping the barrels short could only be achieved at the expense of accuracy and range. (One of the many lessons of the American Civil War was the decisive superiority of rifled artillery over smooth-bore, due to the steadying spin given to the departing shell by the gun barrel's spiral rifling; this effect could not be completely achieved in a short-barrelled gun.) As naval guns grew longer, therefore, turret dimensions increased until turrets were bidding fair to take up the entire beam and make the ship dangerously top-heavy.

Reloading, however, was only one of the problems involved with giant muzzle-loaders. Even with the nineteenth century's transformation of steel making, founding and casting, building a gun strong enough at the breech to take the shattering force of the exploding powder charge required an ungainly weapon twice as thick in the breech as in the barrel – and weighing up to 110 tons in the case of the heaviest muzzle-loaders, the 18-inchers. By the 1870s, therefore, the search was on for a propellant explosive which would, as it were, explode slower, giving the shell an accelerating push rather than an instantaneous punch; and for a method of closing the breech of a gun which would be strong enough to take the stress of firing. The latter need was emphasised in 1879 when one of the turreted

Top: Another of the British 'Admirals', HMS *Benbow* was a test-bed for the 110-ton, 16·25-inch gun (firing an 1,800-lb shell) mounted singly in fore and aft barbettes. Developed some 30 years ahead of its time, this huge calibre was not a success and by the middle 1890s the twin 12-inch mounting had become accepted as the norm for battleship main armament.
Above: The after turret of HMS *Conqueror*.

muzzle-loaders in the British *Thunderer* (sister-ship to *Devastation*) burst on firing. It was the easier of the two to meet, profiting from the advent of breech-loading in land-based artillery: the system of the *interrupted screw* in which the breech-block was first closed on a door-like hinge, then locked into place with a twist which meshed the segmented screw thread of the block with that of the interior of the breech.

By the 1880s, therefore, the turreted muzzle-loader was fast giving place to the lighter, longer breech-loader mounted in barbettes. The propellant was still gunpowder, but the slower-burning 'prism brown' instead of the instantaneous 'black pebble'. By the end of the decade a long-term solution had been found with the patenting of cordite in 1889.

Though the turret and barbette had banished the old fixed broadside for good as far as battleship main armament was concerned, none of the latest gunnery developments could change the fact that the most effective way for a battle fleet to unleash its massed fire-power was, as in the sail era, in line-ahead. Evolving new fleet tactics for steam warships was a painful process, for keeping tight formation in speeds over 10 knots allowed little margin for error. This was demonstrated in June 1875 when the battleship *Vanguard*, making an untimely course change while steaming in fog, was rammed and sunk by her next in line (the latter built, as was still the custom, with a ram bow).

Apart from human error such as this, the new battleships were facing a totally different menace by the middle 1880s. This was the self-propelled torpedo, steadily perfected through the late 1860s and 1870s and first used in action (against the rebel Peruvian monitor *Huascar*) in 1877. The torpedo could be launched from small craft, as was demonstrated in the Russo-Turkish War of 1878 when Russian torpedo-boats sank a Turkish revenue cutter with the new weapon. A British battle fleet (*Alexandra, Agincourt, Swiftsure, Sultan, Temeraire,* and *Achilles*) steamed through the Dardanelles to give the Turks moral support by lying off Constantinople; but the fear of attacks by Russian torpedo-boats caused the fleet's prudent withdrawal to the south side of the Sea of Marmara. This was the first time that a battle fleet shied away from the torpedo menace but, as both World Wars were to prove, not the last.

Together with the increased range of heavy guns, the torpedo effectively ended the steam battleship's brief flirtation with close-range actions and ramming tactics. From the moment that the torpedo menace made itself felt, a new element began to be added to the weaponry of battleships: 'secondary' and even 'tertiary' armament, intended to help beat off torpedo attacks while the heavy-calibre main armament dealt with the enemy's battleships. Other anti-torpedo precautions included watertight compartments and false bottoms, and a skirt of anti-torpedo nets which could be swung out on booms to protect the ship at anchor. When under way these booms were secured slantwise on the ship's side, and their distinctive barred pattern remained an unvarying feature of battleships from the 1880s to the First World War.

The appearance of the British *Collingwood* in 1886 summed up all the revolutionary changes of the past 20 years. *Collingwood* was the first battleship to be built of steel throughout instead of iron, or iron-on-wood. In appearance she was as totally unlike the *Inflexible* of only five years earlier as *Inflexible* had been unlike the *Devastation* of 1871, and as *Devastation* had been unlike the *Warrior* of ten years before that. After *Collingwood* and her sister 'Admirals' of the 1880s, it would be seen that the transitional

By the end of the 1880s the traditional masts and yards were vanishing, like the shrinking tail of a maturing frog. This is HMS *Inflexible* as completed, with a full ship-rig in 1881 . . .

. . . and completely re-rigged in 1890.

years of 'one-off', experimental types were over. Sail-carrying masts and fixed broadsides had gone for good. *Collingwood*'s main armament consisted of four 12-inch breech-loaders, twin-mounted in centreline barbettes, and the secondary armament of 6-inch guns; she also carried torpedo-nets. Over the next 25 years the guns would increase in number and in calibre; their arrangement would vary; the hulls which carried the guns would continue to grow, and their armoured protection to increase. For all that, the basic pattern of the modern battleship had been set.

4. THE PRE-DREADNOUGHTS, 1886–1905

Previous pages: HMS *Revenge*, the only 'Royal Sovereign' to serve in the First World War (completed March 1894). Canvas screens over her open barbettes serve as weather protection for the crews of her 13·5-inch guns.

For 30-odd years in which it became little more than a series of experimental prototypes, from the 1850s to the 1880s, the battleship lost what had always been one of its most valuable attributes: longevity in service. From the moment that Dupuy de Lôme's *Gloire* appeared on the scene, it seemed that every new type of battleship was doomed to be rendered obsolete virtually overnight by the next floating prodigy. Whereas an old-style 'wooden wall' would have been good for at least 50 years' service, very few of the experimental battleships introduced after *Warrior* and her immediate successors retained superior combat value for more than ten years; and from the 1870s onward this fell off to five years or less.

It was from the 1880s that a welcome measure of stability was restored to battleship design, and battleships were built some of which were still to be found in service over 25 years later, at the end of the First World War. With all the fundamental debates over steam power, armoured protection and gun armament resolved by the preceding three decades of experimentation, it became possible to order whole classes of new battleships instead of individual units. Though new developments in weaponry and technology kept coming, this new stability permitted at least a measure of deliberate planning instead of the former haphazard additions to the battle fleets.

Before the next big jump forward in battleship design took place with the launch of Britain's famous *Dreadnought* in February 1906, there was an interlude of nearly 20 years. Over this period 'pre-Dreadnought' battleships, as they are commonly known, regardless of the country for which they were built, retained three distinct features in common:

Main armament: of two barbettes or turrets, forward and aft, normally of two guns per turret – calibres 8-/12-inch.

Secondary armament: invariably of more guns than main armament, mounted in small turrets or casemates in hull sides – calibres 3-/9-inch.

Tertiary armament: again of more guns than secondary armament, with light or no protection – calibres up to 3-inch.

Thus the invariable distinguishing features of the pre-Dreadnought battleship were the proportionally modest, two-turret main armament pioneered by Britain's *Devastation* back in 1871, and a bristling array of secondary and tertiary armament. And the so-called 'Dreadnought revolution' after 1905 stemmed from the growing realisation that secondary and tertiary armaments had become more of a hindrance than a help. Though certainly adding to the battleship's overall repertoire of fire-power, they were a distraction from the battleship's traditional role: a platform for the greatest possible number of heavy guns.

As explained in the previous chapter, secondary and tertiary armaments had been adopted in the 1880s to help counter the torpedo-boat menace. In the 1890s a new type of anti-torpedo-boat light warship entered service, the 'torpedo-boat destroyer', soon referred to by the last word alone for the sake of convenience. It was obvious from the start that destroyers, in beating off enemy torpedo-boat attacks, would be ideally placed to carry out torpedo attacks of their own on the enemy battle line. They were therefore armed with torpedo tubes as well as light guns in the 3–4-inch bracket, and became torpedo-boats themselves. But there could be no absolute guarantee that enemy torpedo-boats or destroyers would be unable to penetrate the defensive destroyer screen. It was therefore considered perfectly reasonable for battleships to retain powerful subsidiary armaments capable of taking out enemy destroyers, even as close as the optimum torpedo-dropping range of a mile or less, while the main armament concentrated on bombarding the enemy battle line.

Though it has always been axiomatic that trying to provide for every situation rarely produces satisfactory results, the pre-Dreadnought's typical multiplicity of armament therefore made sense, at least in theory. It must always be remembered that the pre-Dreadnought's heyday was long before the introduction of the fire control of all guns from a central director – the first step in converting the battleship into a truly integrated weapons system. Whether every gun in the ship hit the target or missed depended on the prowess of the individual gunlayers, and the gunlayers' test was one of the most crucial events in fleet gunnery shoots. As long as gunlayers' firing prevailed – as it did until the eve of the First World War – the separation of battleship fire-power into long, medium, and short-range capacities remained the order of the day.

Providing fire-power of varying ranges for a fleet action in the new torpedo era was only one justification for the pre-Dreadnought's 'multi-layer' armament. It will also be recalled that the battleship's use in bombarding fleets caught at anchor and

Launch of Germany's *Fürst Bismarck* in September 1897. Behind the pageantry lay the phenomenon of Germany's bid for modern sea power – and the mounting tension of the Anglo-German naval building race.

shore strongpoints had always rivalled its use in fleet actions against enemy battle lines at sea. Certainly the destruction of the Spanish fleet in Manila Bay by Commodore George Dewey's American Pacific Squadron, in the Spanish-American War (1 May 1898) indicated that subsidiary armament was of the highest value in the bombardment role.

In the age of sail one of the perennial debates had been whether or not a well-handled heavy frigate could take on a poorly-handled fourth-rate ship of the line; and by the time of the pre-Dreadnoughts, at the end of the nineteenth century, the question had evolved with the ships and was still relevant. Undergoing a similar metamorphosis to the sailing ship of the line, the sailing frigate had grown into the steam cruiser, the heaviest classes of which were armoured. Though the cruiser's primary roles remained those of the sailing frigate, to patrol the sea-lanes in strength and scout for the battle fleet, a rising question was whether or not armoured cruisers were fit to take their place in the line of battle. Despite its antique origins the question really referred to the armoured cruiser's design as a battleship-in-miniature, complete with secondary and tertiary armaments; and these were used to excellent effect at Manila Bay.

Though undeniably helped by wretched Spanish gunnery throughout, Dewey's squadron still had to penetrate Manila Bay under battery fire from Corregidor and El Fraile islands, and attack the Spanish ships (eight in all) as they lay protected by shore batteries at Cavite. The four American cruisers had ample fire-power for the job. Dewey's flagship, the armoured cruiser USS *Olympia* (launched 1892) had a main armament of four 8-inch guns in two twin turrets, a secondary armament of ten 5-inch guns and a tertiary armament of 14 6-pounders – a perfect miniature pre-Dreadnought. Having silenced the island batteries on his entrance into Manila Bay, Dewey approached the Spanish ships where they lay at anchor and destroyed them in four east-to-west passes, using his ships' port and starboard batteries in succession. Without secondary batteries, Dewey's ships would have been deprived of nearly 70 per cent of their fire-power. As it was they suffered only seven men wounded (Spanish guns only scoring five hits) while landing no less than 171 hits on the Spanish ships, not one of which survived.

In passing it may be added that as well as justifying pre-Dreadnought fire-power at

Britain's 'Majestics' were easily distinguishable by their side-by-side funnels. This is HMS *Caesar*, seventh of the class to be completed (January 1898).

Manila Bay, *Olympia* went on to demonstrate the useful longevity recovered by capital ships of her era. She served throughout the First World War (if only on convoy escort duty) and was not finally taken out of commission until 1922 – 30 years after her launch. Her last mission was to bring home the body of the American Unknown Soldier for burial in Washington's Arlington National Cemetery. Apart from Japan's *Mikasa*, *Olympia* is the only surviving heavy warship of the pre-Dreadnought era, lying on public view at Penn's landing, Philadelphia.

Because of her ocean-connected world empire and its unique naval requirements, Britain inevitably fought to keep the lead in pre-Dreadnought battleship construction. Since the days of sail, when the British fleet had frequently to contend with combinations of two or more enemy fleets (Trafalgar being the classic example) the strength of the battle fleet had been maintained to a theoretical 'Two-Power Standard' – the ability to fight and beat the fleets of two hostile powers combined. This ability had of course been largely destroyed by the melting-pot years of 1860–90, in which every new battleship would have been able to beat its latest predecessor with ease. But after the 'Admiral' class battleships of the 1880s of which *Collingwood* was the forerunner, Britain's Naval Defence Act of 1889 sought to recover the Two-Power Standard by ordering a whole squadron of the most powerful new battleships which could be contrived.

The first-fruits of the Naval Defence Act were the seven ships of the 'Royal Sovereign' class (1892–94) – *Royal Sovereign*, *Royal Oak*, *Revenge*, *Ramillies*, *Resolution*, *Repulse* and *Empress of India*. Of these all but *Revenge* had been struck off the effective list and disposed of by 1914, only *Revenge* being retained in service as the oldest British battleship to serve in the First World War. The 'Royal Sovereigns' retained the main armament arrangement of the 'Admirals': four guns in open barbettes, but 13·5-inch guns instead of 12-inch. (As soon as the stocks of 13·5-inch shell had been used up, the guns were relined to take the 12-inch calibre favoured as standard British battleship main armament down to 1910.) The secondary armament consisted of ten single 6-inch guns in casemates, and the tertiary armament of up to 12 3-pounders; there were also two torpedo-tubes, mounted forward below the waterline.

After the muzzle-loading gun, with its short range and flat trajectory, had given place to breech-loaders capable of achieving

French *Jaureguiberry* (1897) with her single-mounted 12-inch main armament and massive 10·8-inch wing turrets. Typical French pre-Dreadnought features: heavy masts, high freeboard and exaggerated sloped sides or 'tumble-home' – nearly all to be found in Russian battleships of the same period.

greater range by firing at higher angles of elevation, it became necessary to armour horizontal surfaces against plunging fire as well as the ship's sides and barbettes. In the 'Royal Sovereigns' the main armour belt of 14–16 inches was therefore supplemented by deck armour 2½–3 inches thick.

The last of the 'Royal Sovereigns' had still to be completed when, in February 1894, the first of the next generation of pre-Dreadnoughts was laid down. This was the 'Majestic' class, completed between December 1895 and April 1898 – *Majestic, Caesar, Hannibal, Illustrious, Jupiter, Magnificent, Mars, Prince George* and *Victorious*. Apart from the archaic side-by-side arrangement of their funnels, the 'Majestics' set the pattern for all succeeding pre-Dreadnoughts and they were unique, the most numerous single class of battleship ever ordered by any navy. The reason for this was the manifest superiority of the 'Majestics' over the 'Royal Sovereigns' which, if prematurely attained by any hostile navy, would clearly liquidate Britain's naval supremacy at a stroke. In every sense the 'Majestics' represented the final end of the years of transition and the true beginning of the modern battleship era. They pioneered the new cordite-firing 12-inch gun and an entirely new look in armoured protection; otherwise, in dimensions and speed, the 'Majestics' were roughly comparable to the 'Royal Sovereigns'.

The new armour consisted of specially hardened (Harveyized) steel, saving the considerable deadweight created merely by adding further layers of conventional steel. The barbettes of the main armament were now topped by armoured turrets 10 inches thick, giving the gun crews an unprecedented degree of protection. The 'brain' of the ship, the command centre, was also given more protection with a 14-inch armoured conning tower, and the deck armour was increased to 4 inches. The secondary armament was increased to 12 6-inch guns and the tertiary armament to 16 12-pounders and 12 3-pounders.

Completed as they were within a six-year period, the 16 'Royal Sovereigns' and 'Majestics' gave Britain an overwhelming lead in modern battleship strength. During the same six years it was obvious that no other naval power was anywhere near matching the British either in numbers or speed of battleship production. Britain's old rival, France, was the most notable example: she was still in the process of adding individual units to her battle fleet, not whole classes, and taking twice as long about it at that. The *Jaureguiberry*, laid down in

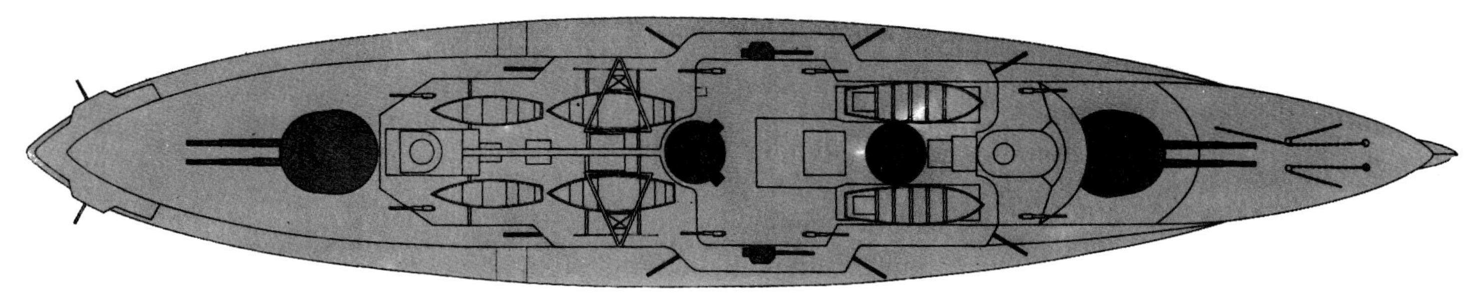

Above : Gun plan of the French *St Louis*, completed February 1900: four 12-inch, ten 5-inch, eight 3·39-inch (below).
Bottom : Tsesarevich (1903), showing the unmistakable stamp of French design and building.

April 1891, was not completed until February 1897, and carried only two 12-inch guns in single mountings; a particularly grave weakness was that her main armour belt did not extend to cover the magazines. *Jaureguiberry*, like her contemporary *Bouvet* (completed in 1898) also carried the pre-Dreadnought imbalance between main and subsidiary armaments to almost ludicrous extremes. The two single 12-inch guns of the main armament were supplemented by two 10·8-inch guns mounted on massive beam sponsons, plus eight 5·5-inch guns. Where *Jaureguiberry* had a tertiary armament of 14 47-mm guns, *Bouvet* had eight 3·9-inchers and ten 3-pounders. The French reply to Britain's 'Majestics' was the three-unit 'St Louis' class: *Charlemagne, Gaulois* and *St Louis* (completed in 1898, 1899 and 1900), which at least finally achieved a four-gun 12-inch main armament and dropped the sponson-mounted 10·8-inchers. Though decisively outnumbered and already obsolescent when they finally entered service, these French pre-Dreadnoughts had one worrying advantage over the 'Majestics' – speed. At 17–18 knots they were nearly 2 knots faster than the British ships.

After the fright which *Duilio* and *Dandolo* had given the British Admiralty in the late 1870s, Italian battleship design had lost direction and the only two Italian contemporaries of the 'Majestics', *Ammiraglio di St Bon* and *Emanuele Filiberto*, were obvious imitations. They took even longer to complete than their French contemporaries, *Ammiraglio di St Bon* not being completed until September 1900 and *Emanuele Filiberto* in April 1902; both had been laid down in 1893. They were distinguished by their low freeboard between waterline and deck, adequate only for Mediterranean sea conditions. The Italians, moreover, opted for the lighter 10-inch gun in order to achieve comparable armoured protection and a speed of 18 knots.

Nor was any real challenge to the British battleship supremacy likely from Russia, whose ships retained the remarkable blend of modernity and inadequacy proclaimed with the experimental *popoffkas* in the 1870s. The *Georgi Pobiedonosets* (completed 1894) was the first warship fitted with electrically-powered turrets and ammunition hoists; her main armament consisted of three twin 12-inch turrets, two of them forward-firing, positioned side by side, and one aft. Her sister-ship *Sinope* (completed 1898) was the first warship with triple-expansion engines. But *Sinope*'s armament was an imbalanced mix of four 8-inch and 12 6-inch guns; and by the time of the Russo-Japanese War in 1904 not even the most modern Russian battleships had been fitted with electric ignition gear to fire the guns, as adopted in all other leading navies. The same contradictions were to be found in *Rostislav*, laid down in 1894 and completed in 1899: the world's first oil-fired battleship, with the eight 6-inch guns of her secondary armament mounted in twin turrets – the last a feature some 30 years ahead of its general adoption by other navies. Yet *Rostislav*'s

main armament consisted only of four 10-inch guns.

As a direct result of the Franco-Russian *entente* the Russians looked to the French for the newest ideas in battleship design, not the British. Russian pre-Dreadnoughts aped the predominating French characteristics: high freeboard and massive masts and funnels which made for top-heaviness, and indifferently distributed armoured protection. In May 1899 the French began work on the prototype of a new Russian pre-Dreadnought class, the other five being built in Russian yards. The prototype was *Tsesarevich*, completed in August 1903, and the Russian copies were *Kniaz Suvorov, Imperator Aleksandr III, Borodino, Orel* and *Slava.* Like their French-derived predecessors *Petropavlovsk, Sevastopol* and *Poltava* (1891–98) these newest Russian battleships included the top-heaviness and exaggerated 'tumble-home', or inward sloping of the hull sides, so characteristic of French design.

Given the rapidly approaching showdown between Russia and Japan, it was unfortunate for the Russians that the Japanese Navy looked to the British, not the French, for the most modern ideas in training and warship design. The Japanese Navy was a prodigy: the newest in the world, commenced only after the 'Meiji Restoration' of 1867–68 had begun Japan's conversion from a medieval to a modern state. To build a modern fleet, Japanese practice was to order prototypes from Britain, then improve on them. The first Japanese battleship was *Fuji*, completed in August 1897 – basically a 'Royal Sovereign' with improved 12-inch armament. From lessons learned during *Fuji*'s construction in England, and her British-built successors *Hatsuse* and *Yashima*, the Japanese laid down the first of their excellent 'Asahi' class battleships in 1897, backbone of the force which pulverised the Russians at Tsushima only seven years later.

Across the Atlantic the United States Navy also began to create a battle fleet in the 1890s. *Indiana, Massachusetts* and *Oregon* (BBs 1, 2 and 3) were inevitably unsatisfactory, the result of trying to get a quart into a pint pot; their hull size was too modest for the four 13-inch guns they carried, and their low freeboard made them unsuitable for Atlantic service. These faults were corrected in *Iowa* (BB4, completed in 1897) which carried four 12-inch guns.

The next eight American pre-Dread-

Top: Indiana (1895), American coast-defence battleship with low freeboard.
Bottom: Kearsarge (1900) with her distinctive 'double-deck' turret arrangement (twin 8-inch atop twin 13-inch) – not a success but repeated, with no better results, in the five 'Virginias' laid down six years later

Germany's first coast-defence battleships. *Above : Heimdall* (1894), with her side-by-side 9·4-inch forward mountings. *Right :* 'Wörth' class *Brandenburg* (1893) with centreline twin 9·4-inch turrets.

noughts were all armed with 13-inch main armament. *Kearsarge* and *Kentucky* (BBs 5 and 6, both completed in 1900) featured a highly unorthodox (and unworkable) experiment: double-deck turrets, with twin 13-inch turrets fore and aft each topped with a twin 8-inch turret. The idea was to save deadweight by making one armoured barbette support two turrets, but as the 8-inch and 13-inch guns were housed by the same structure all it did was prevent the 8-inch guns from being allocated different targets to the main armament. Orthodox twin 13-inch turrets were carried by *Illinois, Wisconsin* and *Alabama* (BBs 7–9, completed in 1900–01). These ships closely resembled Britain's 'Majestics', even to the side-by-side funnels. *Maine, Missouri* and *Ohio* (BBs 10–12, completed in 1902–04) gave the double-decked 13-inch/8-inch combination another try. But all of the subsequent 19 battleships laid down between April 1902 and February 1910 ('Virginia', 'Connecticut', 'South Carolina', 'Delaware', 'Florida' and 'Wyoming' classes, BBs 13–22 and 25–33) reverted to the 12-inch gun as long as it remained the heaviest gun in service with other battleship navies.

Japan and the United States were not alone in gaining 'battleship status' for their navies in the 1890s. The third power to do so was the German Empire, which for the first

20 years after its creation in 1871 seemed content with a small, coast-defence naval force. A move to give more muscle to this lightweight force inherited from the kingdom of Prussia began in August 1889, when the prototype *Siegfried* was launched at Kiel. Like her successors – *Beowulf, Frithjof, Heimdall, Hildebrand* and *Hagen* (completed 1890–94) followed by *Odin* and *Ägir* (completed 1896), *Siegfried*'s modest armament consisted of three 9·4-inch guns in single turrets, one aft and two side by side forward. The 9·4-inch gun was also mounted in the four 'Wörths' (completed 1893–94), but these ships greatly excelled the 'Siegfrieds' in size and fire-power. They carried three twin 9·4-inch turrets, all on the centreline, a secondary armament of eight 4·1-inch and a tertiary armament of eight 3·4-inch. Subsidiary armament was increased still further with the first of the 'Kaiser' class, *Kaiser Friedrich III*, launched in July 1896. The 'Kaisers' featured the conventional two-turret main armament (of four 9·4-inch), a very strong secondary armament of 14 5·9 inch (18 in *Karl der Grosse*, laid down in 1898) and a tertiary armament of 12 3·4-inch.

Thus by 1898 the British were confronted by a German Navy which had completed 12 new battleships in seven years, with two new hulls already launched and another three in hand. In the same period Britain's traditional naval rival, France, had only laid down six new battleships, none of which were anywhere near completion. Of course it was true that these new German battleships were cast strictly in the coast-defence role, which in Germany's case extended to the Russians in the Baltic as well as the British and French in the North Sea and Channel. It was also true that the new German battle fleet was easily outgunned by the Royal Navy. The fact remained that Britain was now faced with a North Sea naval power which was confidently expanding its battle fleet at a pace surpassed only by the British.

British apprehensions about the ultimate strategic function of the new German fleet were confirmed in 1898 by the promulgation of the German Navy Law. This announced the next class of German battleship, the five 'Wittelsbachs', and laid down the planned strength of the German Navy by 1903 at 27 capital ships. As only eight of these (the 'Siegfrieds') were designated as coast-defence ships, and as the allocated force for service overseas consisted only of 20 cruisers, it was obvious that the German fleet was to be concentrated in home waters as a growing rival to the Royal Navy. This was confirmed by the second German Navy Law of 1900, which raised the objective to a strength of 38 battleships and could not be

Below : Kaiser Friedrich III (completed 1898).

Above : HMS *Canopus* (1899), a reduced version of the 'Majestic' design but with funnels fore-and-aft.
Left : Quarter stern view of sister-ship HMS *Goliath* (1900), showing stern gallery and torpedo-net booms.
Top right : 'King Edward VII' class HMS *Hindustan* (1905).
Below right : Gun plans of (*centre*) British 'King Edward VII' class (four 12-inch, four 9·2-inch, ten 6-inch) and (*bottom*) German 'Braunschweig' class (four 11-inch, 14 6·7-inch, 14 3·4-inch).

separated in context from the vicious anti-British propaganda, fomented in Germany during Britain's struggle with the Boers in the South African War (1899–1902).

The British reaction was swift. In addition to the six 'Canopus' class battleships being built to follow the 'Majestics', Britain laid down no less than 14 new battleships – 'Formidable', 'London', 'Queen' and 'Duncan' classes – between 1898 and 1901, and the first four of eight 'King Edward VIIs' in 1902. Germany's unabashed riposte was to lay down five 'Braunschweigs' in 1901–02, followed by the first of five 'Deutschlands' in 1903.

It was against the background of this quickening 'Anglo-German Building Race' that the world's navies were given a demonstration of the brutal realities of modern naval warfare: the Russo-Japanese War of 1904–05, and the clash of the battle fleets at Tsushima.

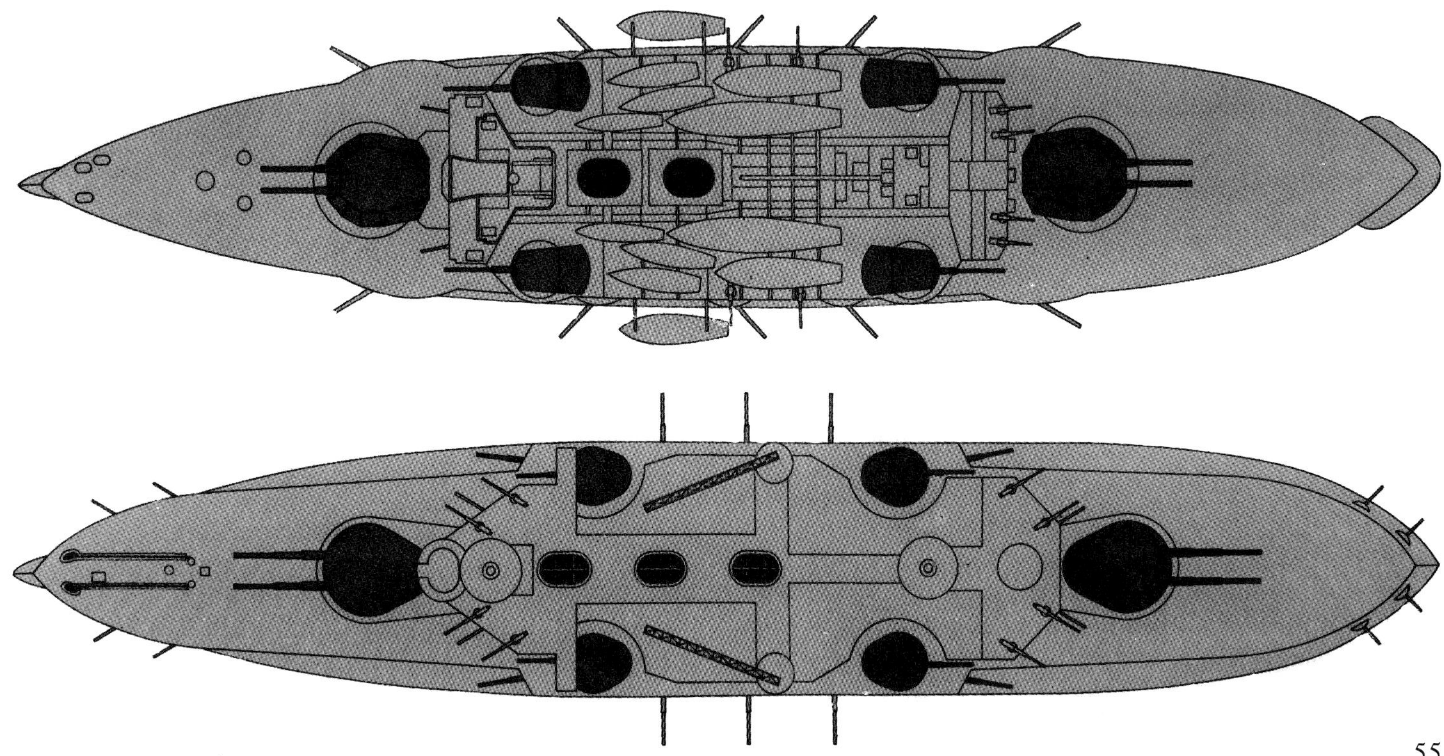

5. THE IMPACT OF TSUSHIMA, 1905

Previous pages: Russia's luckiest battleship in a wholly unlucky war – *Tsesarevich*, which survived the mines and shells of Port Arthur and avoided the disaster of Tsushima by being interned after the Battle of the Yellow Sea (10 August 1904).

THE ISSUE BEHIND the Russo-Japanese War of 1904–05 was the question of which power would hold the monopoly of dominating the northern provinces of the moribund Chinese Empire: Japan or Russia. In the brief but bloody Sino-Japanese War of 1894–95, a victorious Japan had won Formosa, control of a nominally independent Korea, and the Manchurian base of Port Arthur (Lü-shun) – only to be forced, by international pressure brought to bear by Russia, to give up Port Arthur (April 1895). Since then the Russians had occupied Port Arthur by force (December 1897), bullied China into a formal lease of the base to Russia (March 1898) and consistently undermined Japan's dominance over Korea. A Russo-Japanese showdown was inevitable and it was anticipated with confidence by both sides. Japan was determined to recover Port Arthur, relying on her *samurai* tradition and the excellence of her modern, European-moulded armed forces. Russia, eager for a glorious Far Eastern war to quash domestic discontent, was the first of many Western powers to make the mistake of despising the Japanese on racial grounds and discounting their ability to wage effective modern war against Europeans.

Port Arthur was the focus of the war of 1904, which turned on sea power. To eject the Russians from Port Arthur in Manchuria by shipping troops to neighbouring Korea, the Japanese needed to seize and keep command of the sea in order to supply and reinforce their troops, and prevent Russian reinforcements being shipped in to Port Arthur. To frustrate these aims, the Russian naval forces at Port Arthur and Vladivostok would have to operate as wings of the same fleet and keep the initiative from the start; and they believed they could do this with ease. In the words of Rear-Admiral Vitjevt, Chief of Staff of the Russian Far East Fleet, 'Our fleet cannot be beaten by the Japanese Fleet, either in the Gulf of Korea or in the Yellow Sea', and wrote off the Japanese chances of landing troops in Korea as 'absolutely impossible'. In time-honoured style, hubris earned the inevitable penalty of nemesis.

At the end of January 1904 the Russians had seven battleships, six cruisers, 25 destroyers, two torpedo gunboats and two minelayers at Port Arthur, with another four cruisers and 17 torpedo-boats at Vladivostok. In the face of this array, Admiral Heihachiro Togo's Japanese fleet numbered six battleships, 14 cruisers, 19 destroyers and 16 torpedo-boats. Confident in their numerical superiority, which indeed left Togo with no margin for one-sided losses, the Russians at Port Arthur complacently believed that the Japanese would have to be brought to action and would certainly not open hostilities. As a result no precautions were taken to guard against the savage pre-emptive strike, without formal severance of diplomatic relations or declaration of war, which Togo launched at Port Arthur just after midnight on the night of 8–9 February 1904.

Togo's overriding objective was to permit the transfer of the Japanese expeditionary force to Korea and Manchuria by making it impossible for the Port Arthur fleet to put to sea. The aim was to gain numerical superiority – without putting a single Japanese battleship at risk – by sinking or rendering unfit for sea as many Russian battleships as possible. Togo's pre-emptive attack on the Russian fleet has justly been compared with the carrier strike at Pearl Harbor in December 1941; but though the tactical objectives were the same in both cases, the Port Arthur attack went off at half-cock. The opening strike was carried out by torpedo-boats which fired 18 torpedoes into the brightly-lit anchorage, scoring damaging hits on the 12-inch gun battleships *Retvizan* and *Tsesarevich* and the cruiser *Pallada; Retvizan* and *Pallada* had to be beached. At a stroke, Togo was thus presented with a superiority of six Japanese 12-inch gun battleships (*Fuji, Yashima, Hatsuse, Mikasa, Asahi* and *Shikishima*) against three Russian 12-inch gun battleships (*Petropavlovsk, Poltava* and *Sevastopol*) and two 10-inch gun battleships (*Pobieda* and *Peresviet*). But the Japanese torpedo-boats, not being fitted with the newfangled wireless signal apparatus, were unable to summon Togo's intact battle fleet for a decisive follow-up bombardment. By the time Togo attempted this later on the 9th the Russian shore batteries were fully alerted, and Togo withdrew after the battle ensign of his flagship *Mikasa* had twice been brought down by Russian shells.

Yet the vital first trick had been won, and Togo's fleet blockaded Port Arthur while the Japanese Army crossed unmolested into Manchuria and advanced on Port Arthur from the landward. Though badly shaken by the initial Japanese attack the Russians by no means despaired and set about repairing their damaged ships. Togo's attempt to seal them in with 27 blockships was foiled later in February by excellent Russian practice with searchlights and shore bat-

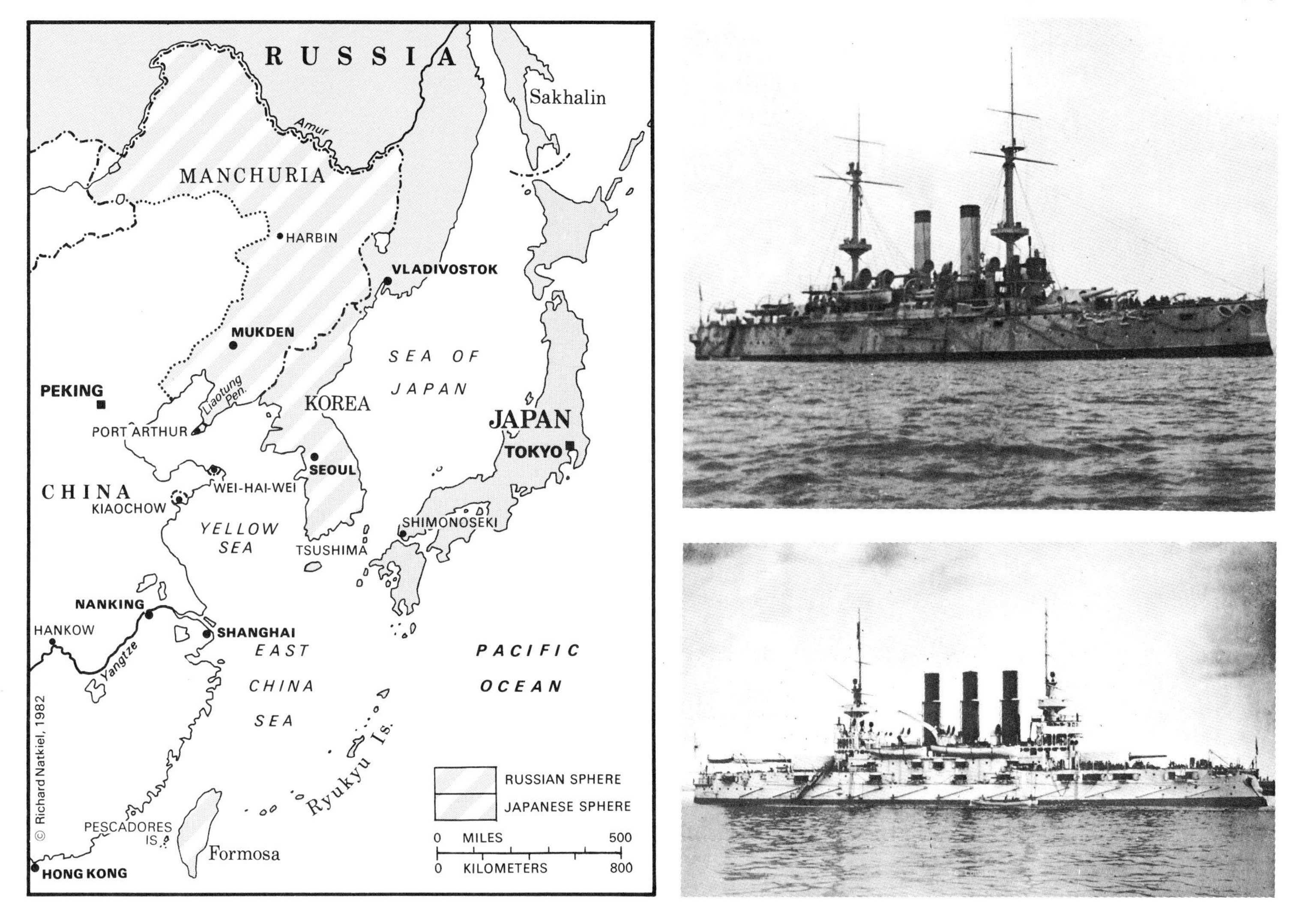

Top left: The main battle zones of the Russo-Japanese War of 1904–05, showing the dominant position of the Russian base at Port Arthur.
Top: The British-built *Fuji*, whose sister-ship *Yashima* was mined and sunk off Port Arthur.
Above: Retvizan, damaged and beached in Togo's first strike at Port Arthur, but salvaged and taken into Japanese service after the war as *Hizen*.

teries. Meanwhile Admiral Stark was made the scapegoat for the setback of 9 February and replaced as C-in-C by Admiral Makarov, the most popular and inspiring leader in the Russian Navy. Makarov's arrival in Port Arthur on 8 March after running the Japanese blockade sent Russian morale soaring, but not for long. On 13 April Makarov was lost when his flagship *Petropavlovsk* sank with immense loss of life after hitting a mine, while *Pobieda* was damaged by another mine. Makarov was succeeded in command by Vitjevt, who knew that even if all the damaged Russian battleships could be perfectly restored to fighting condition, Togo's battle fleet still out-gunned them.

Vitjevt therefore held strictly to the defensive, pinning his hopes on mining the approaches to Port Arthur regardless of international law and the theoretical sanctity of the high seas outside territorial waters. Inglorious though this tactic was, it soon bore dramatic results. On 15 May Togo lost two of his British-built battleships, *Hatsuse* and *Yashima*, to mines laid the previous day. Though Togo had lost his battleship superiority he grimly maintained his blockade, knowing that the Japanese Army was already closing in on Port Arthur from the north. On 23 June the growing urgency of the Russian position was revealed by Vitjevt taking his fleet to sea, under orders to break the Japanese blockade. Togo did the only thing he could and deployed his fleet in battle order across the Russians' course. This resolute sight unnerved Vitjevt and he took his fleet back into Port Arthur. On the night of the 23rd Togo launched another torpedo attack. It scored no hits but *Sevastopol*, manoeuvring to avoid torpedoes, blundered on to a mine and sustained heavy damage. The blockade continued.

By the end of July, with the Japanese siege-lines now drawn so tight around Port Arthur that the Russian fleet was coming under artillery fire from the landward, it was clear that the end was in sight. Vitjevt prepared to break out regardless of losses to take his surviving ships to Vladivostok, and sortied on 10 August with six battleships, four cruisers and eight destroyers. Togo was waiting for him with four battleships, four cruisers, 17 destroyers. The resultant Battle of the Yellow Sea began at the unprecedented range of 14,000 yards in the afternoon of 10 August, Togo declining to hazard his battleships and risk driving the Russians back in to Port Arthur by a rash early engagement. It was not until 17.30 hours that the range came down to 8,000 yards and a general engagement began. For

Togo's flagship *Mikasa* at Tsushima, flying his Nelsonic signal 'The fate of the Empire depends on this event. Let every man do his utmost'.

大勝利
露艦○ワリヤーグ
○コレーツ
二隻ヲ轟沈セシム

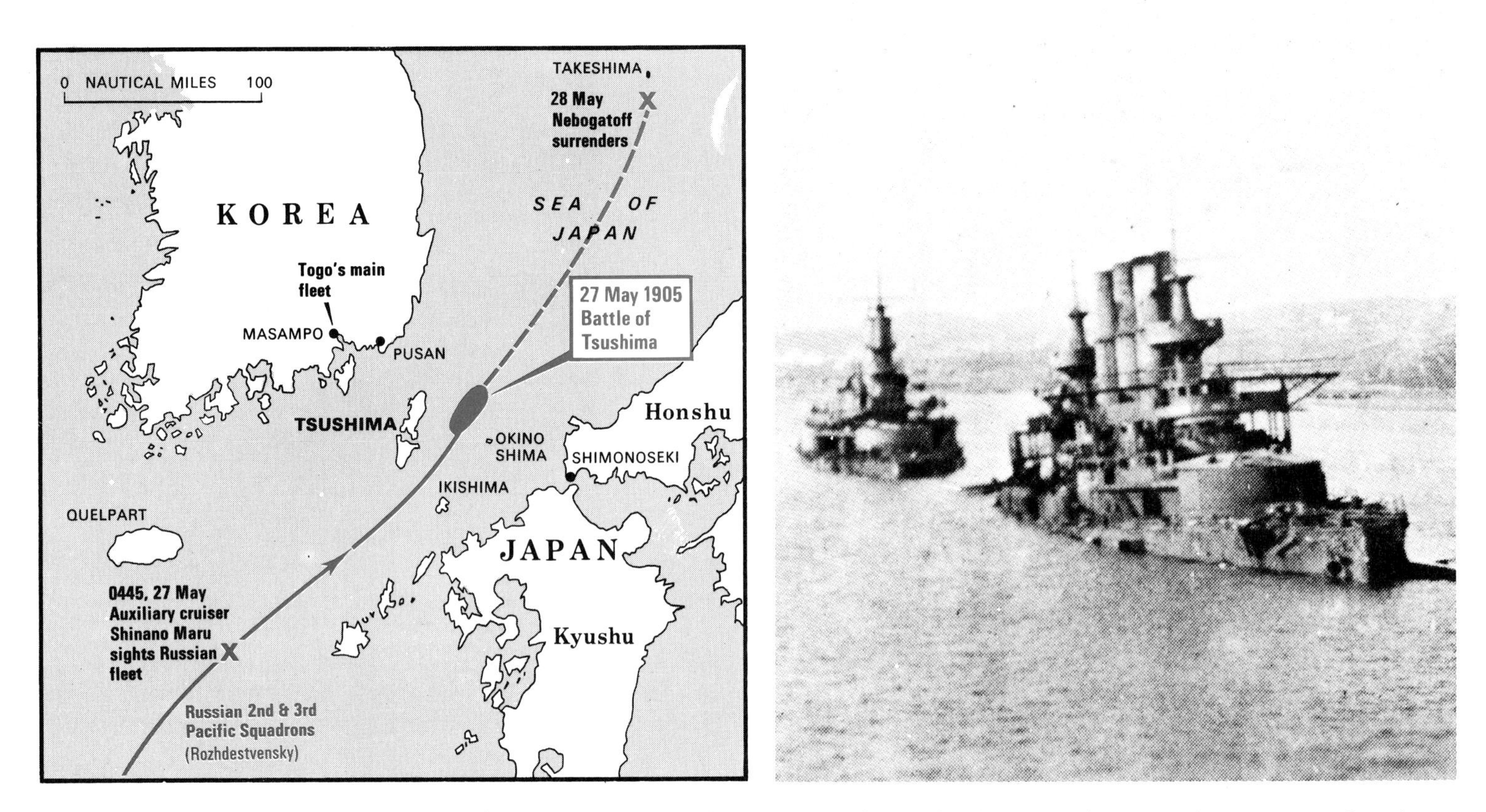

Above right: *Pobieda* and *Peresviet*, scuttled at Port Arthur. Like *Retvizan* they were salvaged and entered Japanese service as *Suwo* and *Sagami*.
Above: Tsushima, the opening phase.
Opposite page: Accurately fed with information by the cruisers shadowing the oncoming Russians, Togo's battle fleet steams out to engage in line-ahead.

an hour the issue hung in the balance, the Russians stoutly maintaining their fire and managing to inflict considerable superficial damage on the Japanese fleet. By 18.40, however, it was all over. Three minutes before two Japanese 12-inch shells had hit Vitjevt's flagship *Tsesarevich*, killing the Admiral, his flag staff, and all ship's executive officers in the conning-tower. With the helm jammed hard over, *Tsesarevich* reeled out of the line and the leaderless fleet broke up in confusion, saved from total destruction only by the falling of darkness. Though badly battered in the action, five battleships, a cruiser and three destroyers fled back to Port Arthur. *Tsesarevich*, two cruisers and a destroyer were interned in neutral ports, another cruiser was beached and destroyed on the Shantung coast, and the cruiser *Novik* was trapped and sunk off Sakhalin (21 August) by a Japanese cruiser squadron.

Though Togo maintained the blockade of Port Arthur with his damaged fleet, the Russians never sortied again. The siege of Port Arthur took its relentless course until, in December, the surviving Russian warships came under the fire of 11-inch Japanese siege howitzers. One by one they were sunk, with the exception of *Sevastopol* which was scuttled in deep water just before the Port Arthur garrison surrendered on 2 January 1905. In the 11 months since the outbreak of war, the Russian Navy had lost seven battleships, seven cruisers, 33 destroyers, torpedo-boats and minelayers sunk, captured, or driven into neutral internment; the Japanese had lost only two battleships, two protected cruisers, two destroyers and four torpedo-boats. They planned to make good their battleship losses by taking possession of the bottomed hulks at Port Arthur, salvaging them for repair and continued service under Japanese colours – *Retvizan* as *Hizen*, *Peresviet* as *Sagami*, *Pobieda* as *Suwo*, *Poltava* as *Tango*.

But the Port Arthur triumph only marked the end of the first phase of the naval war of 1904–05. Togo knew that the captured Russian battleships would not be ready for service before he would have to deal with a new threat. This was the amazing cruise of the Russian Baltic Fleet from the Gulf of Finland round the world to the Tsushima Straits, bent on avenging the humiliations of the Port Arthur campaign.

The cruise of the Baltic Fleet remains one of the most audacious concepts and achievements in the history of modern naval warfare. Spee's war cruise in 1914, the formation of the British Pacific Fleet in 1945 and the despatch of the South Atlantic Task Force

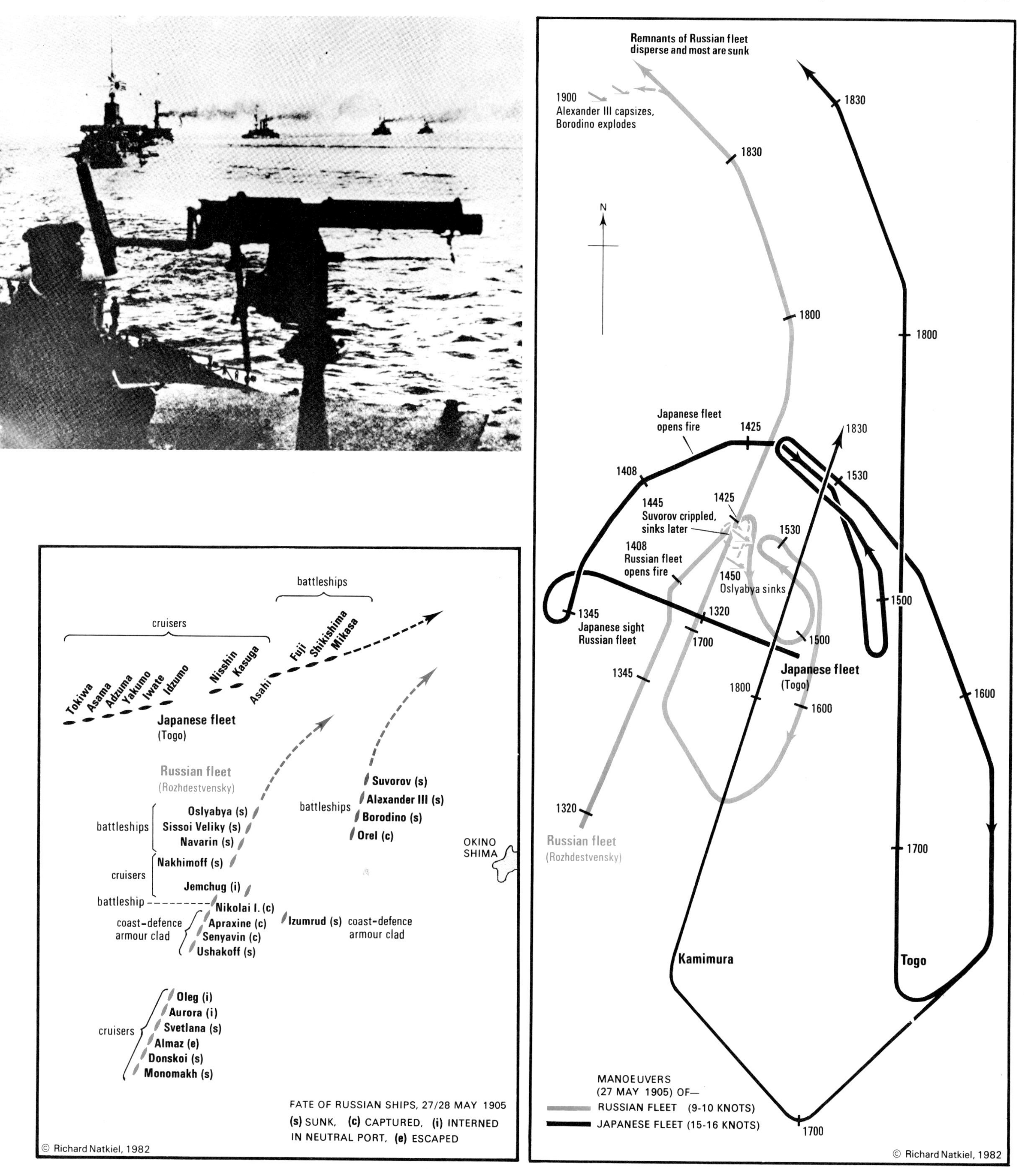

Left and above: Togo's brilliant manoeuvring at Tsushima concentrated the heaviest Japanese fire against Rozhestvensky's leading ships.

in 1982 were nothing by comparison. Even in the age of sail there had been nothing to touch it, with the possible exceptions of the circumnavigations of Drake in 1577–80 and Anson in 1740–44: a voyage 18,000 miles long without a single Russian supply base anywhere along the route, and action against a well-armed, battle-tested enemy fleet waiting at journey's end. And this was achieved by a fleet of steam warships dependent on mountains of coal – not oil fuel, which can be replenished by the simple technique of pumping it along a hose.

The decision to transfer the Baltic Fleet to the Far East was taken on 20 June 1904, when the Port Arthur fleet was still in being,

'Samurai-style' Japanese print of a 6-inch gun crew, with suitably heroic expressions, in the heat of the action.

and the plan envisaged an eventual union of the two fleets in overwhelming strength. The Baltic Fleet command and the whole epic mission were entrusted to Admiral Zinovi Petrovich Rozhestvensky, who after heroic struggles with Tsarist bureaucracy managed to assemble a motley supply fleet to get his warships at least as far as the Indian Ocean. When he received the news of Port Arthur's fall, Rozhestvensky had got no further than Nossi Bé in Madagascar. The voyage out had been a nightmare, starting with a full-blooded fiasco in the North Sea on the night of 22 October, only a week after departure. Panicky Russian gunners fired on British trawlers off the Dogger Bank, believing them to be Japanese torpedo-boats (not such a lunatic assumption as it would appear, given the Japanese Navy's reliance on the products of British shipyards). Fulsome apologies saved the Russians from a fleet action with the British Channel Fleet, which was nevertheless at battle stations as the Russians passed down-Channel. Diplomatic wranglings had attended every coaling stop: at Vigo (1 November 1904), Tangier (6 November), Dakar (16 November), Libreville (1 December), Mossamedes (7 December) and Lüderitz (16 December). The news of the destruction of the Port Arthur Fleet meant that the original plan lay in ruins. And the sailors of the fleet were, from January 1905, increasingly disaffected by the news of domestic workers' unrest at home, heavily censored though the reports were.

Rozhestvensky's decision to press on from Madagascar, hoping to bring the Japanese fleet to action before it could make good the wear and tear of the Port Arthur campaign, was therefore uniquely courageous in view of the difficulties surrounding him at every turn. Those difficulties were increased by the news that he was to be joined by Rear-Admiral Nebogatov's antique squadron which was derided even by optimistic Russians as 'auto-sinkers', and which Rozhestvensky had begged the Russian Ministry of Marine to keep at home. Nebogatov's 'auto-sinkers', which came out through the Mediterranean and Suez Canal, consisted of the old coastal battleship *Imperator Nikolai I*, an armoured cruiser, three coastal defence ships and seven auxiliaries. When they joined Rozhestvensky off Indo-China they became the latest millstone round his woefully tired neck.

It was on the voyage from Madagascar to the Far East (16 March–26 May) that the Russian Navy achieved yet another 'first': the first successful ship-to-ship refuelling carried out while under way. This innovation, the basis of all protracted modern-day fleet operations, was forced on the Russians by the unique demands of the voyage.

Against all odds, Rozhestvensky's 'Second Pacific Fleet' sailed from its last replenishment-stop on the Indo-Chinese coast on 14 May 1905, the final lap reached at last. Its progress was consistently reported all the way up the China Sea, contact being lost on the 25th but regained on the night of the 26th. The latter news was radioed to Togo where he lay at Mesampo Bay on the

Korean coast, planning to engage the Russian fleet as it emerged from the bottleneck of the Tsushima Straits. In addition to his four 12-inch gun battleships (*Fuji, Mikasa, Asahi* and *Shikishima*), Togo's command consisted of eight armoured cruisers, 16 light cruisers, 21 destroyers, and 57 torpedo-boats of all classes.

The Russian fleet had a nominal structure of three squadrons, the best battleships leading: Rozhestvensky's flagship *Kniaz Suvorov, Aleksandr III, Borodino* and *Orel,* all 12-inch gun ships. Close astern came the second squadron: the 10-inch gun battleship *Oslyabya,* followed by two relics better suited to the American Civil War than the pre-Dreadnought era: the turret ironclads *Sissoi Velikiy* and *Navarin.* Bringing up the rear came Nebogatov's *Imperator Nikolai I* with two armoured cruisers, two light cruisers and the three coastal defence ships; and a supply flotilla of four transports, two repair tugs and two hospital ships. The result was an ungainly armada of over 30 ships of all types from 12-inch gun battleship to tugboat. Rozhestvensky's chain of command had not been improved by the death of Rear-Admiral Felkersam on 25 May; to prevent morale slipping further, Rozhestvensky had ordered that Felkersam's flag was to keep flying in *Oslyabya,* as though he were still alive.

Though again outnumbered in battleships, Togo viewed the approaching engagement in an entirely different light to that of the Yellow Sea nine months before. He knew all the major weaknesses in the Russian fleet – they had been the subject of international debate for months. Togo also knew that the fleet he was about to fight was the last one Russia had to send. Like Nelson at Trafalgar, he doubted whether this was an instrument which the enemy knew how to play. Togo therefore planned to exploit the Russian lack of cohesion by keeping the Japanese battle line tightly together, concentrating its joint fire-power against the strongest Russian ships. At the Yellow Sea his powerful 8-inch gun armoured cruisers had operated separately to split the Russian fire; this time they were to go into action in the line of battle, augmenting the weight of heavy shell thrown by the battleships. Togo also planned to use the 5-knot speed advantage of the well-drilled Japanese fleet to pressurise Rozhestvensky's armada by manoeuvre, hopefully bringing about the same confusion which had dissolved Vitjevt's fleet at the crisis of the Yellow Sea action.

By noon on 27 May the Russian fleet had passed the Tsushima Straits in line-ahead, with the supply ships trailing behind Nebogatov's squadron at the rear. The Russians had been shadowed for the past six hours by Japanese cruisers, reporting the Russians' progress by radio. The approach of these cruisers to within 9,000 yards was too tempting for Captain Yung of *Orel,* fourth in line, who opened fire; Nebogatov's squadron followed suit, and 32 rounds were wasted before Rozhestvensky's angry 'cease fire' order was obeyed. This undisciplined outburst at least had the effect of making the Japanese cruisers withdraw, and the Russian ships' companies were sent to dinner.

At this point Rozhestvensky suddenly began a manoeuvre which has baffled historian ever since. He ordered his first and second divisions to make an 8-point (90-degree) turn to starboard. This would have divided the Russian fleet, presumably with the intention of catching the oncoming but still invisible Japanese battle fleet between two fires. It may well be, however, that Rozhestvensky had been touched by a flash of the same intuition which was to come to Jellicoe at Jutland 11 years later (*see p. 114*) and he sensed that this manoeuvre would lay his best battleships in line-ahead across the track of the Japanese battle fleet, ideally placed to concentrate fire on the head of the Japanese line. (This was the tactic known as 'crossing the T'.) In any event, only *Suvorov, Aleksandr III, Borodino* and *Orel* had completed the turn when more Japanese cruisers were sighted, approaching from the north-west. If they were the scouts ahead of Togo's battle fleet, the original course had been right all the time and Rozhestvensky hastily turned back on to it. This left the Russian fleet in two parallel columns, with Rozhestvensky's first division slightly ahead and to starboard of the second and third; and at this moment the leading Japanese battleships at last hove into view, advancing not from the north-west but the north-*east* – in other words, heading straight for the Russian fleet.

When the two fleets sighted each other at 13.45 hours, Rozhestvensky still had the option of edging out to starboard with the first division and threatening Togo with envelopment. Instead he held to his course, most likely intent on reducing the range for the benefit of his ships' lighter guns. This left the initiative to Togo, who proceeded to give a demonstration of fleet handling which for sheer virtuosity has seldom been rivalled. After confirming that the Russian

Togo's battleships open fire; the dense funnel smoke is a reminder that the wind, just as in the days of sail, remained a vital factor in battleship actions until the coming of radar.

fleet was headed by its most powerful battleships with Rozhestvensky's flagship in the van, Togo swept the Japanese battle line across to the Russian left flank. The Japanese line crossed the path of the Russian columns well out of range, then turned in succession to end up ahead of the leading Russian ships on a slightly converging course. Caught off balance, Rozhestvensky attempted to counter by re-forming his fleet in a single line, cutting in ahead of the second division headed by *Oslyabya*. As he did so, *Suvorov* fired her first ranging shots at 9,000 yards – but Rozhestvensky would have been better advised to concentrate on his resumption of the line-ahead. Barging across the path of the rest of the fleet, the first division threw the second and third divisions into angry confusion, with sharp course changes and reductions of speed to avoid collisions. The disarray thus created in the Russian centre and rear only helped Togo in his planned concentration of fire on the strongest Russian ships.

Rozhestvensky showed complete indifference to the confusion into which the centre and rear of his fleet had fallen. He snatched at the opportunity handed to him by Togo's opening manoeuvre: the fixed point at which the Japanese battleships and armoured cruisers were turning in succession. In the opening ten minutes of the battle (13.45–55) this point became the focus of unexpectedly accurate Russian fire. Togo's flagship *Mikasa* and her sister-ship *Shikishima* were hit by several 6-inch and 12-inch shells; Nebogatov's *Nikolai I*, firing with equal accuracy, landed 10-inch hits on the armoured cruisers *Asama* and *Nishin* and forced them out of the line. A lucky hit at this moment could have had far-reaching results for the Russians, because Togo's custom was to command in the old style, out in the open on the wing of his bridge. He was hit in the thigh by a splinter hurled by an exploding shell but never even turned round, stoically waiting for the moment when his ships' superior speed would take them out of range of the Russian centre and rear and allow his 12-inch gunners to concentrate on the Russian van.

The fleeting Russian opportunity soon passed. By 14.00 hours the Japanese line, settled on its converging course, was out of range of the Russian rear and a torrent of 12-inch, 8-inch and 6-inch shells broke on Rozhestvensky's leading ships, the Japanese battleships concentrating on *Suvorov*, the armoured cruisers on *Oslyabya*. 'I had never imagined anything like it. Shells seemed to be pouring upon us incessantly, one after the other,' wrote one of Rozhest-

vensky's surviving staff officers later. 'It seemed as if these were mines, not shells, which were striking the ship's side and falling on the deck. They burst as soon as they touched anything – the moment they encountered the least impediment in their flight.' These were instantaneously-fused shells filled with *shimose*, an improved Japanese explosive; their effect was to wreck the upperworks of the Russian ships, killing the crews of the secondary and tertiary armaments and starting innumerable fires.

Rozhestvensky lost the battle between 14.00 and 14.20 hours when, while he still had signalling apparatus and a flagship under control, he failed to swing to port. This would have 'crossed the T' of the Japanese rear and at least enable the Russians to do to the Japanese armoured cruisers what Togo's fleet was doing to them. At 14.30, blazing above the waterline, her mainmast gone and helm jammed by a hit in the stern, *Suvorov* swung helplessly out of the line; *Oslyabya* was in similar plight. By 15.00 Rozhestvensky, repeatedly wounded, had been driven from his conning-tower to shelter with his staff in a midships 6-inch gun turret; the stricken *Suvorov* was being circled by the Russian line with *Aleksandr III* and *Borodino* in the lead, forced by another Japanese change of course to shy away to the south-east.

Oslyabya sank at about 15.30, rent open by repeated hits at the waterline – the first modern battleship to be sunk by gunfire. Half an hour later *Aleksandr III* was also forced out of the line, burning furiously. The action now degenerated into a wildly confused but wholly one-sided slaughter, with Togo engaging and disengaging at will and picking his targets with ruthless efficiency, each time with overwhelming firepower. Dazed and incoherent from his wounds, Rozhestvensky transferred to the destroyer *Buiny* at 17.30 but he no longer had a cohesive fleet to command. Half an hour later *Aleksandr III* capsized and sank, shattered by the fire of Togo's battleships; about 19.00 *Borodino* blew up and sank when a 12-inch shell exploded in her magazine. *Suvorov* was finished off at 19.20 by Japanese torpedo-boats, her heroic gunners hitting back to the last with the only 75-mm gun still able to fire. When Togo came in for the kill on the morning of the 28th, Nebogatov was left in command of the remnants which had joined him, but he knew that their exhausted crews were incapable of fair resistance, and surrendered. At 16.50 that afternoon the destroyer *Biedovyi*, into which Rozhestvensky had made his second shift of flag, also surrendered; and Togo's victory was complete.

So ended the first fleet action of the modern battleship era – and, it should be noted, the last to be fought purely in two dimensions, ship to ship, without molestation from naval aircraft above or submarines below. Tsushima remains the only battleship fleet action to end with an *entire battle fleet* sunk or captured. Only one Russian cruiser and two destroyers escaped to reach Vladivostok; three other cruisers escaped to neutral ports and were interned. Togo's losses were only three torpedo-boats sunk, 117 killed and 583 wounded. Known Russian losses were 4,830 killed, 5,917 captured and 1,862 missing; no figures were ever reached for the wretched wounded.

Tsushima re-stated the battleship's predominance in fleet actions at sea, and above all the devastating effect of long-range heavy-calibre gunfire. At the same time the battle was only the dramatic finale to a naval war which had also showed the battleship's vulnerability to torpedoes and mines. All these lessons were avidly studied and applied, with varying success, to the new generations of battleships already taking shape in the west: the Dreadnoughts.

6. THE DREADNOUGHT BATTLESHIP, 1905–1914

BY 1905, THE YEAR OF TSUSHIMA, the battleship had remained substantially unchanged for 15 years: four-gun main armament, heavy secondary and tertiary batteries, around 15,000 tons displacement, powered by coal-fired triple-expansion engines, maximum speed 15–18 knots. But by the outbreak of the First World War nine years later this format had been rendered hopelessly obsolete. The introduction of the Dreadnought type, named from the first of the new breed to enter service, had raised the battleship to an entirely new plane of development.

In itself the 'Dreadnought Revolution' of 1905–14 was not so remarkable; there had been many such improvements since the first ironclads had appeared 50 years before. It was the *combination* of new features which made HMS *Dreadnought* such a nonpareil when launched in February 1906: not just more powerful armament, not just heavier armour, not just far more efficient machinery delivering far greater speed, but all of them at a stroke.

The Dreadnought concept sprang from the uneasy feeling that the battleship, in the prevailing format of the 1890s and early 1900s, was being prevented from doing full justice to itself by basic faults in design and combat theory. It made no sense to mount ever-increasing numbers of guns able to cripple an enemy at short range, within range of his torpedoes, when a more generous allocation of heavy guns would enable the enemy to be destroyed at long range, outside the range of his torpedoes. Armament was therefore the essence of the Dreadnought concept: the scrapping of secondary batteries to produce an 'all big-gun' battleship. With a doubled allocation of heavy guns went better armoured protection and more speed. The new formula first took definitive form in a much-discussed article by an Italian, General Vittorio Cuniberti – 'An Ideal Warship for the British Navy', which appeared in *Jane's Fighting Ships* (1903).

Cuniberti's suggestions were music to the ears of the British Admiral Sir John Fisher, a tireless crusader in the Royal Navy for maximum efficiency, battle-worthiness and fire-power. When Fisher became First Sea Lord on 21 October 1904 – Trafalgar Day – he set in motion a spate of much-needed

Previous pages: The after 15-inch guns of the British super-Dreadnought HMS *Queen Elizabeth* (1915).
Right: HMS *Lord Nelson* (1908). Though she and her sister-ship *Agamemnon* were completed after *Dreadnought*, they were the most powerful of the British pre-Dreadnoughts, with a mixed armament of four 12-inch, ten 9·2-inch and 24 12-pounders and ten 3-pounders.
Below: Gun plan of HMS *Dreadnought* (1906), showing the awkward wing turrets and overzealous purge of all secondary armament which were the most serious flaws of Britain's 'first generation' Dreadnoughts.

reforms, aimed at a fundamental regrouping of the navy to permit a concentration of its most powerful ships in home waters. Obsessed with the increasing challenge represented by the ever-growing German fleet, he knew that it would only be a matter of time before battleships of the Cuniberti type were built by other navies. In the spring of 1905 it was learned that the Japanese had started the ball rolling, laying down a 20,000-ton monster which would be armed with 12 12-inch guns. Appalled at the prospect of Germany following suit and producing a battle fleet of ships with three times the fire-power of Britain's 'King Edward VIIs', Fisher overbore all opposition. On 2 October 1905 Britain's first 'all big-gun' battleship was laid down at Portsmouth, her name, HMS *Dreadnought*, being derived from Fisher's personal motto – 'Fear God and Dread Nought'.

Dreadnought's revolutionary features may best be assessed by comparing them with contemporary pre-Dreadnoughts:

Dimensions	**Mikasa (J)**	**Braunschweig (G)**	**King Ed. VII (GB)**	**Dreadnought (GB)**
Displacement	15,200 tons	13,200 tons	15,700 tons	17,110 tons
Length	415 ft	398·5 ft	425 ft	490 ft
Beam	75·5 ft	72·75 ft	78 ft	82 ft
Draught	28·25 ft	25 ft	24·5 ft	26·6 ft
Armament				
Main	4×12 in	4×11 in	4×12 in	10×12 in
Secondary	14×6 in	14×6·7 in	10×6 in	—
Tertiary	20×12 pdr	14×3·4 in	14×3 pdr	24×12 pdr
Torpedoes	4×18 in	6×17·7 in	4×18 in	5×18 in
Armour				
Main belt	9-4 in	8·75-4 in	9-4 in	11-4 in
Barbettes/ Turrets	10-8 in	10-6 in	12-6 in	11 in
Decks	3 in	3 in	2·5-1 in	3-1·5 in
Machinery				
Type	2-shaft triple-exp.	3-shaft triple-exp.	2-shaft triple-exp.	4-shaft turbines
Horsepower	15,000	16,000	18,000	23,000
Speed	18 kts	18 kts	18·5 kts	21 kts
Complement	935	691	777	773

Massed pre-Dreadnoughts of the British Fleet dressed overall for the 1907 Royal Review – but already rendered obsolete by the debut of *Dreadnought*.

Right : The bristling assortment of gun calibres mounted in the 'Lord Nelson' class *Agamemnon* (1908).
Inset : Completed only a year later but streets ahead in heavy-calibre hitting power: the 'Bellerophon' class Dreadnought HMS *Temeraire*, with ten 12-inch guns to *Agamemnon*'s modest four.

The novelty of *Dreadnought*'s 12-inch gun broadside lay in the turret arrangement: from no matter on what bearing she might have to engage a pre-Dreadnought, she would always be able to throw at least double the weight of 12-inch shell. *Dreadnought*'s other virtues included the freedom from vibration conferred by turbine engines. The latter novelty had been demonstrated at the Diamond Jubilee Naval Review of 1897 by the speedboat *Turbinia* of Charles Parsons, the first vessel in the world to exceed 30 knots. With turbine power, *Dreadnought* became the first battleship to break the 20-knot barrier – though not the first to burn oil fuel. That honour belonged to the Russian pre-Dreadnought *Rostislav*, completed seven years before *Dreadnought*.

Fisher nevertheless had to defend *Dreadnought* against a storm of opposition. The weightiest objection was that she did indeed make every other battleship in the world redundant – including those of Britain. The Royal Navy's pre-Dreadnought battle fleet had been the strongest in the world, and its strength was still growing. Only five months before *Dreadnought* had been laid down, work had started on *Lord Nelson* and *Agamemnon*, which had set new standards in pre-Dreadnought fire-power. The 'Lord Nelsons' were armed with four 12-inch, ten 9·2-inch, 24 12-pounders and ten 3-pounders. But now, with *Dreadnought*, British naval supremacy was no more: if the German Navy started to build Dreadnoughts, which it obviously would, they would be competing on level terms.

The answer to this was that Britain remained the world's master shipbuilder, unmatched in speed and expertise by any other naval power. Even today, with all the advantages of prefabrication and advanced construction techniques, *Dreadnought* remains the all-time record beater for speed of construction with a warship of her class: only 366 days from laying-down to trials. It was this ability, added to the vital advantage of having snatched the lead in producing Dreadnoughts, which guaranteed that Britain's battleship supremacy could be preserved.

And so it proved. It was not until the summer of 1907 that Germany laid down her first Dreadnoughts: *Rheinland* (1 June), *Posen* (11 June), *Nassau* (22 July) and *Westfalen* (12 August). These retained the favourite German 11-inch gun, but in six twin turrets, two on the centreline and the other four back-to-back amidships. But by the time work started on *Westfalen* in

Top: USS *Michigan* (1910), with eight centreline 12-inch guns. The vastly superior centreline turret arrangement enabled her, though mounting one less turret, to fire the same broadside as Britain's *Dreadnought* – handicapped as the latter was in broadside fire by always having one wing turret blanked off by the mass of the superstructure.
Above: French pre-Dreadnought *Danton* and (centre) *Courbet*. The latter (completed 1913) was name-ship of the belated first class of French Dreadnoughts.

August 1907, Britain had already launched *Bellerophon*, her second Dreadnought; and *Temeraire* followed on 24 August, with work proceeding on *Superb*, and *Collingwood*. *St Vincent* was laid down in December 1907 and *Vanguard* in April 1908. *Nassau* was the first of the 'Westfalens' to be completed, in October 1909. By then Britain already had five Dreadnoughts to Germany's one: *Dreadnought*, *Bellerophon*, *Temeraire*, *Superb*, and *St Vincent*.

The Japanese had precipitated *Dreadnought*'s design by laying down *Aki* and *Satsuma* in March and May 1905, but these ships when completed were not true Dreadnoughts with a uniform main armament. The immense weight problem created by the eight 12-inch turrets of the original design proved insuperable and the ships were eventually completed with a hybrid armament (*Satsuma* in March 1909, *Aki* in March 1911). They were armed with a centreline twin 12-inch turret fore and aft, and six twin 10-inch turrets amidships. The first true Japanese Dreadnoughts were *Settsu* and *Kawachi*, laid down in January and April 1909. Their turret arrangement naturally owed much to *Aki* and *Satsuma*: a centreline twin 12-inch turret fore and aft, and four more amidships, two back to back on each side.

The United States Navy introduced an entirely novel feature with the 'South Carolina' class battleships – *Michigan* and *South Carolina*, both laid down in December 1906. This was a reduced number of turrets (four twin 12-inch) but all of them on the centreline, two forward and two aft. The great advantage of an all-centreline turret arrangement was that it enabled the entire main armament to be fired in broadside, which was not possible in the case of battleships with wing turrets. The latter only enjoyed a crushing superiority when approaching head-on, which was at best a fleeting advantage. Thus *Dreadnought*, approaching *South Carolina* head-on, would have been able to open fire with six guns to the American's four; but in broadside fire, with one or the other of *Dreadnought*'s wing turrets blanked off by the superstructure, the two ships' fire-power would be identical. All American battleships built after the 'South Carolina' class retained the all-centreline main armament, which the British did not adopt until the 'Orion' class of 1909–10. The 'South Carolinas' were, however, technically kept in the pre-Dreadnought speed bracket by their coal-burning reciprocating engines, delivering a maximum speed of only 18½ knots.

Hamstrung as ever by the prolonged construction time of its shipyards, the

French Navy had painfully begun work on a pre-Dreadnought fleet with the ten battleships of the 'République', 'Vérité' and 'Danton' classes, laid down between December 1901 and July 1908. The first French Dreadnoughts were the four battleships of the 'Courbet' class (*Courbet*, *Jean Bart*, *Paris* and *France*). Their armament was six twin 12-inch turrets, two superimposed fore and aft and two in wing mountings. The latter feature, plus the intervening increase in gun sizes, meant that they were outclassed by all contemporary Dreadnoughts by the time of their completion in 1913–14.

The Italian Navy suffered from the same lengthy construction time, with its inevitable tendency to built-in obsolescence, as the French. The last Italian pre-Dreadnoughts were the four ships of the 'Regina Elena' class (*Regina Elena*, *Napoli*, *Roma* and *Vittorio Emmanuele*), all laid down in 1901–03 but not completed until 1907–08. Though designed by General Cuniberti, father of the Dreadnought concept, they were hopelessly outgunned: only two 12-inch guns and 12 8-inch. They were, however, built for speed, with fine lines and much use of high-tensile steel to save deadweight, and their coal-burning triple-expansion engines could deliver 21 knots. The first Italian Dreadnought was *Dante Alighieri*, laid down in June 1909. She introduced an entirely new gun arrangement: the triple turret mounting. Together with all-centreline arrangement, the triple turret was destined to remain the standard armament of all 'last generation' battleships of Second World War vintage, with the exception of Britain's 'King George V' class and HMS *Vanguard*. Designed for broadside fire, with no wing turrets, *Dante Alighieri* could throw 12 12-inch shells to *Dreadnought*'s ten – but like the French 'Courbets' she was not completed until 1913. She was, however, powered by coal-burning turbines and had a speed of 22·75 knots.

Top: Sacrificing armament and protection for high speed – Italy's *Regina Elena* (1907). *Above:* Enter the centreline *triple* turret mounting: *Dante Alighieri* (1913), Italy's first Dreadnought and one of the most innovative of them all.

Italy's main rival before 1914, the Austro-Hungarian Empire, was the first to build Dreadnoughts with centreline triple 12-inch turrets in superimposed arrangement. These were the excellent 'Viribus Unitis' battleships: *Viribus Unitis*, *Tegetthof*, *Prinz Eugen* and *Szent Istvan*, completed in 1912–14. Using superimposed turrets made for shorter hull length (469 feet, against *Dante Alighieri*'s 519 feet) and greater manoeuvrability to offset their 2-knot inferiority in speed. To out-gun the 'Viribus Unitis' class battleships the Italian designers, versatile as ever, came up with the 'Conte di Cavour' class laid down in 1910: *Conte di Cavour*, *Giulio Cesare* and *Leonardo da Vinci*.

These moved up to a unique compromise of midships and superimposed turret arrangements: triple 12-inch turrets forward, midships and aft, with the fore and after turrets superimposed by a two-gun 12-inch turret – 13 12-inch guns in all.

Because of its murderous battleship losses in the recent war with Japan, no other navy in the world was better placed to take advantage of the Dreadnought revolution than that of Russia. All that was left was an assorted handful of pre-Dreadnought types which in no way constituted a balanced fleet. There were only three surviving Russian pre-Dreadnoughts which had been completed after 1900: *Tsesarevich* (released from internment after the Russo-Japanese War), *Slava* (last of the 'Suvorov' class immolated at Tsushima) and the most famous Russian pre-Dreadnought of them all, *Kniaz Potemkin*, immortalised by Eisenstein's film *Battleship Potemkin*. After her crew had mutinied in the Revolution of June 1905, *Potemkin* had wandered irresolutely round the Black Sea before being interned at Constanza in Rumania. Returning to Russian service on 9 August 1906, St Pantaleimon's Day, *Potemkin* was rechristened *Pantaleimon*.

After the Revolution work was resumed on four pre-Dreadnoughts which had been laid down in 1903: *Svatitoi Evstafi* and *Ioann Zlatoust* (roughly equivalent to Britain's 'King Edward VIIs') and *Imperator Pavel I* and *Andrei Pervozanni*, the latter pair, with their turreted 8-inch secondary armament, more reminiscent of the British 'Lord Nelsons' than anything else. All four were finally completed in 1910, the year after the first four Russian Dreadnoughts had been laid down (all on the same day, 13 July). These were *Gangut, Petropavlovsk, Sevastopol* and *Poltava*, and they were intended to be the first stage of a massive fleet rebuilding programme lasting until 1930.

Given this grandiose long-term goal, it was all the more unfortunate that the 'Ganguts' were such obvious copies of Italy's experimental *Dante Alighieri*. They were armed with four triple 12-inch turrets dotted along a gangling 600 ft-long hull, instead of the superimposed arrangement being adopted by other navies. They also carried their secondary battery of 24 4·7-inch guns in single sponson mountings rather than twin turrets; and their unnecessary use of high-tension steel delayed their completion until 1914–15. The same gun arrangement was chosen for Russia's next three Dreadnoughts: *Imperatritsa Maria, Imperatritsa Ekaterina II* and *Imperator Aleksandr III*, laid down in 1911. All seven ships were powered by oil-burning turbines with the 'Ganguts', at 23 knots, having a 2-knot speed advantage over the 'Imperatritsa Marias'.

By 1909 the British were paying the penalty for having initiated the Dreadnought building-race with Germany in such haste. Their marvellous building capacity had given the Royal Navy an operational, all-Dreadnought battle squadron before Germany had more than one in service. But this had only been achieved by sticking to the original 10-gun layout, flawed as it was by the use of wing turrets, with a resultant delay in superimposing turrets in the style pioneered by the Americans. To make matters more embarrassing, foreign navies ordering Dreadnoughts from British yards began to order battleships with at least nominal superiority to those being built for the Royal Navy. In 1907, only a year after *Dreadnought*'s completion, the Vickers' yard at Barrow laid down two such ships for Brazil. These were *Minas Geraes* and *São Paolo*, with six twin 12-inch turrets to the five mounted by British Dreadnoughts. *Minas Geraes* and *São Paolo*, briefly the most powerful battleships in the world, were a straightforward cross between *Dreadnought* and the American 'South Carolinas' – wing turrets *and* superimposed centreline turrets fore and aft.

Britain began to move tentatively towards centreline armament and superimposed turrets with *Neptune* (laid down in January 1909) and *Colossus* and *Hercules* (July 1909). These retained wing turrets, but the after

Italy's *Conte di Cavour* (1915), showing her novel turret arrangement: forward twin 12-inch turret superimposed over a triple 12-inch turret.

Viribus Unitis, at right of picture, joins the Austrian fleet in 1912 (pre-Dreadnought *Zrinyi*, of 1911, at centre).

pair of turrets was superimposed. The first all-centreline British Dreadnought was *Orion*, laid down in November 1909: forward and aft turret pairs superimposed, with a fifth turret abaft the funnel. Three sister-ships, *Conqueror*, *Monarch* and *Thunderer*, were laid down in April 1910.

The 'Orions' again demonstrated the conservatism of British battleship design, especially its reluctance to experiment with multiple turret mountings to achieve heavier salvos per turret. They nevertheless marked the beginning of the 'second generation' of Dreadnoughts: onward and upward from the 12-inch gun to the 13·5-inch. *Orion* and *Thunderer* also served as test-beds for the new system of fire control: director firing, with all turrets obeying data passed from a central director instead of relying on the individual gunlayers. This was the brain-child of British naval gunnery's temperamental genius, Admiral Sir Percy Scott – a man scarcely less controversial and certainly far more disliked than Fisher himself. Scott had to fight all the way against the inert conservatism of HMS *Excellent*, the Royal Navy's gunnery school at Whale Island, before his idea was put to the test. On 13 December 1912 a shoot was arranged on terms reminiscent of the tug-of-war between *Rattler* and *Alecto* in 1845. *Thunderer* was fitted with an experimental director, *Orion* relied on gunlayers' firing, and both ships were required to fire for three minutes at 9,000 yards' range while steaming at 12 knots. The result was a triumph for director firing, with *Thunderer* scoring six times as many hits as *Orion*. Even so, getting the new equipment into production was a painfully slow process and by the outbreak of war in August 1914 only eight British battleships had been fitted with directors for their main armament.

The 'Orions' were the last class of British battleship laid down before Fisher left the Admiralty in 1910, but by then his work was done: the 'building race' with Germany had become a major public and political obsession and there could be no question of slackening the pace. The 'Orions' were followed by four slightly enlarged successors, all laid down between January and March 1911: *King George V*, *Centurion*, *Ajax* and *Audacious*. The four 'Iron Dukes' laid down in 1912 – *Benbow*, *Emperor of India*, *Iron Duke* and *Marlborough* – expanded the 'Orion' formula still further, adding a powerful secondary battery of 6-inch guns in 12 single mountings. It had not been long before the original *Dreadnought*'s flyweight subsidiary armament of 24 12-pounders had been criticised as an inadequate answer to the torpedo-boat menace. All subsequent British battleship classes had featured a gradual return to a full secondary battery. The gun most favoured for this purpose, until the re-introduction of the 6-inch by the 'Iron Dukes', had been the 4-inch quick-firer.

Built at Vickers', Barrow, for Brazil: the mighty *Minas Geraes* (12 12-inch guns) on trials in 1910.

The only ship of her class to have completed trials and working-up by the summer of 1914, *Iron Duke* was inevitably chosen to be flagship of the British Grand Fleet, the most powerful British 'super-Dreadnought' afloat. But it was already known that the reign of the 'Iron Dukes' would be brief, for the first of the five splendid 'Queen Elizabeths' – eight 15-inch guns, burning oil fuel only for the first time, designed for 24 knots – had already been launched, *Queen Elizabeth* in October 1913 and *Warspite* in the following month.

German Dreadnought development had inevitably followed the pace set by the British: content to emulate rather than innovate, and so avoid costly failures. After the 'Westfalens' came the 'Helgolands', laid down in 1908–09: *Ostfriesland, Thüringen, Helgoland* and *Oldenburg*. These had the same basic design as the 'Westfalens' (two wing turrets on each side) but moved up from the 11-inch gun to the 12-inch. Superimposed turrets and all-centreline armament began to creep in with the 'Kaisers', laid down in 1910: *Kaiser, Prinz Regent Luitpold, König Albert, Kaiserin* and *Friederich der Grosse*, trimmer versions of the British *Neptune*. The British 'Orions' were patiently matched by the 'Königs', laid down in 1911: *König, Grosser Kurfürst, Markgraf* and *Kronprinz*, though these ships retained the 12-inch gun and did not move up to 13·5-inch. Finally there came the German equivalents of the British 'Queen Elizabeths', the 15-inch gun 'Bayerns', the first two of which (*Bayern* and *Baden*) were also launched in 1913.

Yet there was one vital difference between Britain's Dreadnoughts and their German counterparts. Fisher's favourite dictum may have been 'Speed is armour', but his German rival, Grand-Admiral von Tirpitz, never modified his insistence on 'unsinkable gun platforms'. When it came to providing the latter, German battleship designers had the easier task. Despite their new battle fleet's grandiloquent title of *Hochsee Flotte* – the 'High Seas Fleet' – in the Imperial German Navy crews lived ashore in barracks and only manned their ships when a sortie was imminent. With German battleship design, internal protection in the form of watertight partitions and compartments came first; there was no need to incorporate open messdecks which must remain habitable for weeks on end, as in the Royal Navy. And increasing German care with protection was certainly reflected in the allocation of armour plate:

Ship	Main belt	Barbettes/ turrets	Decks	Control tower
Dreadnought WESTFALEN	11-4 in 11·5-4 in	11 in 11 in	3-1·5 in 4 in	— 12 in
St Vincent HELGOLAND	10-5 in 11·75-4 in	9-5 in 11 in	3-1·5 in 3 in	— 12 in
Orion KAISER	12-8 in 13·75-7·75 in	11 in 11·75 in	4-1 in 3 in	11 in 13·75 in
King George V KÖNIG	12-8 in 14-10 in	11 in 14 in	4-1 in 4·5 in	11 in 14 in

By 1914 the term 'Dreadnought' was becoming old hat; the new paragon was the 'super-Dreadnought', a description commonly used for any battleship with guns heavier than 12-inch, or with more than ten 12-inch guns. In its new incarnation, the battleship had become the most revered international military status symbol and was destined to remain so until the coming of the nuclear bomb 30 years later. Super-Dreadnoughts were being ordered by every state with hopes of cutting a dash as a world sea power – Brazil, Argentina, Chile, Turkey – whether or not those states had a hope of paying for the ships when completed.

Nearly all such customers applied for their wonder-warships to be built in Britain; and nothing says more for the dominance

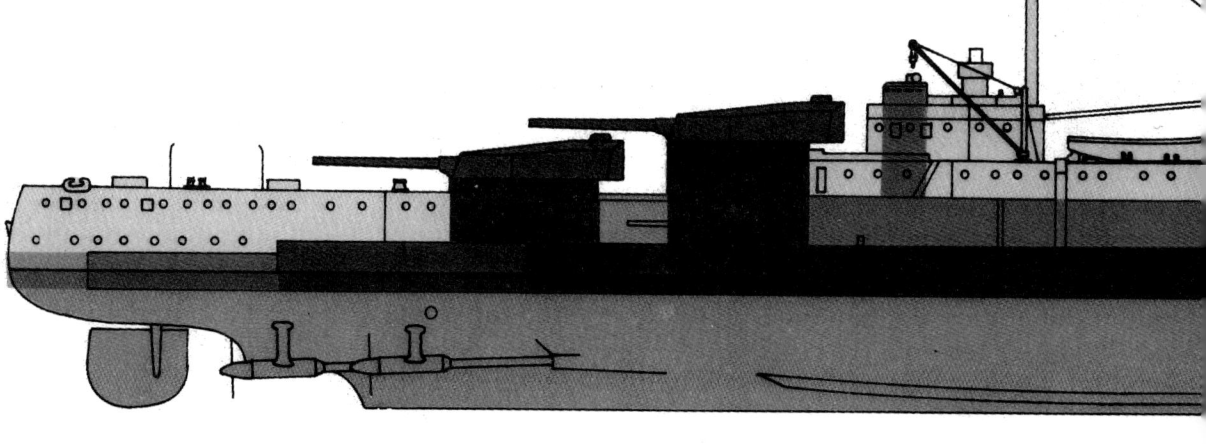

Main belt and barbette turret armour distribution in *Queen Elizabeth*: main belt 13/16-inch, turrets 13/11-inch.

of the British shipbuilding industry in those years than the fact that Britain was able to supply all foreign needs while maintaining her lead in the battleship 'building race' with Germany. By 1914 Britain had 20 completed Dreadnoughts and super-Dreadnoughts to Germany's 17. But those who had studied recent naval history knew that this gave Britain little cause for complacency. It was only nine years since the Japanese Navy had emerged as absolute victor over a fleet whose superiority in numbers had vanished within months. In 1914 the mine and the torpedo both remained a deadly threat to the mightiest super-Dreadnought afloat.

Yet never from the start had the Dreadnought story been limited to battleships alone: it had thrown off an entirely new breed of heavy warship whose future was to develop in parallel with that of the battleship over the next 30 years. These new ships were considered a vital element in the Dreadnought battle fleets of both Britain and Germany. Fisher, their originator, exultantly called them the 'New Testament ships', fulfilling the 'Old Testament' promise of the battleship: the battle-cruisers.

Top : The super-Dreadnought HMS *Erin*, of ten 13·5-inch guns (built for Turkey as *Reshadieh*) in dry dock. The repair hulk alongside is the hull of the old ironclad *Algiers* (formerly *Triumph*).
Above : How the inevitable clash of the battle fleets was popularly imagined before the First World War: the German High Seas Fleet in perfect visibility, steaming in line-ahead on battle manoeuvres with broadsides blazing.

7. THE BATTLE CRUISER, 1905-1914

THE INFLUENCE OF THE Russo-Japanese War was never more clearly shown than with the concept of the battle-cruiser. The British had taken the keenest interest in the Russo-Japanese naval conflict, with the Royal Navy's Captain Pakenham observing the Battle of Tsushima from the vantage-point of Togo's flagship *Mikasa* (in a deck chair out on the open quarterdeck, thereby gaining great 'face'). Pakenham's detailed reports on the battle described the way in which Togo had used his armoured cruiser squadron in close collaboration with the battleships, and the punishment from heavy Russian shells which the armoured cruisers had suffered during their sterling service in the action. The first battle-cruisers, laid down in Britain only nine months after Tsushima, were designed with the proven advantages and disadvantages of Togo's armoured cruisers very much in mind. What the Dreadnought concept sought to do for the traditional role of the battleship, the battle-cruiser concept sought to do for the traditional role of the cruiser.

As in the days of sail, when it had been carried out by frigates, the cruiser's role was twofold. In peacetime, cruisers were the ideal ships of force with which to patrol the sea-lanes and generally 'show the flag'; in wartime cruisers retained this role, on the lookout above all else for enemy surface raiders preying on commerce. But the cruiser's other role, no less important, was to scout ahead of the battle fleet, searching out the enemy and keeping in touch for as long as possible, sending back information on the enemy's numbers, types of ship in company, speed and heading. And the cruiser's prerequisite was therefore speed, to keep out of trouble while gathering this vital information and passing it to the battle fleet.

Armoured cruisers, as distinct from unarmoured 'light' and moderately-armoured or 'protected' cruisers, were developed specifically to prevent enemy cruiser scouts from doing their job, and to survive under enemy fire while pressing their own reconnaissance. Armoured cruisers carried the heaviest main armament (usually 8/9-inch) of any warship type other than battleships. Their average armoured protection was 6–8 inches and their speed a clear 5 knots higher (at 21–23 knots) than the fastest battleships of the day. As we have seen in the case of USS *Olympia* *(see p. 47)* the armoured cruiser of the pre-Dreadnought era was virtually a fast, miniature battleship, and could certainly do a battleship's job in the straightforward role of bombarding shore targets. Until the matter was actually put to the test in the Russo-Japanese War, therefore, there was much debate over whether or not armoured cruisers could or should 'take their place in the line' with the battle fleet.

Certainly the evidence of the Port Arthur and Tsushima campaigns yielded no clear-cut answers; it seemed that 'what was gained on the roundabout was lost on the swings'. Armoured cruisers operating in company apart from the battleships, as in the Yellow Sea action, obviously had a vital role to play as the fast scouting wing of the battle fleet. On the other hand the same armoured cruisers, manoeuvring in the actual battle line at Tsushima, played a no less vital role in augmenting the fire-power of the battleships. Their manifest weakness was their vulnerability to heavy-calibre gunfire – yet if more armour were added to overcome this vulnerability, the armoured cruiser's essential speed advantage would be lost.

When within months of Tsushima Admiral Fisher was planning HMS *Dreadnought*, with her 'all big-gun' armament and speed of over 20 knots, he accepted that this combination would, once in widespread service, render the armoured cruiser wholly obsolete. What Fisher was *not* prepared to sacrifice were the invaluable services which the armoured cruiser had proved itself capable of providing in action. It was to guarantee the continued provision of those services in the new Dreadnought era that the 'battle-cruiser' was conceived, with Fisher as its most enthusiastic champion.

Described in simplest terms the battle-cruiser was a 'super-cruiser': the fastest heavy warship bar none, with the same speed advantage over the Dreadnought battleship that the armoured cruiser had enjoyed over the pre-Dreadnought battleship. The battle-cruiser was given 'battleship-sized' uniform armament, to overwhelm enemy cruisers at maximum range, to run down and annihilate the fastest enemy surface raider which tried to cut loose on the mercantile sea-lanes. And the battle-cruiser was allocated enough armoured protection to enable it to reconnoitre within gunnery range of the enemy battle fleet, further than any armoured cruiser had dared to venture. With a squadron of battle-cruisers in company, a Dreadnought battle fleet would indeed be able to 'Fear God and Dread Nought'.

Such was the battle-cruiser, in Fisher's dreams – yet the type was always a warship

Previous pages: First of the new breed – Britain's HMS *Invincible* (1908), unloaded and riding high in the water.

Massive bow waves and dense drifts of black funnel smoke: British battle-cruisers *Indomitable* and *Inflexible* push for their top speed of 25 knots.

more of the heart than of the head. Its blend of speed, dash and hitting-power overwhelmed the senses, all too easily obscuring its biggest design flaw: lightness of armour to guarantee speed. 'Speed is armour!' Fisher grandly proclaimed – but speed is not armour. As First Lord of the Admiralty (1911–15) Winston Churchill enthusiastically called the Royal Navy's battle-cruiser fleet an 'incomparable command'. The grim combat experience of the First World War had revealed the truth of the matter by the time Churchill came to write *The World Crisis* in 1930:

> To put the value of a first-class battleship into a vessel which cannot stand the pounding of a heavy action is a false policy. It is far better to spend the extra money and have what you really want. The battle-cruiser, in other words, should be superseded by the fast battleship, ie fast strongest ship, in spite of her cost.

But the truth of the matter still lay concealed when the first three battle-cruisers were laid down at the beginning of the Dreadnought era in 1906.

The first three battle-cruisers were HMS *Invincible, Indomitable* and *Inflexible,* laid down in February–April 1906 and completed in 1908. Their designer, Sir Philip Watts, had been required to produce a 25-knot warship capable of mounting eight 12-inch guns and standing up to 12-inch shellfire at a range of 9,000 yards. The first two conditions were met, the 'Invincibles' having the same wing-turret 12-inch arrangement as *Dreadnought* and four-shaft turbines; but armoured protection was a more doubtful matter. It has never been safe to assume that warships will always fight at an arbitrary range fixed on at design stage, and at Tsushima ships *had* engaged at ranges over 9,000 yards, when all but the most heavily armoured warships are vulnerable to plunging shellfire. The 'Invincibles' owed their speed to undeniable economy in armoured protection: 6-inch belt, $2\frac{1}{2}$–1-inch decks, and only 7 inches on the turrets where contemporary Dreadnoughts had 11 inches.

The most serious hidden fault, not exposed before the battle experience of the First World War, was the failure to prevent a cordite flash in the turret from travelling down the turret shaft to explode the massed cordite charges in the magazine. And the Royal Navy's treatment of cordite was amazingly casual. One of Britain's greatest exponents of naval gunnery, Admiral of the

German reply to the new British challenge: the excellently protected ($9\frac{1}{2}$-inch maximum armour) battle-cruiser *Von der Tann* (1910).

Fleet Lord Fraser of North Cape, recalled in later life that when he was completing his Long Gunnery Course at HMS *Excellent* in 1912 there had been little or no instruction on the touchiness of cordite. On one occasion Fraser was conducted round a magazine packed with cordite charges, by the light of a naked candle; on another he watched in disbelief while cordite charges were dried in front of a galley fire. Nor did the British protect their cordite charges in brass canisters, as the Germans did: they used silk bags instead.

The rapid completion of the three 'Invincibles' gave Britain a comfortable early lead in battle-cruiser construction, and this was extended by 'leaking' the false information that their main armament would be no heavier than 9·2-inch, then the heaviest gun carried by conventional armoured cruisers. Misled by this, German designers produced the armoured cruiser *Blücher*, completed in 1909, with 12 8·2-inch guns. But they more than atoned for this initial error with *Von der Tann*, the first true German battle-cruiser, laid down in March 1908 and completed in September 1910. *Von der Tann* was only marginally slower than the 'Invincibles' (24·8 knots), and was in fact the first turbine-powered German capital ship. Armed with eight 11-inch guns, she aped the Dreadnought-style turret arrangement with midships turrets out on the beam. But *Von der Tann*'s armoured protection was greatly superior to that of the 'Invincibles': 9·5–4-inch belt, 2·5-inch decks, and 9 inches on the turrets. This protection was very well distributed, especially below the waterline, and *Von der Tann*'s $9\frac{1}{2}$ extra feet across the beam also made her a steadier gun platform than the 'Invincibles'.

There were political objections to adding three more British battle-cruisers to the 1908 Naval Estimates, and costs were kept down by duplicating all the essential features of the 'Invincibles'. In the event only one new battle-cruiser was sanctioned: *Indefatigable*, with *New Zealand* and *Australia* paid for by the Dominions whose name they bore. *Indefatigable* was laid down in February 1909 and completed in February 1911. Both *Australia* and *New Zealand* were laid down in June 1910 and completed in 1912–13.

Germany's next two battle-cruisers were *Moltke* and *Goeben*, laid down in December 1908 and December 1910 respectively and completed in 1911 and 1912. Unlike the British 'Indefatigables' they were a definite

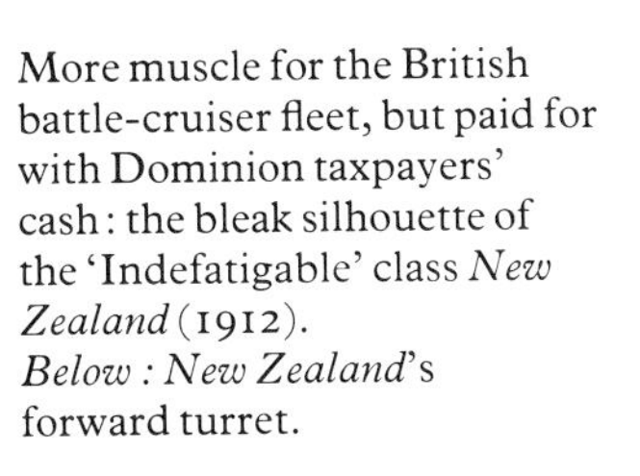

More muscle for the British battle-cruiser fleet, but paid for with Dominion taxpayers' cash: the bleak silhouette of the 'Indefatigable' class *New Zealand* (1912).
Below: New Zealand's forward turret.

Enlarged versions of *Von der Tann*: Germany's *Moltke* (*above*) and *Goeben* (*below*), with maximum armoured protection raised to 11 inches on the belt.

improvement on their predecessors, especially in armour and watertight compartmentation. Their belt armour was raised to 11 inches (nearly double that of the six British battle-cruisers) and their turret armour to 10 inches, all without dropping below the 25-knot speed level. The worst fault of the German battle-cruisers was their low freeboard, making them extremely 'wet' ships at high speed. This fault was tackled in the altered design of the 'one-off' *Seydlitz*, laid down in February 1911 and completed in May 1913, which was given a raised forecastle. Ton for ton her protection, both external and internal, was second to none; her armour alone amounted to 31 per cent of her total tonnage displacement.

It was a very different story with the next three British battle-cruisers, which were designed to emulate the increased fire-power of the 'Orion' class battleships. These were *Lion*, *Princess Royal* and *Queen Mary*, which had the centreline 13–5-inch turret arrangement of the 'Orions' with a central 'Q' turret amidships. All existing restrictions on battle-cruiser dimensions and tonnage were abandoned to produce the 27 knots delivered by the 'Lions':

Ship	**Orion**	**Lion**
Loaded displacement	25,870 tons	29,680 tons
Length	545 ft	660 ft
Beam	88 ft	88·5 ft
Draught	28·75 ft	28·83 ft
Horsepower	27,000 hp	70,000 hp
Speed	21 knots	27 knots

Yet the maximum armour thickness in the 'Lions', belt armour and turrets, was only 9 inches and the armour of the 'Lions' accounted for only 23 per cent of the total tonnage displacement, against the 31 per cent in *Seydlitz*. Amid the general marvelling over the superlative size, speed and grace of the 'Lions', this ominous fact received little attention.

Germany's next battle-cruisers were *Derfflinger* and *Lützow*, laid down in 1912, followed by *Hindenburg* in 1913. These were the last three battle-cruisers completed for the Imperial German Navy and as usual they were admirably protected within and without. Though the 'Lions' had a marginal advantage in speed and a higher freeboard the 'Derfflingers' were the steadier gun-platforms, being 7 feet broader in the beam. They were handsome ships, with eight 12-inch guns in superimposed twin turrets fore and aft.

Thus by 1912 the only two navies to have built separate battle-cruiser squadrons were those of Britain and Germany. Though the new ships had naturally been closely studied by all sea powers of the 'Dreadnought league', the Austrian, French and Italian navies were still concentrating on bringing in their first Dreadnought battleships and did not build battle-cruisers. As with Dreadnought battleships, Britain ap-

Above: Arguably the toughest of all 'first generation' battle-cruisers: Germany's *Seydlitz*.

parently had a commanding lead in battle-cruisers by the end of 1912, with five ships completed (*Invincible, Inflexible, Indomitable, Indefatigable* and *New Zealand*) to Germany's three (*Von der Tann, Moltke* and *Goeben*). Britain's advantage in numbers was reinforced by superior battle-cruiser fire-power, with 12-inch guns against 11-inch in the completed battle-cruisers and 13·5-inch against 12-inch in the ships approaching completion. But of the two battle-cruiser navies it was the German, not the British, which had managed to achieve adequate protection without sacrificing speed. This meant that the German Navy, in the course of its 'building race' with the British, had come closest to producing battle-cruisers which were really *fast battleships*, which by the end of 1912 had already emerged as the latest phenomenon.

In 1911 the United States Navy had laid down *Texas* and *New York* (BBs 34 and 35), the first 20-knot Dreadnought battleships armed with 14-inch guns. But in the preceding year Japan had ordered a new battle-cruiser from Britain which, to the profound embarrassment of her builders, clearly outclassed any British battleship or battle-cruiser built or building. This was *Kongo*, nominally a 27·5-knot battle-cruiser with maximum armoured protection of 9 inches, but armed with eight 14-inch guns in centreline twin turrets. *Kongo* was laid down at the Vickers' yard, Barrow in January 1911 and launched in May 1912, by which time three sister-ships (*Hiei, Haruna* and *Kirishima*) were already building in Japan.

Britain could obviously count herself extremely lucky that it was her ally Japan which had come up with *Kongo* and not Germany; her 14-inch armament trumped the latest British move up to 13·5-inch and made energetic counter-moves essential. The first of these was to overhaul the design of the 'Lion' class battle-cruisers, so clearly outclassed by *Kongo*. The result was *Tiger*, laid down in June 1912 a month after *Kongo* was launched at Barrow. *Tiger* was given the same turret arrangement as *Kongo*, with the awkward midships 'Q' turret moved aft, and a clear knot of superior speed (28–29 knots). But *Tiger* was never seen as more than a stop-gap. Britain's Naval Programme for 1912 ordered the creation of an entirely novel 'Fast Squadron' to be armed not with 14-inch but 15-inch guns. Already referred to on page 78, the first of these ships, *Queen Elizabeth* and *Warspite*, were laid down four months after *Tiger* (October 1912); *Valiant, Barham* and *Malaya* were laid down in 1913 and a sixth ship of the same class, *Agincourt*, was cancelled in 1914. With their 13-inch armour, eight 15-inch guns in superimposed twin turrets fore and aft, and speed of 24 knots, the 'Queen Elizabeths' were the first true fast battleships.

The only other Dreadnought navies to react so energetically to the new standards

Top left: What Churchill called the 'splendid cats' at sea: British battle-cruiser squadron in 1911.
Above: The ship which stood the whole battle-cruiser concept on its head by heralding the fast battleship: Japan's British-built *Kongo* (eight 14-inch guns, $27\frac{1}{2}$ knots) on trials in 1913.

set by the United States and Japan were those of Russia and Germany. To counter the four Japanese 'Kongos', the Russians laid down four 'Borodino' class battle-cruisers on 19 December 1912. These adopted the three-gun turret introduced for the 'Gangut' and 'Imperatritsa Maria' class battleships, but with 14-inch instead of 12-inch guns. The turret arrangement was the same as that used in the 'Ganguts' – but the armour was increased to 12 inches and the speed to 26·5 knots, which would have made the 'Borodinos' fast battleships rather than battle-cruisers. All four were launched in 1915–16, but work on them had been stopped before the Revolution of 1917.

The German reaction was determined by confidence in the protection built in to the existing battle-cruisers, which made it unnecessary to build a rival fast battleship squadron in emulation of Britain's 'Queen Elizabeths'. The German 'Bayern' class battleships (of which the first two were *Bayern* and *Baden*) were therefore not envisaged as a rival 'fast squadron' but as the first stage in giving the German battle fleet 15-inch fire-power.

By the outbreak of the First World War in August 1914, Britain already had nine battle-cruisers in service to Germany's four. It had, however, taken barely six years to recognise that Fisher's original battle-cruiser format had been seriously flawed. In its primary role as 'super-scout' for the battle fleet, there was clearly little in the battle-cruiser's repertoire which could not be more securely performed by the fast battleship. On the other hand the battle-cruiser still had the advantage of speed, and remained the world's fastest heavy warship; the battle-cruiser was clearly unsurpassed in the role of commerce protection against enemy surface raiders. All that remained was the test of battle, to prove or disprove the theoretical advantage of superior speed and fire-power over inferior protection.

8. DREADNOUGHTS AT WAR, 1914-1918

ON THE OUTBREAK OF WAR in August 1914, emergency measures taken in Britain immediately altered the balance of capital ships further in Britain's favour. This was brought about by the seizure or purchase of battleships which had been ordered by foreign powers, and which were approaching completion.

On Clydebank there was the splendid *Almirante Latorre*, laid down for Chile in November 1911: a lengthened copy of *Iron Duke*, but with ten 14-inch guns instead of 13·5-inch. She was purchased for the Royal Navy after work had been suspended on the outbreak of war, and eventually joined the British Grand Fleet as *Canada* in the autumn of 1915. (Britain was also given the option of buying her sister-ship *Almirante Cochrane*, laid down in 1913; but the option was not taken up before 1917, and then only to complete *Almirante Cochrane* as the aircraft-carrier HMS *Eagle*.)

Given the pro-German regime of Turkey, the two super-Dreadnoughts being completed for that country were a very different matter. *Reshadieh* was a superb ship, an improved 'King George V' with ten 13·5-inch guns. Though certainly awe-inspiring, *Sultan Osman I* was arguably the weirdest prodigy thrown up by the international Dreadnought mania of the past five years. She had been ordered by Brazil in 1911 as *Rio de Janeiro* but purchased by Turkey in January 1914, and she was the result of the Brazilian obsession to own the battleship with the world's biggest broadside. And so she did: no less than 14 12-inch guns in seven centreline turrets, with 20 6-inch guns in her secondary battery. But it would have made no sense to have handed *Reshadieh* and *Sultan Osman I* to customers who, considering the imminence of war by the end of July 1914, could well be using their purchases against the manufacturers within weeks. As Churchill put it in *The World Crisis*, 'The Turkish battleships were vital for us. With a margin of only seven Dreadnoughts [over Germany] we could not afford to do without these fine ships.' On 2 August 1914 both ships were occupied at bayonet point as they lay waiting for their Turkish crews to take possession. Both were rapidly completed for Royal Naval Service, *Reshadieh* as HMS *Erin* and *Sultan Osman I* as HMS *Agincourt*.

Though Turkey remained neutral for another two months, the British take-over of her fine new ships had immediate and dramatic results in the Mediterranean, where the British Admiralty was hoping to open the war with a crushing battle-cruiser victory. For the past 18 months the German battle-cruiser *Goeben* with the light cruiser *Breslau* in company had been showing the flag, commanded since October 1913 by Rear-Admiral Wilhelm Souchon. *Goeben*'s presence had resulted in three British battle-cruisers, *Indefatigable*, *Indomitable* and *Inflexible*, being sent out to the Mediterranean Fleet, which also had four armoured cruisers, four light cruisers and 16 destroyers. Based in the central Mediterranean, on Malta, the British were therefore well placed to intercept *Goeben* whether she tried to break up the Adriatic to the Austrian fleet base at Pola, or came west to try accounts with the French in the western Mediterranean. In fact she came west, and the first shots in the naval war of 1914–18 were fired in the early hours of 4 August when *Goeben* bombarded the French Algerian port of Philippeville with 15 11-inch rounds. As *Goeben* headed east for a pre-arranged rendezvous with *Breslau*, *Indefatigable* and *Indomitable* sighted her just after 10.30 hours the same morning.

Previous pages: Fast battleships of the British 5th Battle Squadron – *Valiant*, led by *Malaya* and *Barham*. All three were to give sterling service in two world wars.
Below: Rival flagships of the British Grand Fleet and German High Seas Fleet – HMS *Iron Duke* and (*bottom*) the 'Kaiser' class *Friedrich der Grosse*.

HMS *Agincourt*, with her record-breaking broadside of 14 12-inch guns, leads the Grand Fleet's 4th Battle Squadron. Built as *Rio de Janeiro* for Brazil, she was purchased by Turkey and completed as *Sultan Osman I* and taken over by the British in August 1914. Her nickname in British service was 'Gin Palace'.

The British Admiral Milne was, however, restrained from immediate action on two counts. This was the first war in which radio communications made it possible for politicians to interfere with naval commanders at sea, and the last in which the combatant powers observed the diplomatic niceties down to the last minutes of peace. When *Goeben* was sighted Germany and France were technically at war, but the ensuing British ultimatum to Germany still had 13½ hours to run. Milne was therefore ordered to shadow *Goeben* but not attack until the ultimatum ran out at midnight, and the result was a long and exhausting chase through the afternoon. By 16.36 *Goeben*, the newest of the three battle-cruisers, had run out of sight of her pursuers, though only by straining her boilers to the verge of catastrophe and killing four of her stokers from scalds and burns.

Though humiliating for the British, *Goeben*'s escape need have been only temporary and Milne had plenty of chances still to intercept and engage; he had Rear-Admiral Troubridge patrolling the mouth of the Adriatic with four armoured cruisers, and for the moment *Goeben*'s need to replenish coal was as urgent as in the British battle-cruisers. (The first of Fisher's 'New Testament ships' still relied predominantly on 'Old Testament' coal.) Souchon coaled at Messina (5–6 August), Milne at Malta. Unfortunately Milne had no idea that Souchon was already under orders to head for Constantinople; *Goeben* was to be placed at Turkey's disposal in atonement for the treacherous British seizure of *Reshadieh* and *Sultan Osman I*. Milne was given no clue to this effect by the British Admiralty, but he *was* ordered not to risk driving neutral Italy into the German camp by heading into Italian territorial waters.

The last real chance of bringing *Goeben* to action was lost in the early hours of 7 August, when Troubridge declined to intercept her with his four armoured cruisers – believing that *Goeben* could out-gun the lot of them. In fact the 9·2-inch, 7·5-inch and 6-inch guns of the armoured cruisers could have thrown a combined broadside of 8,680 lb, against the 6,870-lb combined broadside of *Goeben* and *Breslau* – if they lived long enough to reach optimum range, which the experience of Tsushima suggested was unlikely. Agonising though it was, Troubridge's decision not to fight was certainly understandable by the standards of 1914. Not before the Battle of the River Plate (13 December 1939) did a well-handled light

Frustrated by the diplomatic niceties at the outbreak of the war – British battle-cruisers *Indefatigable (left)* and *Indomitable (right)*. *Below : Goeben*, their elusive German quarry.

cruiser force, operating in two divisions to split the enemy's fire, dare take on a 'super-cruiser' armed with battleship-sized guns. *Goeben* was therefore allowed to steam on to Constantinople, passing the Dardanelles on the evening of 10 August. There, transferred to Turkish service as *Yavuz Sultan Selim*, the only German capital ship to serve outside the North Sea theatre in the First World War hampered Allied naval planning in the Black Sea and eastern Mediterranean for the next four years.

The humiliation of the British battle-cruisers in the Mediterranean was wiped out a fortnight later by the Battle of the Heligoland Bight. This action was brought about by the British penetration of the Bight with two light cruisers and two destroyer flotillas. Their mission was to curtail the German destroyer patrols in the Bight which, as reported by British submarines, had become routine by the last week of August. But when the British warships entered the Bight on 28 August they were promptly 'jumped' by a much larger German force, which concentrated six German light cruisers against two British. Another British humiliation seemed inevitable until Vice-Admiral Sir David Beatty, sent south from the Humber with the battle-cruisers *Lion*, *Princess Royal*, *Queen Mary*, *Invincible* and *New Zealand*, made the decision to intervene. He did this in complete ignorance of the possible whereabouts of German minefields, submarines, or even of heavy units of the German battle fleet, knowing full well that he was risking his superb force for a minor tactical objective. But the gamble came off. The battered British light forces withdrew without losing a single ship, while the German light cruisers *Ariadne* and *Köln* were shattered and quickly sunk by the battle-cruisers' 12-inch and 13·5-inch shells. A third German light cruiser, *Mainz*, was sunk by the light cruisers and destroyers, and three others were sent limping back to Wilhelmshaven with severe damage.

Though won against the flimsiest opposition, the Heligoland Bight victory was a heartening fillip to British morale at a moment when the German Army was marching full-tilt on Paris and the British Expeditionary Force retreating from Mons. But there were to be no more such gambles. Beatty's battle-cruiser fleet had not been built to play Russian roulette amid German minefields, and the main characteristic of the British Grand Fleet in the first months of the war was growing awareness of its weakness, not strength. The Dreadnought fleet had been built at breakneck speed and the short-term need to provide money for the new ships had eclipsed a no less urgent long-term need. This was the provision of secure bases from which the fleet would operate in time of war. No such bases had been provided for the Grand Fleet by the outbreak of the First World War and they did not take shape until the middle of 1915: at Scapa Flow in the Orkneys for the battle fleet and at Rosyth on the Firth of Forth for Beatty's battle-cruisers. The Russian fleet in Port Arthur, ten years before, had actually been better protected than was Admiral Sir John Jellicoe's Grand Fleet in 1914–15.

As a result the world's strongest battle fleet was, for the first six months of the war, subject to panicky withdrawals from its war station, brought about by fears of torpedo attack and minefields laid by German submarines. The Grand Fleet's U-boat neurosis was implanted by the sobering discovery, in the very first week of the war, that U-boats could reach Scapa Flow. On 8 August the Grand Fleet's 2nd Battle Squadron was sighted out at sea off Fair Isle, midway between the Shetlands and Orkneys, by two U-boats – and the 'Orion' class *Monarch* had a narrow escape from a torpedo fired at her. One of the culprits, *U-15*, was rammed and sunk by the light cruiser *Birmingham* on the following day; but the psychological damage had been done. The British could not know, and were never to learn until after the war, that German Naval Intelligence had not the slightest suspicion of Scapa Flow's nakedness at the outbreak of war in 1914. Nor did German Naval Intelligence learn – though timely air reconnaissance by its Zeppelin airships would have unmasked it – of the humiliating panic which swept the Grand Fleet on 1 September 1914.

The cause of the trouble was most probably an innocent seal poking its head out of the water – but whatever it was, it was reported as a submarine periscope, and the Grand Fleet rushed for the safety of the open sea. For the next four days – while the outcome of the war hung in the balance with the approach of the First Battle of the Marne – the Grand Fleet hovered uncertainly at sea before Admiral Jellicoe withdrew its main body to Loch Ewe on the *west* coast of Scotland – and kept it there until 22 September. But the German High Seas Fleet did not sortie to sever Britain's supply-channel across the Dover Narrows. If Jellicoe was hag-ridden by fears of losing

The first Dreadnought casualty of the First World War: 'King George V' class HMS *Audacious* sinking after being mined off Northern Ireland on 27 October 1914.

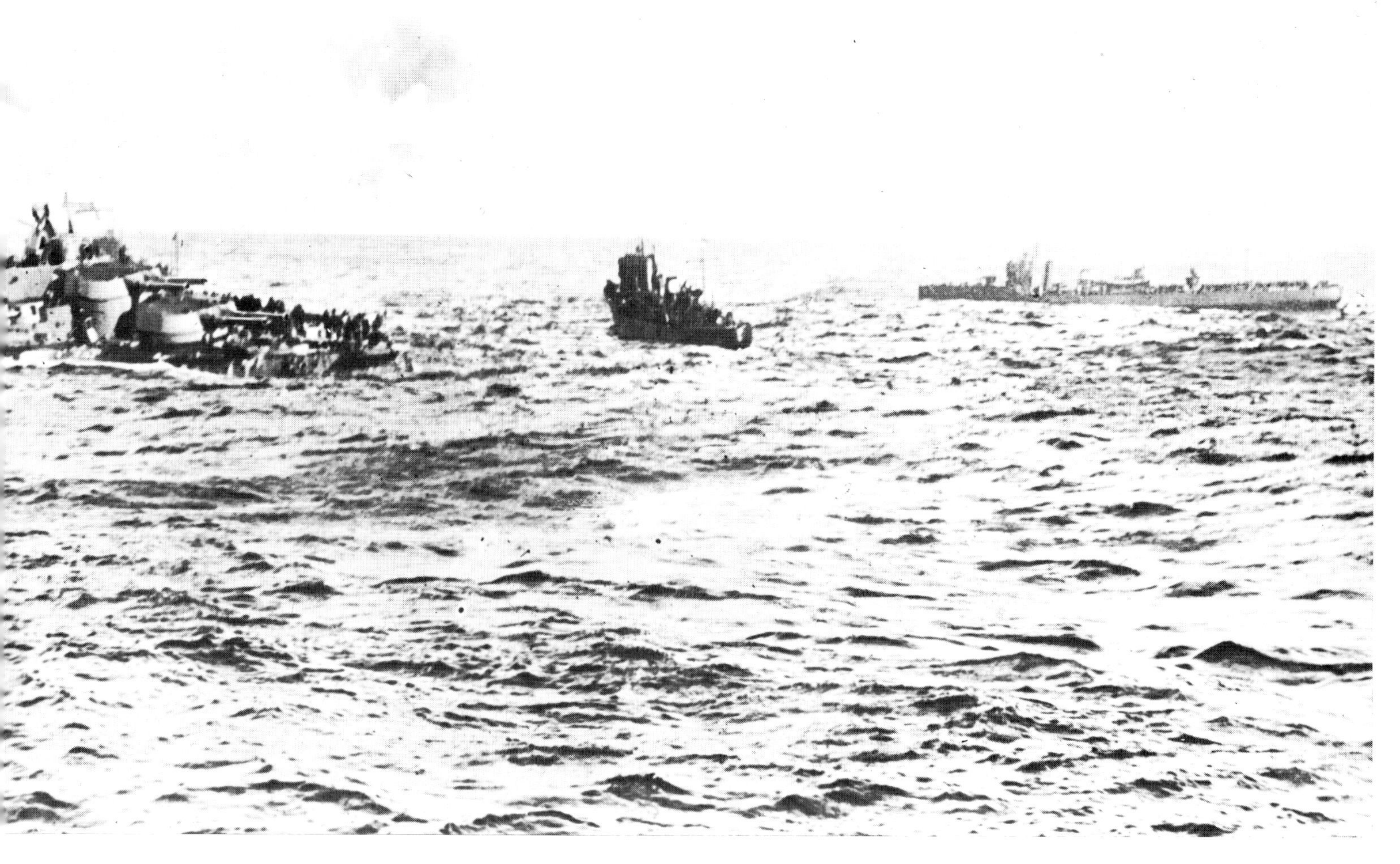

the Grand Fleet's slender superiority, similar fears existed in Germany. Untimely German battleship losses would only render Britain's battleship superiority absolute.

Thus the opening month of the First World War confirmed a basic lesson learned in the Russo-Japanese conflict ten years before. Contrary to outward appearances and public expectation, mere superiority in battleships, the supreme goal of the past decade, now seemed illusory and dangerously fragile. The mine and the submarine presented the strongest Dreadnought battle fleet with even greater dangers than fireships had presented to the wooden sailing battleships of old. And the reality behind the mine/submarine fear was soon revealed. The light cruiser *Pathfinder* was torpedoed and sunk by *U-21* on 5 September, and the old cruisers *Aboukir*, *Hogue* and *Cressy* were sunk in a single hour by *U-9* on the 22nd. The first British Dreadnought lost in the war was the 'King George V' class *Audacious*, sunk (very largely because of inadequate internal protection and damage control facilities) after striking a mine on 27 October. Only ten days after this disaster another false U-boat panic convulsed the Scapa Flow anchorage, followed by a second tactical withdrawal of the Grand Fleet by Jellicoe – this time 300 miles south-east to Lough Swilly on the Northern Irish coast. It seemed to many that the traditional assessment of naval supremacy by the strength of battle fleets had been rendered virtually meaningless by the new weapons. 'We are hunted about the sea', lamented an officer in Beatty's flagship *Lion*, 'and have nowhere we can rest.'

Only time would show that this was not the case – time, and the eventual conversion of Scapa Flow and Rosyth into truly secure bases. The American naval historian Alfred Thayer Mahan, who died in December 1914, had revealed the potency of the 'fleet in being' – the ability of a weaker fleet to immobilise, by its very existence, a stronger enemy. The doctrine of the 'fleet in being' applied just as much to stronger fleets as to weaker enemies, and until the Grand Fleet and its battle-cruiser arm had been given secure bases from which to operate, Jellicoe's caution was fully justified. It was not exploited by the German High Seas Fleet because the Kaiser, daunted by the British battle-cruiser foray into Heligoland Bight on 28 August, ignored the urgings of Tirpitz and issued strict orders that the German fleet was not to be unnecessarily exposed.

During this initial phase of mutual

Top : Shattered by the British battle-cruisers at the Falklands – the armoured cruiser *Scharnhorst*, Spee's flagship. *Above :* German memorial montage of Spee and his 'South Seas Squadron'.

caution, there was plenty of naval activity outside the North Sea war zone in August-December 1914. Unlike the Second World War, the First was a global conflict right from the start, with the British, French, Russian and Japanese naval allies hunting German raiding cruisers in Indian and Pacific waters. The German aim was to disrupt the Allied attempts to ship colonial troops from the Orient and Pacific to the cockpit of the war in France. The biggest menace was Vice-Admiral Graf von Spee's cruiser squadron (two armoured and three light cruisers) based on the Chinese treaty port of Tsingtau, which put to sea on the outbreak of war. After detaching the light cruiser *Emden* to pursue an outstandingly successful lone war cruise in Indian waters, Spee's force set off south-east across the Pacific. The Allies sought to catch him with a scatter of dispositions including pre-Dreadnought battleships sent out from home and the new battle-cruiser *Australia*, which began the war as flagship of the Australian Navy. Spee not only eluded the lot but was reinforced by the light cruiser *Dresden*, and on 1 November 1914 crushed a motley British cruiser force under Rear-Admiral Cradock off Coronel on the Chilean coast. This disaster, the first British naval defeat in more than a century, caused consternation in Whitehall because Cradock was supposed to be operating with the pre-Dreadnought *Canopus* in company. But Cradock had been mistakenly informed that *Canopus* was capable of no more than 12 knots, and had pushed forward to bring Spee to action without the dubious assistance of the old battleship.

The British Admiralty's reaction was to detach the battle-cruisers *Invincible* and *Inflexible* from the Grand Fleet and rush them out to the South Atlantic to liquidate Spee's force. *Canopus* was ordered to be immobilised in Port Stanley to help beat off the attack on the British Falkland Islands which Spee, with the Pacific closed to him by the Allied hunting groups closing in from the west, was expected to make. Vice-Admiral Sir Doveton Sturdee arrived at

Port Stanley with *Invincible* and *Inflexible* on the morning of 7 December. The British ships were still coaling after their long voyage when, at 07.50 hours on the following morning, Spee's scouts were sighted from a lookout post on Sapper Hill. Very luckily for the British, Spee had not arrived off the Falklands with a fully concentrated force – otherwise he could have commanded the harbour exit and concentrated his fire on each British warship as it came out. Nor had Spee been given the slightest warning that British battle-cruisers were anywhere closer to him than the Mediterranean. These considerations, plus the fact that over an hour passed before German lookouts got their first sight of Dreadnought-type tripod masts in Stanley, gave Sturdee the time to break off coaling and raise steam for sea.

The Battle of the Falkland Islands was opened at 09.20 by *Canopus* while the armoured cruiser *Gneisenau* and light cruiser *Nürnberg* were still carrying out their reconnaissance of Stanley. *Canopus* opened fire at 11,500 yards with her two 12-inch turrets. She had been preparing for a practice shot that morning – and thereby hung a tale:

> The after turret's crew, in order to get one up on their deadly rivals in the fore turret, crept out privily by night and loaded with practice shell. Next morning they found it was a real battle and there was no time to unload. The result of this naughtiness was very interesting; the *Gneisenau* was well outside our extreme range, and live shell from my turret, the fore turret, burst on impact with the water, while those from the after turret ricochetted and *one of them scored a hit.*

Apart from being a revealing sidelight on pre-Dreadnought gunnery ethics, the incident caused Spee to abandon his planned bombardment of Stanley and run from what he still believed to be a battle squadron, from which he had every chance of escaping. It was not until 11.00 that Spee realised the truth: that he was being chased by a pair of *battle-cruisers* which, with their 5-knot speed advantage, were bound to

Wyllie's painting of the British battle-cruisers in action at the Falklands. The long range proved especially testing and did not reflect well on British gunnery; it took a combined total of 1,174 rounds to sink *Scharnhorst* and *Gneisenau*.

By far the filthiest job in the pre-oil fuel era: the grimy ordeal of coaling ship.

overhaul him by early afternoon. *Inflexible* and *Invincible* opened fire at extreme range (16,500 yards) just before 12.50. By this time Spee was running on a course allowing only two 12-inch turrets per ship to bear on him and had also, in time-honoured style, seized the more advantageous wind gauge. This was not the weather gauge, as in the days of sail, but the lee, guaranteeing that the British range-tankers and gunlayers (neither battle-cruisers was fitted for director firing) would experience maximum difficulty from their own funnel and cordite smoke. As soon as the battle-cruisers began to get the range (about 13.20) Spee bravely ordered his light cruisers *Leipzig*, *Nürnberg* and *Dresden* to break away and try to escape, while he engaged the battle-cruisers with the armoured cruisers *Scharnhorst* and *Gneisenau*.

Sturdee's most urgent mission was to destroy *Scharnhorst* and *Gneisenau*, the crack gunnery ships of the Imperial German Navy – and to do it quickly and painlessly so that *Invincible* and *Inflexible* could return to service with the Grand Fleet. This meant avoiding damage from the formidable batteries of the German armoured cruisers – eight 8·2-inch guns and six 5·9-inch guns per ship. These scored no less than 22 hits on Sturdee's flagship *Invincible*, which speaks volumes for the excellence of German gunnery in Spee's squadron and his momentary success in closing the range on his massive pursuers.

Sturdee held all the trumps in fire-power and superior speed, and had the sense not to throw them away by playing the enemy's game. But his repeated manoeuvring to keep the range as long as possible, cancelling Spee's gallant efforts to get in close, meant that the inevitable destruction of *Scharnhorst* and *Gneisenau* took a very long time. It was further protracted by the bravery with which the Germans fought their ships to the last. *Scharnhorst* rolled over and sank at 16.17 but *Gneisenau* fought on until 18.00, when she was scuttled on her captain's orders. Both Spee and Captain Maerker of *Gneisenau* were lost with their ships; there were no survivors from *Scharnhorst*, and only 190 out of *Gneisenau*'s complement of 850. Sturdee's victory was rounded out by the sinking of *Nürnberg* by the cruiser *Kent* (at 19.27) and of *Leipzig* by the cruisers *Cornwall* and *Glasgow* (at 20.35). Only *Dresden* escaped the slaughter, to court internment in Chile and be scuttled three months later (14 March 1915) after being run to earth by *Kent* and *Glasgow*.

Sturdee had won his battle in resounding style and avenged the humiliation of Coronel, but he was lucky that there were no other heavy German cruisers at large. Though German gunnery had been superb throughout the action, the British battle-cruisers had fired off most of their 12-inch ammunition, nearly 600 rounds per ship – not the best of omens for the longed-for clash with the High Seas Fleet. Though the Admiralty made the most of the undeniable problems besetting Sturdee's gunners throughout the Falklands battle – smoke, the long range, and the energetic ship manoeuvres – these were not a complete excuse for the indifferent British heavy-calibre gunnery practice. Improved accuracy could only come as a result of more intensive heavy-calibre practice shoots. By the end of 1914, however, Fisher could claim that Heligoland Bight and the Falklands had amply vindicated the battle-cruiser in its role as 'super-scout' and destroyer of enemy raiding cruisers. Only the crucial question of how battle-cruisers would stand up to enemy heavy-calibre fire remained to be put to the test.

This confrontation occurred within three months of the Battle of the Falklands, as a result of a new tactical initiative by the High Seas Fleet. Its commander, Admiral von Ingenohl, was encouraged by the absence of *Invincible* and *Inflexible* in the South Atlantic to attempt to convert this temporary advantage into a permanent one by ambushing portions of the Grand Fleet. The plan was to send out a battle-cruiser force to bombard towns on the English East Coast, at the same time laying minefields over which, hopefully, the British battle-cruisers and battle fleet would be drawn as they hastened south to intercept.

On 3 November 1914 seven German cruisers and three battle-cruisers shelled Yarmouth and Gorleston for half an hour, then withdrew unmolested. Virtually no damage was done (most of the German shells landed on the beaches) and it was certainly a costly experiment, as the cruiser *Yorck* was sunk by a mine on the threshold

Below left: Eve of the Falklands action – the British cruiser *Kent*, with battle-cruisers *Inflexible* and *Invincible*, getting up steam in Port Stanley before setting out to engage Spee's force.
Bottom left: Taken from the flagship *Invincible* – *Inflexible* opening fire on *Scharnhorst* and *Gneisenau*.
Below: The Battle of the Falkland Islands, which vindicated the battle-cruiser as the ultimate 'cruiser destroyer'.

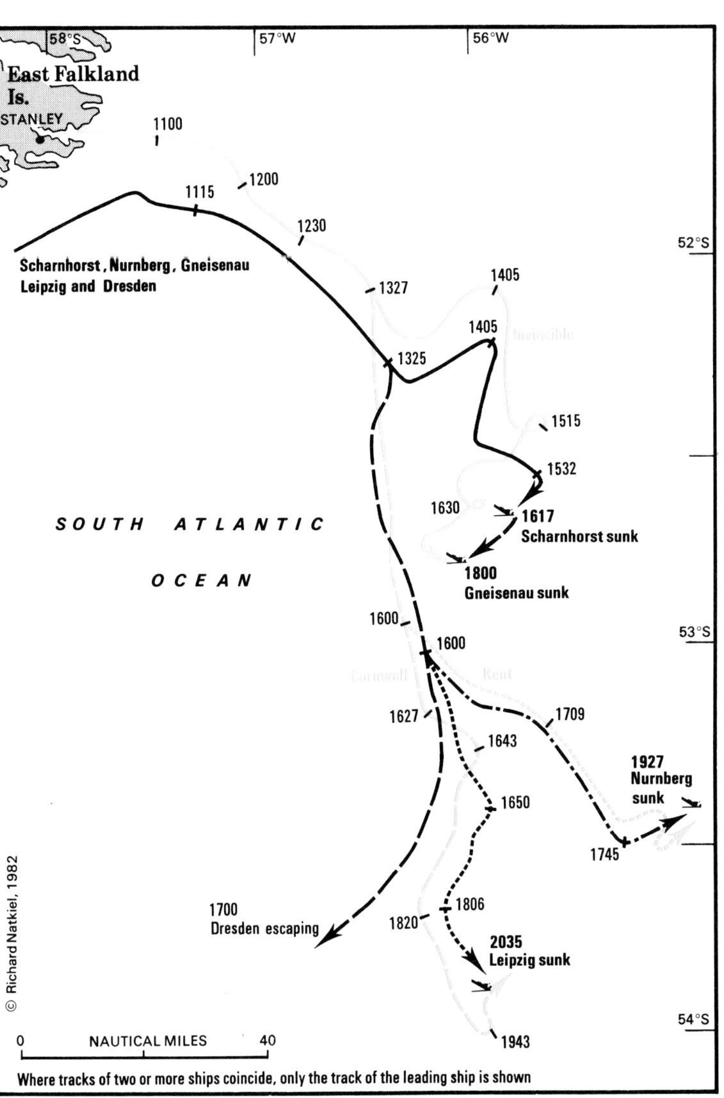

Inflexible's stark silhouette dominates the horizon as German survivors from *Gneisenau* await rescue after their ship was sunk, by scuttling, at 18.00 hours.

of the Jade Bay anchorage at Wilhelmshaven. Ingenohl was nevertheless encouraged by the southward rush of Beatty's battle-cruisers in a vain attempt to cut off the raiders. He planned a full-scale raid for December, this time with the German battle fleet in support. Admiral Franz von Hipper's battle-cruisers were again to act as bait, with *Derfflinger* and *Von der Tann* bombarding Scarborough and Whitby, *Seydlitz*, *Moltke* and the heavy cruiser *Blücher* bombarding Hartlepool. The cruiser *Kolberg* would meanwhile lay a minefield in the expected path of the British, while all three battle squadrons of the High Seas Fleet would be laying in wait in the central North Sea. If Beatty's battle-cruisers missed the mines, Hipper's retreating force would lead Beatty into the jaws of the High Seas Fleet. The operation was planned for dawn on 16 December.

For the first time, however, the British were able to use a new 'secret weapon': radio intelligence, listening-in to the orders being passed to the units of the High Seas Fleet as it prepared for sea. This intelligence, provided by the Admiralty's top-secret 'Room 40', offered the chance of preparing an ambush for the would-be ambushers. But two important pieces of the puzzle were missing: the precise objective of the German battle-cruiser attack, and the fact that the German battle fleet was coming out. And the Admiralty made the first of many fateful errors destined to be repeated throughout the First and Second World Wars, culminating in the PQ.17 disaster of July 1942 (*see p. 151*). Instead of contenting itself with passing all available intelligence to the appropriate C-in-C – the 'man on the spot' who would have to do all the actual fighting (in this case Jellicoe) and letting him make his own dispositions – the Admiralty laid down too rigid an operational framework to cope with unexpected circumstances. In December 1914 this took the form of instructing Jellicoe to send only one of his battle squadrons south (Vice-Admiral Warrender's 2nd Battle Squadron, of six Dreadnoughts) instead of the entire Grand Fleet.

The result was one of the most fascinating 'might-have-beens' of the First World War at sea, with the British Admiralty having unwittingly presented the High Seas Fleet with precisely the favourable conditions for which the Germans yearned. Beatty's four battle-cruisers and Warrender's six Dreadnoughts were to rendezvous off the Dogger Bank before dawn on the 16th, poised to crush Hipper's battle-cruisers as they withdrew from their hit-and-run raid. But advancing against Beatty and Warrender – though ignorant of their presence – was Ingenohl with the High Seas Fleet, 14 Dreadnoughts and eight pre-Dreadnoughts which, counting Hipper's four battle-cruisers, gave the Germans an advantage of nearly three to one: 26 German capital ships against ten British.

Confusion and mistakes on both sides dominated the events of the 16th, which began in pitch darkness at 05.15 hours when the destroyer screens of Warrender's 2nd Battle Squadron collided with that of the High Seas Fleet. Cowed by fears of a torpedo attack by the British destroyers, which he also believed to be escorting the entire Grand Fleet, Ingenohl ordered the High Seas Fleet to head back to base at 05.30. His destroyers failed to identify the true strength of the British force while Warrender, no better served by his own destroyers, carried on to his planned rendezvous with Beatty. But Beatty had meanwhile set off in pursuit of what he believed to be a cruiser/destroyer force, unaware that this was in fact the rearguard of the entire High Seas Fleet. The British were saved from a second impending disaster by the news, shortly before 09.00, that Scarborough was being bombarded by Hipper's battle-cruisers – now left completely unsupported by Ingenohl's withdrawal. It was now the German battle-cruisers, not the British, which were in danger of being cut off and annihilated.

Hipper's force had carried out its raid with telling effect. *Derfflinger* and *Von der Tann* poured 500 shells into Scarborough between 08.00 and 08.30, causing considerable damage but mercifully light casualties. Only 17 were killed, including a baby and two other children – a gift for British 'hate' propaganda, which wasted no time in branding the entire German Navy as 'the baby-killers of Scarborough'. West Hartlepool suffered far more heavily from the 1,150 shells fired by *Seydlitz*, *Moltke* and *Blücher* (08.10–08.52). This was a naval base protected by coastal guns, but of the 102 killed and 467 wounded military/naval casualties only totalled 16 killed and 43 wounded. Finally, Whitby received a 10-minute, 50-round bombardment (09.00–09.10) from *Derfflinger* and *Von der Tann* as they headed north from Scarborough to join the other battle-cruisers before heading for home.

With Beatty and Warrender closing in on him, the retreating Hipper was saved by three factors. The first was deteriorating weather, with rain squalls making accurate sightings increasingly difficult. This was compounded by imprecise orders from the British admirals to their cruiser/destroyer scouts, and the unimaginative interpretation of those orders by the cruiser/destroyer commanders. Commodore Goodenough's light cruiser squadron, screening Beatty's battle-cruisers, sighted Hipper's screen at 11.25. Unwilling to have all his scouts drawn into premature action, Beatty ordered his light cruisers to resume their scouting stations. He intended this to apply to only half Goodenough's force, assuming that the two ships actually in contact would keep shadowing the Germans. But Goodenough chose to obey Beatty's order to the letter, and ordered all four of his ships to fall back, breaking off contact and causing a priceless opportunity to be lost. Warrender's force briefly sighted the German screen at 12.15, but these two fleeting contacts enabled Hipper to alter course and win through to base.

This Scarborough/Hartlepool raid of December 1914 must be seen as one of the most extraordinary episodes in modern naval history. It was brought about by each of the rival fleets being avid for a battle which never took place; it saw each fleet escape disaster by the narrowest of margins; and it left each fleet to count the cost in identical mood: angry frustration at a great opportunity lost. The plain truth was that before the coming of air reconnaissance backed by radar, even the mightiest Dreadnought afloat was a fair-weather weapon,

Ammunitioning ship in the Grand Fleet: 15-inch shells come aboard from the lighter.

The German battle-cruiser *Seydlitz* . . .

with its effectiveness governed by what its lookouts and gunlayers could actually see. Thirty years later, with search and gunnery radar grafted on to battleship technology, and flag-hoist signalling replaced by the ship-to-ship voice radio, it would be a very different story. But in the early years of the First World War these flaws in reconnaissance and communication were crucial and bore heaviest on the biggest battle fleets. Certainly the British admirals, while hoping to excel Togo's achievements with a battle fleet taking up over five times as much sea as the Japanese fleet of 1904–05, had not learned to cope with these problems.

Jellicoe's sense of the narrowness of the Grand Fleet's escape on 16 December was compounded by his worries about the Grand Fleet's frail numerical superiority over the High Seas Fleet. He had to count ships refitting in dock, and new ships not yet fully worked-up to combat efficiency, as temporarily lost to him. On 17 January 1915 he was forced to report that he reckoned the existing balance at only 19 British Dreadnoughts and seven pre-Dreadnoughts ('King Edward VIIs') to 16 German Dreadnoughts and 20 pre-Dreadnoughts. Jellicoe was also worried by the fact that the High Seas Fleet had a bigger destroyer force than the Grand Fleet, giving the Germans greater security as well as the ability to launch decisive torpedo attacks. 'The menace of so large a number of torpedo boat destroyers attacking cannot however possibly be regarded without the certainty of heavy losses in the Battle Line', he reported on 4 December 1914. If so attacked, Jellicoe continued, the Grand Fleet would have no option but to turn away, regardless of its numerical superiority on paper. 'Again and again,' comments the German Official History, 'the fear of German mines, submarines, and torpedo boats deterred (the British) from taking a firm grip'.

All these deficiencies were revealed in the Battle of the Dogger Bank, the clash between the British and German battle-cruisers on 24 January 1915. This came about because of the German keenness to continue the strategy behind the Scarborough Raid, sharpened by a reconnaissance in force by Beatty in the southern North Sea on 19 January. Ingenohl ordered a similar German sweep towards the Dogger Bank for 23–24 January: Hipper with *Seydlitz*, *Moltke*, *Derfflinger* and the heavy cruiser *Blücher*. For this reconnaissance, Ingenohl considered it unnecessary to sail the battle fleet in support of Hipper. German preparations for sea were again detected by the British 'Room 40' at Whitehall, but once again the Admiralty decided to leave interception to Beatty and the battle-cruisers: *Lion*, *Tiger*, *Princess Royal*, *New Zealand* and *Indomitable*. A near-perfect interception resulted, and by 07.30 hours on the 24th Beatty was presented with a greatly outnumbered German force, caught by surprise and forced to run for home in excellent visibility.

Hipper was not only caught with no hope of support from the German battle fleet; his squadron was also hampered by *Blücher*'s lumbering top speed of 23 knots, 4 knots slower than the British battle-cruisers. But if Hipper's incubus was *Blücher*, Beatty's turned out to be the new battle-cruiser *Tiger*. She was the only British battle-cruiser to have been fitted for director firing by January 1915, but this advantage was easily cancelled by other faults, including the rawness of her crew. *Tiger*'s trouble was bad gunnery (this was the first time she had ever fired at a moving target) and worse judgement. As the British closed to maximum range, Beatty intended each of his ships to engage her opposite number in the fleeing German line – but

. . . and how she looked after the ordeal of Jutland, battered and riven in dry dock after struggling home with decks awash.

Tiger joined *Lion* in firing at Hipper's flagship *Seydlitz*, which left *Moltke* free to range on *Lion*. To make matters worse, *Tiger*'s spotters marked down *Lion*'s shell splashes as their own, when in fact *Tiger*'s shells were falling over 3,000 yards past their target.

The resulting concentration of unpleasantly accurate German fire resulted in *Seydlitz* and *Derfflinger* scoring one 11-inch and two 12-inch direct hits on *Lion* between 10.01 and 10.18, an hour after the British had fired their first shots at extreme range. The damage to *Lion* was crippling, silencing two of her dynamos and contaminating an oil feed tank. There was soon nothing for it but to stop the port engine, and by 10.54 the frustrated Beatty had fallen two miles behind the rest of his command. With no electricity for searchlight or radio morse signals, Beatty had to rely on flag hoists to communicate with his ships. This need not have mattered. By 10.54 *Blücher* had taken a terrible battering from the rearmost British ships and was obviously doomed (though her crew fought to the last with the same gallantry shown by their comrades at the Falklands). It should have been clear to Beatty's second-in-command (Rear-Admiral Moore, in *New Zealand*) that his duty was to leave *Blücher* and press on after the three German battle-cruisers, which had taken several hits on their upperworks. Beatty, however, tried to carry on directing the battle from two miles astern, with unhappy results: Moore was obliged to keep looking over his shoulder and attempting to decipher his C-in-C's signals, instead of concentrating on finishing off Hipper.

At this crucial moment another false submarine report fatally distracted Beatty, who later reported that he 'personally observed the wash of a periscope 2 points on our starboard bow'. (There were in fact no U-boats within 60 miles of the battle zone, and what Beatty saw was probably a spent torpedo, surfacing at the end of its run, from a German destroyer.) Believing that a multiple U-boat attack was imminent, Beatty did exactly what Jellicoe would have done and ordered his ships to turn away from the threat. This was long before it was learned, in the Second World War, that a safer parry was to turn *towards* the torpedoes, which made 'combing' (steering between) their tracks easier.

The 90° turn to port ordered by Beatty carried the British battle-cruisers across Hipper's wake, but Beatty did his best to head them back into action. 'COURSE N.E.', he signalled, then 'ATTACK THE REAR OF THE ENEMY'. Unhappily the second signal was hoisted while the first was still flying, giving Moore the impression that he was to attack the rear German ships bearing north-east. Beatty's last effort to hoist Nelson's favourite signal, 'ENGAGE THE ENEMY MORE CLOSELY' was

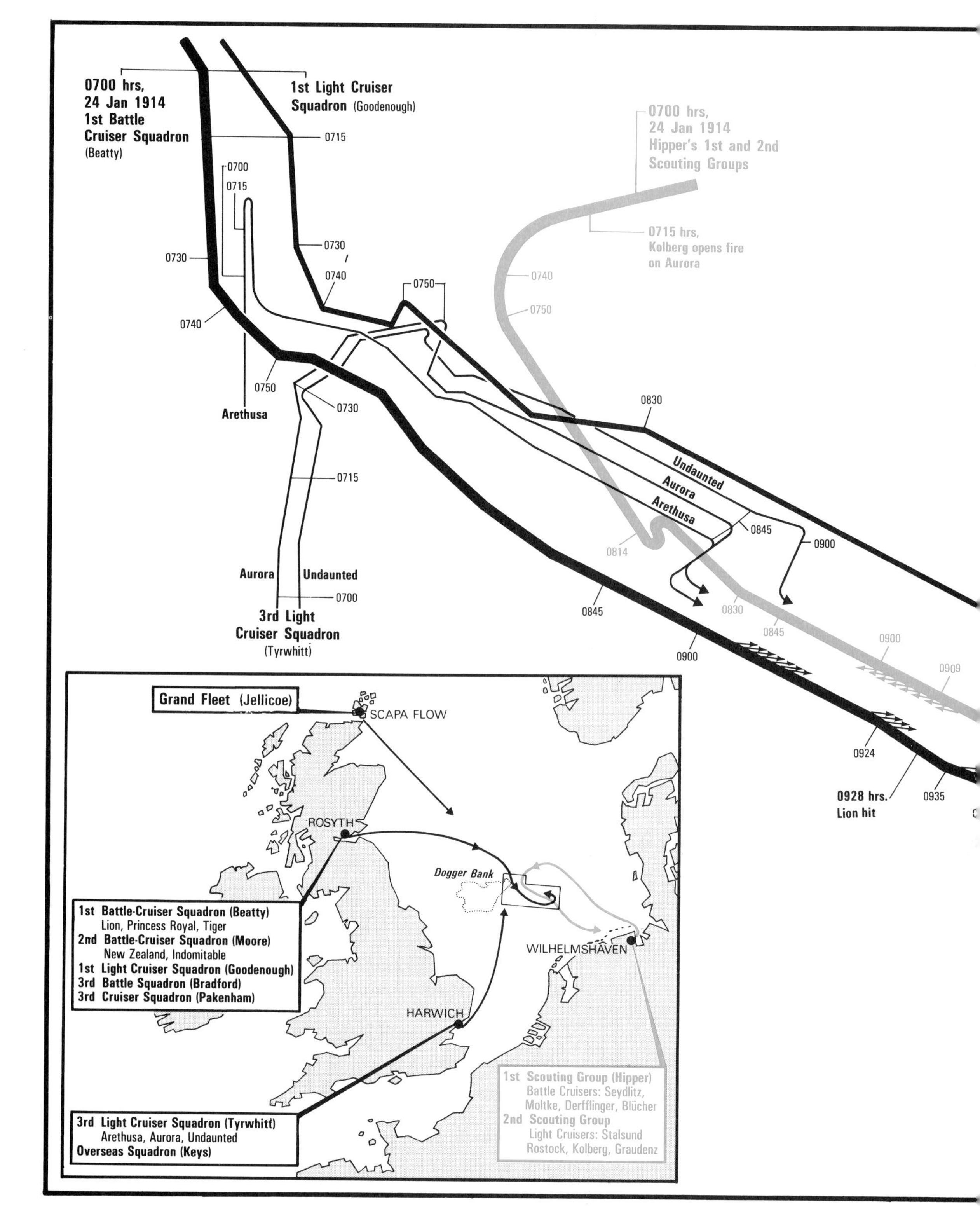

foiled by this signal having been removed from the book during 'improvements' to the signal code. It had been replaced by 'KEEP NEARER THE ENEMY', but by the time this was hoisted in *Lion* it could not be read. The result was that Moore abandoned the pursuit of Hipper and concentrated on the only target lying on the bearing ordered by Beatty: the hapless *Blücher*. She finally rolled over and sank at 12.10, the picture of her on her beam ends with ant-like survivors scrambling over her hull resulting in one of the most famous photographs of the First World War. Beatty frantically transferred to the destroyer *Attack* when he saw what Moore was doing, but by the time he arrived on the scene Hipper was at least 12 miles away and there was nothing for it but to head for home.

The British Press exulted over the Dogger Bank 'victory', claiming that the victims of the Scarborough Raid had been avenged by the Germans' precipitate flight and abandonment of *Blücher* to her doom. But in British naval circles there were vicious post-mortems over this latest missed opportunity, which had let three damaged ships escape. Flames 200 ft high had been seen roaring from the after turret of *Seydlitz*, the result of a 13.5-inch hit by *Lion* at 09.50. This had pierced the barbette armour and the flash had penetrated the magazine

Left : Blücher, the hybrid German heavy armoured cruiser whose lagging speed brought about her demise in the Dogger Bank action (*below*).

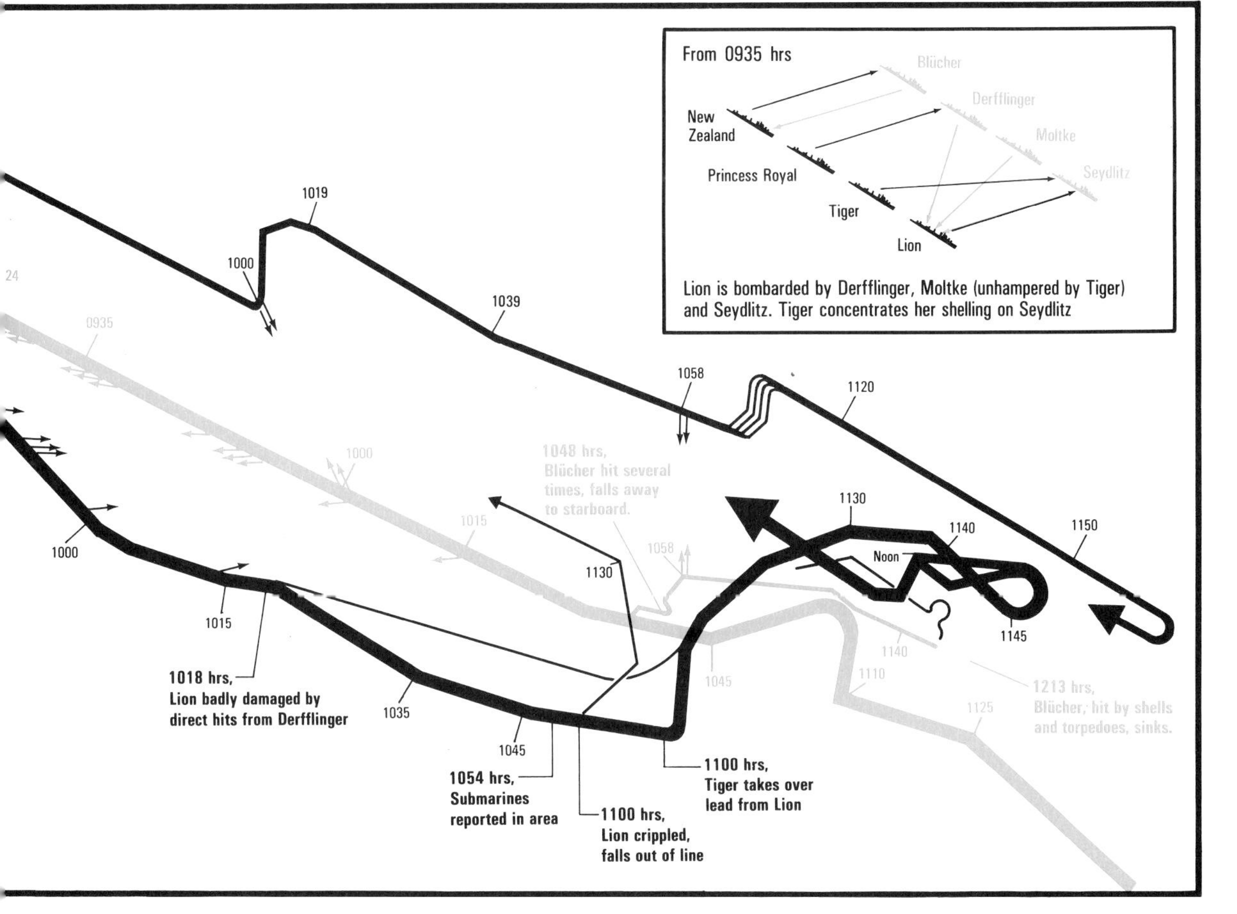

handing-rooms of both after turrets. *Seydlitz* was only saved by the prompt flooding of the after magazines, but 159 men died. Chastened by this experience, the German Naval Command ordered the immediate installation of anti-flash partitions to limit the spread of flash caused by enemy shells. The fact that the Germans but not the British took these measures after Dogger Bank was to have profound results at Jutland in the following year. The most predictable aftermath of Dogger Bank was a prolonged period of inactivity as both sides took stock of the experience of the battle.

Though the Anglo-German confrontation across the North Sea remained the dramatic centrepiece of the war at sea, the Mediterranean/Black Sea theatre had seen no lack of battleship action since the escape of *Goeben* and *Breslau* to Constantinople in August 1914. *Goeben*'s transfer to Turkish service as *Yavuz Sultan Selim* was quickly arranged (*Breslau* became *Midilli*) on 16 August. *Sultan Selim* immediately became a 'one-ship 'fleet in being', dominating Allied naval dispositions as no other single German warship was to do until *Tirpitz* in 1942–44. Based on Constantinople, *Sultan Selim* was the latest instance of the Dreadnought myth and its power, mesmerising the Russian Black Fleet of pre-Dread-

Goeben and *Breslau*, whose presence at Constantinople dominated the Allied deployments in the eastern Mediterranean from start to finish of the war.

noughts – *Georgi Pobiedonosets*, *Sinope*, *Tri Sviatitelia*, *Pantaleimon*, *Rostislav*, *Sviatitoi Evstafi* and *Ioann Zlatoust* – based on Sevastopol. In addition to depriving the Russian Black Sea Fleet of any freedom of action, *Sultan Selim* kept the British battle-cruisers *Indefatigable* and *Indomitable* watching the Dardanelles until the end of 1914.

Sultan Selim became the only single battleship to embarrass its owners into going to war when Souchon took her into the Black Sea and bombarded Sevastopol (29 October 1914). *Georgi Pobiedonosets*, by 1914 little more than a floating headquarters ship for the Black Sea Fleet staff, joined the Sevastopol shore batteries in a spirited counter-bombardment which landed two 12-inch hits on *Sultan Selim*; but Souchon was still able to bombard Novorossiisk and Odessa before returning to Constantinople. The result was the Russian declaration of war on Turkey (1 November) which ended the vacillating Turkish neutrality prevailing since August. The Russians used their pre-Dreadnoughts to cover mine-laying operations off the Bosphorus, but this failed to prevent *Sultan Selim* from making another sortie in the third week of November. This time the Russian Black Sea Fleet sailed to intercept and the result was an indecisive action on 18 November off Sarych Point, the southernmost extremity of the Crimea.

Confronted as she was by five battleships (*Sviatitoi Evstafi*, *Ioann Zlatoust*, *Tri Sviatitelia*, *Pantaleimon* and *Rostislav*), *Sultan Selim* did well to escape. (This she owed to her superior speed, another partial justification of the battle-cruiser concept.) The Sarych Point action was another testimonial for the toughness of German construction, for *Sultan Selim* was hit 14 times and was still able to disengage and return safely to base. Two of these hits were 12-inch shells from *Pantaleimon* (formerly *Potemkin*); *Sviatitoi Evstafi* scored at least one 12-inch hit but was hit four times in return. The observation of these hits, none of which caused more than superficial damage, had tremendous results because the British Admiralty accepted Russian assurances that *Sultan Selim* had sustained heavy damage. *Indomitable* and six destroyers were promptly withdrawn from their watch on the Dardanelles, where the outer Turkish forts had been treated to an Anglo-French bombardment lasting ten minutes on 3 November. The combined belief that *Sultan Selim* was neutralised, and that the Dardanelles forts could easily be destroyed by heavy naval gunnery, led to the conception of the plan to knock Turkey clean out of the war by striking through the Dardanelles. And the result was the tragedy of Gallipoli, prefaced by the failure of an all-naval attempt to force the Dardanelles in March 1915.

The strategy behind the Dardanelles assault was perfectly sound; it was the tactical methods chosen which were at fault, particularly the doomed attempt to force the straits by warships alone after all surprise had been lost. This was attempted because no troops were available to land and secure the Turkish forts which the warships were to bombard. It was also obvious that the straits would be mined, but the difficulty of sweeping a safe path for the bombarding warships, under Turkish fire from the shore, was fatally under-estimated. But the real trouble was 'bombardment mania': the failure to grasp that prolonged bombardment of the enemy's positions merely warned him that an attack was coming. This error was the crux of the deadlock on the Western Front which the Dardanelles plan was supposed to break by a swift and decisive blow. And it derived from the impressive volume of heavy-calibre naval fire-power produced by listing all available British and French pre-Dreadnoughts; deciding that – mines or no mines – these ships could be regarded as expendable; and committing them to attack commanded by admirals who knew that even if the ships *were* expendable, their crews were not. As a final example of the breezy assumption of what an easy job it would be, the British sent out the new fast battleship *Queen Elizabeth* to calibrate her guns by firing at the Turkish forts – a priceless new heavy unit sent to achieve full combat efficiency in the death-trap of a mined strait.

In short, the Anglo-French battleships which attacked the Dardanelles forts in February–March 1915 were set an impossible task. Admiral Carden, commanding the Mediterranean Fleet, set about bombarding the outer forts on 19 February only to be forced to break off because of bad weather. By the first week of March the outer forts had been fairly battered, but the improvised minesweeping force – civilian North Sea trawlermen recruited by the Admiralty – was being driven back from the straits by the fire of mobile Turkish howitzer batteries ashore: elusive targets impossible for the battleships to liquidate. Carden was replaced on 15 March by Vice-Admiral de Robeck, who on 18 March led 18 French and British battleships into the straits. It was learned after the war that the battleships' majestic approach had pushed Turkish morale almost to breaking-point – but the ships failed to knock out any of the guns covering the minefield; *Bouvet*, *Ocean* and *Irresistible* were sunk by mines in an area believed to be swept and safe; *Inflexible* was badly damaged by another mine, and *Gaulois* and *Suffren* had taken heavy punishment from gunfire. For de Robeck these setbacks were ample for a seven-hour action, and he withdrew. After three days' indecision de Robeck decided that the all-naval plan was dead – that even if warships *could* be pushed through the Narrows of the Dardanelles to the Sea of Marmora, their frail line of communication to the Mediterranean would still be dominated by the Turkish shore guns. Any renewed assult must therefore proceed with troops landed to clear the Gallipoli peninsula – but the Turks were given another month before the Gallipoli invasion force was ready.

The Gallipoli landings of 25 April were a ghastly example of how not to carry out an opposed landing on difficult terrain under the covering fire of a powerful fleet. With air reconnaissance still in its infancy, neither the assault troops nor the warships

Sent out from Britain to calibrate her 15-inch guns in bombardments of the Dardanelles forts: HMS *Queen Elizabeth*.

supposed to be giving them covering fire were supplied with detailed maps of the terrain. Ship-to-shore communications consisted of messages sent in boats. Logistic back-up was virtually non-existent and the warships were required to put the troops ashore, supply them with essentials such as water, and provide fire support. Within 48 hours of carnage the assault troops were pinned down in their beach-heads while the warships searched unavailingly for the almost invisible Turkish strongpoints on the heights. Yet the seizure of five separate beach-heads on Gallipoli momentarily shook the Turks' confidence. To bolster it *Sultan Selim* came down from Constantinople on 27 April, only to retire after coming under long-range fire from *Queen Elizabeth*. The British battleship's indirect fire over the intervening land mass of Gallipoli, first attempted on 5 March during the bombardment of the Narrows forts, marked the first attempt at marrying air reconnaissance to conventional surface fire-power. Inevitably hampered by the lack of direct air-to-ship communication, it was nevertheless a tremendous morale-booster for the troops.

But as the army waited for reinforcements before resuming the Gallipoli offensive, the naval picture was transformed by the arrival of the first U-boat off the Dardanelles. This was the redoubtable *U-21* of *Kapitänleutnant* Otto Hersing who had torpedoed *Pathfinder*, the first British warship sunk by a U-boat, back in September 1914. Penetrating the milling swarm of shipping off the beaches on 25 May, Hersing missed the British pre-Dreadnoughts *Swiftsure* and *Vengeance* with his first torpedoes but sank *Triumph* with a single torpedo after a two-hour stalk. Hersing then dived and lay 'bottomed' for the next 48 hours, re-emerging on the 27th to sink *Majestic* before making good his escape. This latest disaster occurred a bare fortnight after *Goliath* had been torpedoed and sunk in a surprise attack by a German-manned Turkish destroyer (on the night of 12 May) which had prompted the immediate recall of *Queen Elizabeth* to home waters.

Since their costly repulse on 18 March, the battleships of the Dardanelles had been brutally exposed to the triple menace of mine, surface torpedo and submarine torpedo; and Hersing's two kills in the last

Beatty's battle-cruisers in action at Jutland

A highly fanciful German depiction of the 'Skagerrak victory', as the narrow escape of Jutland was remembered in Germany.

week of May prompted the immediate withdrawal of the Allied battleships to Port Mudros on the island of Lemnos. They took no part in the final throw on Gallipoli: the landings at Suvla Bay on 6–7 August, which achieved no more than the establishment of another useless beach-head. The military stalemate continued until the decision was taken to evacuate Gallipoli in December. Though fire-eating plans for a renewed direct naval assault up the straits continued to be put forward virtually until the last minute, the inability of the troops to break out and clear the Gallipoli peninsula nullified all these urgings. It was not the first time that battleship fire-power had been set at nought by mine and torpedo, and it would certainly not be the last. But seldom if ever were battleships called upon to attempt a more impossible task than those of the Dardanelles.

The year 1916 came in with Germany bidding high for victory by land and sea – with General von Falkenhayn's strategy for 'bleeding the French Army white' at Verdun, and with plans for resumption of the 'naval ambush' strategy by more aggressive use of the High Seas Fleet. The latter received a new commander in January 1916: Admiral Reinhard Scheer, who had always deplored the caution which had robbed Germany of naval victories at the time of the Scarborough Raid and the Dogger Bank action. Scheer was undaunted by the powerful reinforcements which, while the High Seas Fleet had only been increased by the new battle-cruiser *Lützow*, had added the 14-inch gun *Canada* and the 15-inch gun *Queen Elizabeth*, *Barham*, *Valiant*, *Warspite*, *Malaya*, *Revenge*, and *Royal Oak* to the Grand Fleet. He was still determined to succeed where his predecessors had failed, and use Hipper's battle-cruisers to lure weaker sections of the British fleet within range of the German battle fleet. For 1916, however, Scheer planned to use his naval Zeppelins for air reconnaissance with patrol-lines of U-boats, sent out ahead, to act as the concealed 'front line' of the German surface ships. For their part, the British were now using seaplane-carriers in unavailing raids on the Zeppelin bases in Schleswig-Holstein and as airborne scouts for the fleet. The naval 'campaign' of 1916 in the North Sea was the first uncertain test of naval aviation.

This campaign was crowned on 31 May 1916 by the Battle of Jutland, the full-scale fleet engagement which the High Seas Fleet had never intended to fight. Jutland was the outcome of four months of sparring in the

North Sea which had begun with Scheer trying to draw out the British cruiser/destroyer force based on Harwich. After three tentative sorties in February and March, Scheer ordered a full-scale sortie to open with his battle-cruisers bombarding Lowestoft and Yarmouth (25 April). This opened badly when *Seydlitz* limped home after striking a mine off the Friesian Islands. Hipper was ill and the battle-cruisers were commanded by the ultra-cautious Rear-Admiral Bödicker, who found himself confronting three light cruisers and 18 destroyers of the Harwich Force in overwhelming strength. Bödicker, however, cancelled the strike at Yarmouth and fell back on the battle fleet as soon as he had completed a ten-minute bombardment of Lowestoft, whereupon Scheer ordered the High Seas Fleet home. Bödicker had passed up the chance of doing to the British what they had done to Spee at the Falklands, but at least Scheer knew that the British reaction to a show of force off the East Coast was as quick as in 1914–15. For his next foray he planned to use a strike at Sunderland, 200 miles closer to the Grand Fleet's northern bases, as bait for Beatty's battle-cruisers.

Scheer intended to launch this operation only after positioning U-boat patrol lines south of the Grand Fleet's bases, and after his Zeppelins had reported that the British were not already at sea. Originally timed for 17 May, the operation had to be put back to the end of May because of the time needed to complete repairs to *Seydlitz*. By then bad weather had made it impossible for the Zeppelins to fly, so Scheer opted for his back-up plan: a more easterly sortie, with the Jutland coast of Denmark shielding the starboard flank of the High Seas Fleet. Knowing that his U-boats would reach the end of their endurance on 1 June, he sailed at 02.30 hours on the 31st, preceded by Hipper.

The usual excellent work by 'Room 40' in Whitehall deduced that another German sortie was imminent and both Jellicoe and Beatty were at sea by the time Scheer cleared the Jade. But a needless misunderstanding caused the Admiralty to inform Jellicoe at 12.30 that Scheer's call-sign was still coming from the Jade. In fact Scheer used a different call-sign when he put to sea, as 'Room 40' could have told the Admiralty's Director of Operations if asked. As a result neither Jellicoe nor Beatty was given any notion that the German battle fleet had followed Hipper's force to sea, and the rendezvous between Jellicoe and Beatty was made unnecessarily late in the day. This should not have mattered too much because Beatty's force was far stronger than it had been at the Dogger Bank. In addition to *Lion*, *Queen Mary*, *Princess Royal*, *Tiger*, *New Zealand* and *Indefatigable*, Beatty could also call on the four new 'Queen Elizabeths' of the 5th Battle Squadron: *Barham*, *Valiant*, *Warspite* and *Malaya*. The 5th Battle Squadron had been temporarily swapped for Rear-Admiral Hood's 3rd Battle-cruiser Squadron (*Invincible*, *Inflexible* and *Indomitable*), which was operating with the main British battle fleet on the 31st. Yet Hipper also had two more battle-cruisers than at the Dogger Bank – the new *Lützow* and *Von der Tann*. As well as improved odds against them (six to five instead of five to three) the German battle-cruisers had the advantage, unknown to the British, of the anti-flash precautions installed since the Dogger Bank action.

Contact between the British and German battle-cruiser screens was made at 14.15, just after Beatty had turned north towards his planned rendezvous with Jellicoe. Given the record of past frustrations it was not surprising that Beatty did not wait for 5th Battle Squadron (Rear-Admiral Evan-Thomas) to close up, but headed straight in to engage. Hipper obediently headed south-

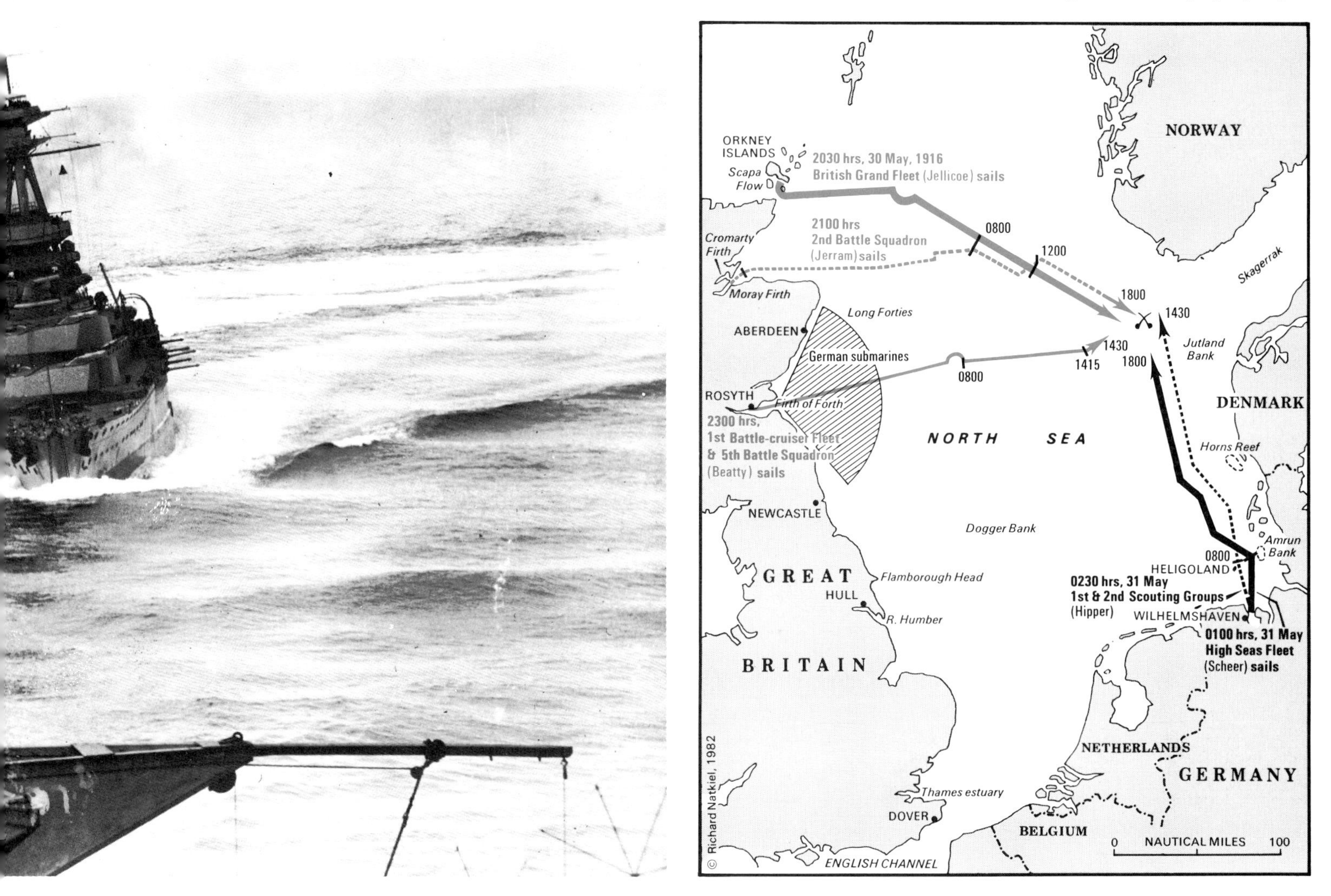

Above left: HMS *Royal Oak* at action stations, making a sharp turn to port with the 6-inch guns of her secondary armament bristling on both flanks.
Above: The North Sea theatre on the eve of Jutland, and the converging of the fleets.

east to lure Beatty within range of Scheer and the battle fleet, and at 15.47 the running fight between the battle-cruisers, the opening phase of the Battle of Jutland, began at a range of 15,500 yards. General visibility was good, but once again the Germans had won the best wind gauge and had picked a course on which smoke would most impair British gunnery.

This opening 'run to the south' ended at 16.38 when the British sighted the oncoming German battle fleet and turned to lure it within Jellicoe's grasp. It was the first naval action in which warships tried to use air reconnaissance, the latter facility being provided by the British seaplane-carrier *Engadine*. Flight-Lt Rutland ('Rutland of Jutland', as he was subsequently known) was airborne between 15.08 and 15.48, when a broken fuel pipe ended his flight. Low clouds forced him to fly at only 900 ft, unable to observe the two fleets simultaneously; but he did report three times on Hipper's opening moves, and it was not his fault that the primitive communications of the day prevented his reports from being passed direct to Beatty in *Lion*. The seaplanes played no further part in the action, largely because *Engadine* was too slow.

Beatty's opening rush was made in the belief that Hipper was on his own, but the British soon found that they had caught a Tartar. German gunnery was excellent from the outset and was helped by the British making the same mistake as at the Dogger Bank: leaving an enemy ship 'unfired-at', in this case *Derfflinger*, second ship in Hipper's line. This enabled the German battle-cruisers to score four times as many hits than the British in the first half-hour (about 14 German hits to three British). At 16.00 *Lion*'s central 'Q' turret was ripped open by a single shell, igniting the cordite charges in the hoist. Total disaster was only averted by the heroism of the mortally-wounded turret officer, who managed to order the magazine flooded before he died. Beatty's rearmost ship, *Indefatigable*, had no such luck. Two minutes later she was pulverised by three shells from *Von der Tann*, blowing up and sinking in less than three minutes.

Within minutes of *Indefatigable*'s loss, Evan-Thomas brought 5th Battle Squadron into action and had begun to land hits on *Von der Tann* and *Moltke* by 16.16; but Hipper's line continued to shoot superbly. At one point *Princess Royal* vanished in an enormous cloud of smoke and spray and Beatty, believing her lost, made his famous comment that 'There seems to be something wrong with our bloody ships today'. Well he might. After a five-minute battering from both *Seydlitz* and *Derfflinger*, *Queen Mary* blew up and sank at 16.26. But this second triumph brought no easement to Hipper. He had already sacrificed speed to give his gunners more stability, steaming at 18 knots to Beatty's 25. While certainly improving German gunnery, this nevertheless allowed 5th Battle Squadron to close on the Germans from the rear while Beatty forged ahead to cut them off from base. By 16.30 the British were getting the better of a spirited destroyer action between the battle-cruiser lines; and within ten minutes of *Queen Mary*'s loss Hipper was turning away eastward to avoid a torpedo attack.

At this point the situation was transformed as Goodenough's light cruiser squadron, gloriously atoning for its fateful error in December 1914, sighted and reported the approach of Scheer's battle fleet from the south. This turned the battle inside out. It was now Beatty's task to draw the Germans north – *and do it without allowing Hipper to sight the British battle fleet in time to warn Scheer*. The actual turn north was clumsily executed, with the British battle-cruisers turning 15 minutes before 5th Battle Squadron. This left 5th Battle Squadron, obediently turning in succession, to endure heavy fire from Scheer's leading battleships for some 30 minutes. Luckily for the four 'Queen Elizabeths', however, the gunnery of the German battle fleet was nowhere near as accurate as that of Hipper's battle-cruisers, while the gunnery of 5th Battle Squadron scored damaging hits on Scheer's three leading ships (*König*, *Grosser Kurfürst* and *Markgraf*). But the 'run to the north' (17.00–18.00) was a tactical triumph for Beatty. A second engagement plastered Hipper's force with a total of 16 hits (two more than had been inflicted during the run south). Much more important, it nudged Hipper so far to the east that Scheer received no warning that Jellicoe's mighty fleet of 24 Dreadnoughts was sweeping down on him.

When Jellicoe received Goodenough's sighting report of 16.38 he was only 50 miles away, and by 17.00 felt confident enough to signal to the Admiralty 'FLEET ACTION IS IMMINENT'. But Jellicoe's problems were immense. Though there were barely three hours of clear daylight left, he had to keep his speed down to 18 knots to ensure that the Grand Fleet kept station: six columns in line-abreast, with four battleships in each. Before he sighted Scheer he would have to deploy these columns into a single line-ahead, which would, depending on the bearing of the German fleet, have to be done by the left, centre or right. Because of banks of mist compounded by gun and funnel smoke, visibility was deteriorating by the minute; by 18.00 it was less than 6 miles. Once again, it all came down to what the human eye could actually see.

This would not have mattered if Jellicoe had been constantly and accurately informed of the Germans' bearing by his scouts, but he was not. Only a scatter of cryptic and often conflicting reports reached *Iron Duke* from Goodenough, Beatty and Evan-Thomas. As late as 18.06, five minutes after the battered *Lion* had been sighted from *Iron Duke*, Jellicoe was still desperately signalling for the vital bearing of Scheer's approach. Not until 18.10 did a lifting of the mist enable Beatty to report the German battle fleet approaching from the S.S.W. Knowing that further delay would certainly catch the Grand Fleet undeployed, Jellicoe had to decide at once on which column the deployment should be made. It took him some 20 seconds of intense thought, staring in silence at the compass. The wrong decision would have placed the Grand Fleet right under the guns of Scheer's line, wide open to concentrated German fire as it deployed – but Jellicoe's decision to deploy on the port wing column, ordered at 18.15, was inspired. It laid the Grand Fleet's 24 battleships in an immense, concave arc right across the head of Scheer's oncoming line: the most extensive, most successful 'crossing of the T' in naval history.

Carried out at the temporarily reduced speed of 14 knots, the Grand Fleet's majestic deployment coincided with violent action in the 'No Man's Land' between the fleets. The German light cruiser *Wiesbaden* was battered to a cripple by Hood's 3rd Battle-cruiser Squadron as Hood strove to join Beatty's force. The British cruiser *Defence* blew up and sank under crushing fire from Hipper's battle-cruisers and Scheer's 3rd Battle Squadron. *Warspite* was forced to limp home, saved again by her armour, after circling helplessly with a jammed rudder under concentrated German fire, taking 13 hits from the head of the German line. By 18.25 Hipper's five battle-cruisers were suffering heavy punishment from the seven battle-cruisers of Beatty and Hood when a salvo from *Derfflinger* smashed through *Invincible*'s 'Q' turret. The flash

Top : Beatty's flagship *Lion* at full speed, seconds away from her near-disastrous hit.
Left : Lion is bracketed by heavy German shells, and finally (*right*) a dense blur between her masts indicates the famous hit on 'Q' turret.

reached the magazine and a colossal explosion blew *Invincible* in half (18.34). The gallant Hood was not among the six survivors out of over 1,000 officers and men.

Invincible's shattering end, however, brought little joy to the High Seas Fleet, which by 18.30 was confronted by the most awesome sight in battleship history: the entire northern horizon ablaze with the broadside fire of 24 Dreadnoughts. No Ger- who saw it ever forgot it, and the results were profound. Two and a half years later, with the Allies advancing into Belgium and the war obviously lost, the memory of that blazing horizon would induce the men of the High Seas Fleet to mutiny rather than face it again. At 18.35, thinking only of escape, Scheer ordered an emergency manoeuvre which the British Grand Fleet Battle Orders had rejected as impracticable. This was the *gefechtkehrtwendung*, 'battle turn-away', in which each ship in the line followed the ship immediately astern in a 180° turn. It was brilliantly executed. Within four minutes, by 18.39, the High Seas Fleet was vanishing westward into the mist while Jellicoe headed the Grand Fleet south to get between Scheer and his base.

In the tense minutes after Scheer's withdrawal, the cruiser scouts of both sides fell down on the job and left the rival commanders without accurate information on the bearing of the other's battle fleet. This tempted Scheer to try a move which, as he admitted later, would have justified his sacking if he had tried it in peacetime manoeuvres. At 18.52 he ordered a second *kehrtwendung*, reversing course and steering back to the east. Scheer's aim seems to have been to get back to eastward of Jellicoe by 'crossing the British T' and mauling the rear of Jellicoe's line as he went. But the

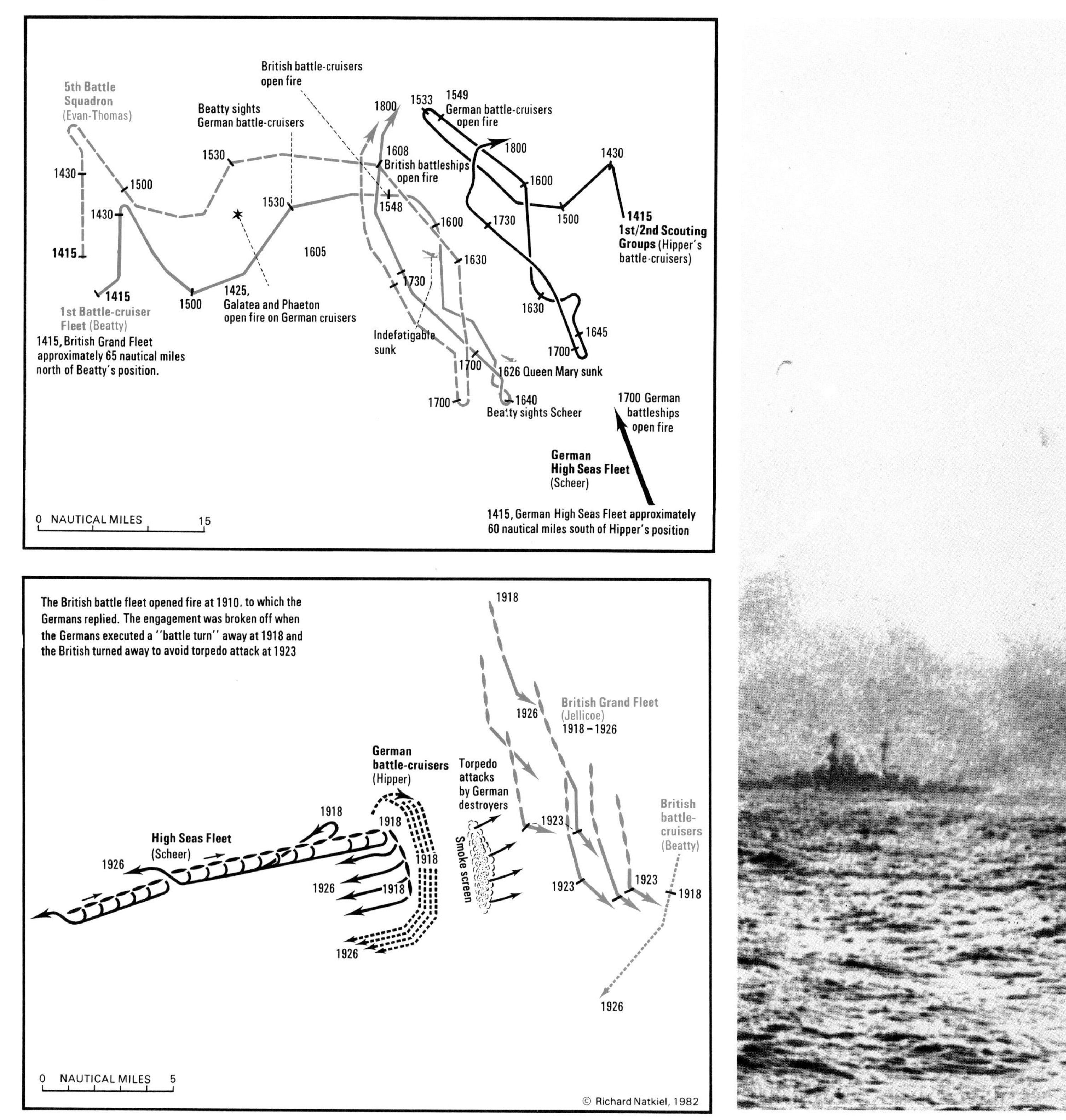

Top: The battle-cruiser action which opened the Battle of Jutland (31 May 1916).
Above: The second clash of the battle fleets at Jutland.

Grand Fleet was not as far south as Scheer believed, and by 19.04 the German line emerged from the mist heading straight for the centre of the British line. A second brief but intense fleet action ensued from 19.10 to 19.35, which saw the imperilled High Seas Fleet take its heaviest punishment. Hipper's battle-cruisers came off worst. At 19.13 Scheer ordered their deliberate sacrifice in an all-out closing and ramming attack, only to reprieve the battle-cruisers from their 'death-ride' by substituting a massed destroyer torpedo attack. As they attacked, the German destroyers laid a dense smokescreen under cover of which Scheer ordered a third *kehrtwendung*. Jellicoe's reflex turn to port, away from the German destroyer attacks, enabled Scheer to complete his disengagement and by 19.35 the High Seas fleet was steaming away to the south-west.

By 19.45 the Grand Fleet's prospects could hardly have looked better. It had brought the High Seas Fleet to action after nearly two frustrating years; the Germans had twice turned and run; they were now cut off from their base, and Jellicoe confidently expected a second 'Glorious First of June' on the following morning. This did not happen because the High Seas Fleet had

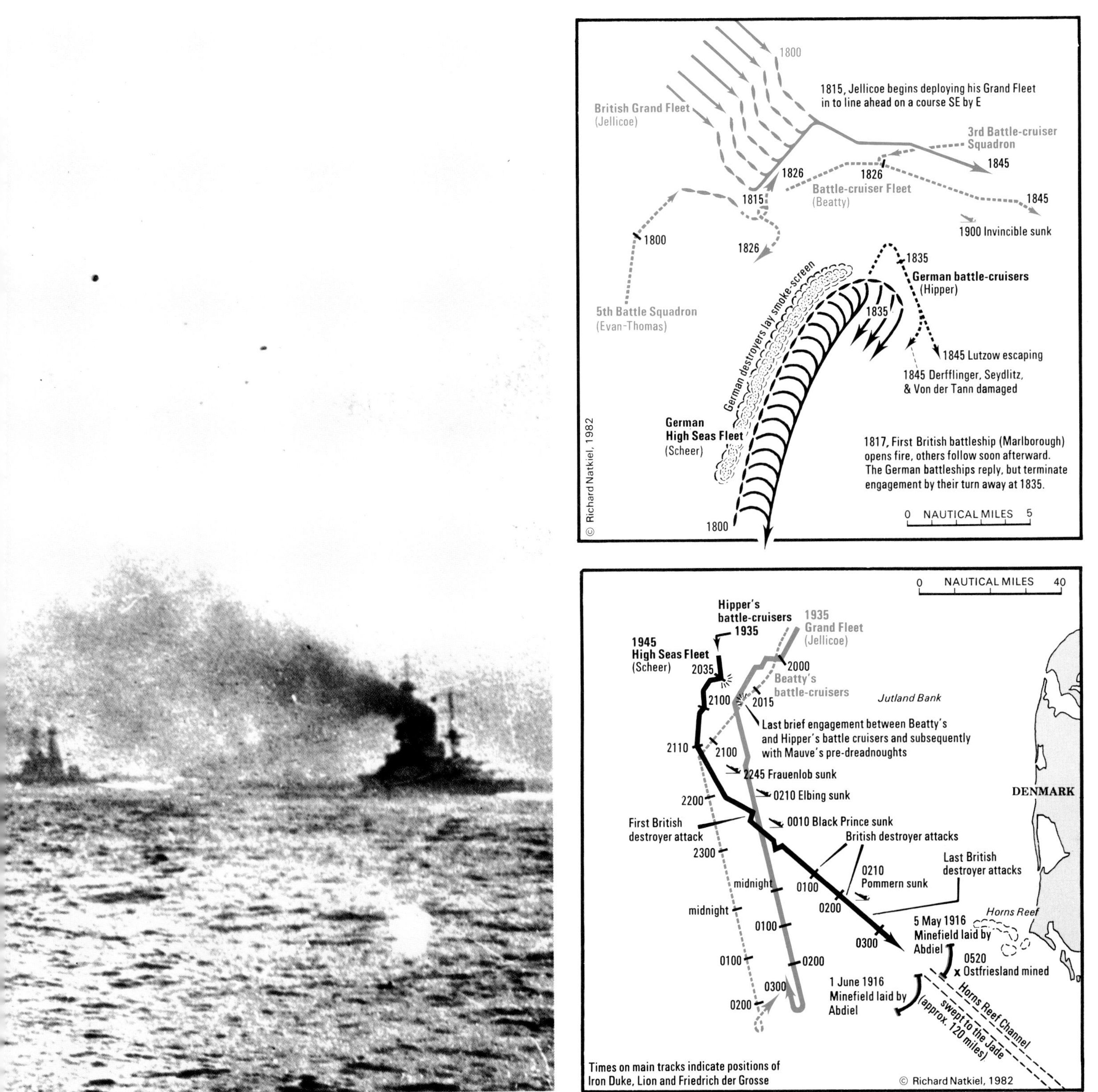

one more surprise in store: it was trained for night manoeuvre and combat, and the Grand Fleet was not. In excellent discipline, held together by Scheer's repeated order '*DURCHALTEN!*' ('Stand on'), the High Seas Fleet steamed straight through the rear of the Grand Fleet under cover of darkness, passing through just after midnight on a direct course to the Jade. As this happened, the Germans crushed frantic British attempts to turn them back, sinking five British destroyers and the armoured cruiser *Black Prince*. German losses were limited to one destroyer, the light cruisers *Frauenlob*, *Rostock* and *Elbing*, and the pre-Dreadnought battleship *Pommern*, which blew up and sank after a destroyer torpedo attack at 02.10 on 1 June. (This was the first and only German battleship lost in the First World War.) The Germans' superior night-fighting tactics were aided by their use of coloured lights, which made it easy to distinguish the white-light signals used by the British. The confused attempts of the British to illuminate the scene relied on searchlights, but these only gave the Germans an easy target when burned. The German Navy had adopted starshells, which lit up the target without instantly revealing the ship which had fired them.

Top: The first fleet action at Jutland and *(above)* the night action in which the High Seas Fleet steamed through the rear of the Grand Fleet to escape from Jellicoe's trap.
Centre: How the smoke and murk of Jutland looked from the Grand Fleet's viewpoint – *Iron Duke* heads the British 4th Battle Squadron, followed by *Royal Oak* and *Superb*.

So it was, against all odds, that the High Seas Fleet came home, leaving the Grand Fleet empty-handed on the morning of 1 June. Never again were battle fleets of comparable size to meet in action, a fact which makes Jutland the great climacteric of the battleship era. How, given that fact, should Jutland be assessed?

Certainly Jutland was not a second Trafalgar – *and could never have been.* Trafalgar had been a stand-up fight, in perfect battle conditions, *against an enemy prepared to battle it out.* This was never the case at Jutland. As with his predecessors in command, Scheer had sortied in hopes of cutting the Grand Fleet down to size, not fighting the whole of it. It takes two to make a fight, and Scheer very correctly turned and ran as soon as he realised the enormity of his peril. Though Scheer's error after his first *kehrtwendung* gave Jellicoe a second chance, the smaller High Seas Fleet was easier to manoeuvre out of trouble than the more cumbersome Grand Fleet.

Then again, the collision of the fleets at Jutland only took place, and followed the course it did, because of the bad visibility. Here is the supreme proof that the super-Dreadnought of the First World War was a fair-weather weapon. In lamenting that they had been robbed of a second Trafalgar by this bad visibility the British fell into a double error, forgetting both the inevitability of a German retreat *and the fact that in good visibility they would never have brought the High Seas Fleet to action at all.*

For his part Jellicoe, like Sturdee at the Falklands, refused to throw away his advantages and court outright defeat by taking risks. The Grand Fleet's moment of greatest danger was the big torpedo attack launched to cover Scheer's second retreat. This was carried out by 13 destroyers carrying a total of 58 torpedoes, of which only 31 were fired. At least ten of these arrived in the British line, and it was a mercy that none hit. *Marlborough*, for instance, was near-missed by three torpedoes, one passing ahead, one astern, and one clean under the ship – and this was less than half an hour after *Marlborough* had been hit by a torpedo probably fired by *Wiesbaden*. This incident had made Jellicoe all the more alert to the torpedo danger, not to mention the possibility of mines being sown in his path if he pursued Scheer too closely.

With one side determined to break off and retreat and the other side determined to avoid casualties, all this made Jutland no ordinary battle. Who won it? In strictly material and human terms the Germans had a good case for claiming victory. The Grand Fleet lost 6,097 officers and men killed (out of 60,000); the High Seas Fleet lost 2,551 (out of 36,000). The Grand Fleet lost three battle-cruisers, three armoured cruisers and eight destroyers and torpedo-boats. The High Seas Fleet lost one pre-Dreadnought, one battle-cruiser (*Lützow*, which had to be abandoned and sunk), four light cruisers and five destroyers and torpedo-boats. But what *is* victory? The Grand Fleet not only 'held the field of battle' on the morning of 1 June: it was also ready and eager to renew the action, which the High Seas Fleet was not. Of the latter's battle-cruisers only

The tragedy of the British battle-cruisers at Jutland – *Invincible*, blown in half by the explosion of her midships magazines, with the destroyer *Badger* searching for survivors.

Despite German claims of victory in the 'Skagerrak' battle, damage and casualties were not wholly one-sided. This picture was taken through one of the heavy-calibre shell holes rent in *Derfflinger*'s armour.

Moltke was remotely battle-worthy; *Von der Tann* had had all her guns knocked out while *Derfflinger* and *Seydlitz* had survived only by excellent damage control and counter-flooding, struggling home with decks awash. Prolonged repairs were needed to the battleships *König*, *Markgraf* and *Grosser Kurfürst*, while the High Seas Fleet was left with only six cruisers to Jellicoe's 30. It was two months before the High Seas Fleet was ready for sea in full remaining strength. There was much truth in the derisive British cartoon run by *Punch* after Jutland, showing a patriotic German family being frantically waved away from the barred gates of Wilhelmshaven dockyard: 'Can't we see our victorious fleet?' 'No, you can't. Nobody can!'

When it came to matériel the British certainly had more to put right after Jutland than the Germans, with proper anti-flash precautions top of the list. There was also the uncertain quality of British shell, which tended to break up instead of penetrating at angles of less than 90°. In general, however, British fire control had tended to improve during the battle, while German gunnery noticeably deteriorated. One of the enduring Jutland myths, springing from the loss of the three British battle-cruisers, has been that Jutland revealed severe inadequacies in the Grand Fleet's armour. This is not true: the battle-cruisers blew up because of spreading flash, not because of German shells exploding in their magazines.

Another Jutland myth is that after the battle the High Seas Fleet cowered in port for the rest of the war. In fact neither Scheer nor Hipper who replaced him in August 1918 ever abandoned faith in the 'ambush' plan, and the High Seas Fleet made three sorties after Jutland: in August 1916, October 1916 and April 1918. With Scheer's instinct to caution and early retreat naturally sharpened by memories of Jutland, these sorties only resulted in more frustration for the Grand Fleet. The decisive factor in the post-Jutland months was the gaining of overwhelming superiority by the Grand Fleet: the last two 15-inch 'Revenge' class battleships (*Ramillies* and *Resolution*), the battle-cruisers *Repulse* and *Renown* (six 15-inch guns each), the light battle-cruisers *Glorious* and *Courageous* (four 15-inch guns each), and the five American battleships (*New York*, *Texas*, *Wyoming*, *Delaware* and *Florida*) which joined the Grand Fleet as the 6th Battle Squadron in 1917–18. The only comparable additions to the High Seas Fleet after Jutland were the 15-inch *Baden* and *Bayern* and the last 'Derfflinger' class battle-cruiser, *Hindenburg*.

Hopelessly outnumbered though it remained after Jutland, the High Seas Fleet *had* won a victory of sorts at that battle – and not merely the tactical 'points victory' of sinking more British ships than German ships lost. Scheer had kept his battle fleet in being, able to protect the minelayers and torpedo flotillas which kept the Grand Fleet's blockade a distant one. And as long as the High Seas Fleet remained in being, able to prevent the British from sealing off the main U-boat bases on the North Sea coast, the Grand Fleet dared not disperse its attendant destroyers to fight the most effective German naval coup of the war: the unrestricted U-boat offensive of 1917–18.

The true legacy of Jutland, a sight never before witnessed in the history of naval warfare: the German High Seas Fleet steams tamely in to surrender, with magazines emptied and even the breech-blocks of the guns removed.

After the British saved themselves from this supreme threat by the introduction of convoy, Germany was left with no other choice than to stake all on the great spring offensive on the Western Front of spring 1918. When this was held and broken in the summer of 1918 and the Allied armies began to push the beaten German Army back, it was small wonder that the men of the High Seas Fleet mutinied rather than be sacrificed in a useless gesture. Hipper ordered what would have been the Fleet's last sortie for 29 October, when negotiations for an armistice had already begun – but the men would have none of it. And the most obvious feature of the High Seas Fleet mutiny was the dominant role played by the crews whose ships had suffered worst at Jutland: *Von der Tann*, *Derfflinger*, *König*, *Markgraf*. The traumatic memory of that blazing horizon at Jutland, two years and four months before, had indeed burned deep.

Though the war of the British and German Dreadnought fleets had been mostly one of watch and ward, the terms of the 1918 Armistice left no doubt of the vital role those fleets had played. The High Seas

The end – in the case of *Baden*, even her scuttling in Scapa Flow (21 June 1919) was a failure. She was refloated and repaired, put through exhaustive trials to compare her with her British contemporary *Revenge*, and was finally sunk as a gunnery target in 1921.

Fleet was required to empty its magazines, remove the breech-blocks from its guns, and surrender unconditionally to the Grand Fleet at sea. The surrender took place on 21 November 1918, a sunny day only slightly marred (for the British) by mist. (The Germans had been hoping for a fog to cloak their humiliation.) The Grand Fleet was at battle stations as the High Seas Fleet hove into view, yearning for the beaten enemy to opt after all for a defiant battle to the death rather than the unprecedented disgrace of tame surrender. Beatty deployed the 370 warships of his Fleet in two parallel lines, 8 miles long and 6 miles apart: the most impressive deployment in the history of the battleship. Led by the British light cruiser *Cardiff*, the newest and most powerful units of the High Seas Fleet steamed sullenly between the watching lines: nine battleships, five battle-cruisers, seven light cruisers and 49 destroyers. For the first and last time, in conditions which would have been unthinkable four years before, the rival fleets saw each other in their entirety.

The German surrender was not, in fact, the last act: this took place on 21 June 1919 when the captive High Seas Fleet, interned in Scapa Flow, scuttled itself rather than be handed over to the victorious Allies, under the terms of the peace treaty which would seal Germany's post-war fate. In German eyes at least, this was partial atonement for the previous act of surrender. For never before, even in the fall of Napoleon, had the battle fleet of a defeated nation been required to yield itself up to a rival which had failed to crush it in battle.

The scuttling of the High Seas Fleet was the dramatic but final postscript to the 'battleship war' of 1914–18. In all naval theatres a total of 36 pre-Dreadnoughts, Dreadnoughts and battle-cruisers had been lost by the time of the Armistice in November 1918:

Old coast-defence battleships, monitors and pre-Dreadnoughts	25
Dreadnought battleships	7
Battle-cruisers	4
Total capital ship losses	36

Capital ship losses by nationality:	
Austria–Hungary	3
France	4
Germany	2
Great Britain	17
Italy	3
Japan	1
Russia	4
Turkey	2

Analysis of losses by cause:	
Gunfire	4
Mine	8
Surface torpedo	5
Submarine torpedo	10
Spontaneous ammunition explosion (not in action)	7
Scuttled	2

The latter figures vividly illustrate the long-term questions hanging over the battleship's future at the close of the First World War. Here was the world's most powerful naval weapon, whose *raison d'être* was the might and menace of its big guns – and yet (scuttling excepted) fewer battleships and battle-cruisers had been sunk by gunfire than by any other cause. The submarine stood revealed as the most effective challenge to the battleship's traditional domination of surface naval warfare; sea power had, in short, been extended from two dimensions to three. And over the next 20 years a fourth dimension would be added with yet another warship revolution: the coming of the aircraft-carrier.

9. THE SHADOW OF THE SUPER-DREADNOUGHT, 1919-1939

Previous pages: Germany's *Bismarck*, when completed in the early spring of 1941, was the strongest, fastest battleship in the world. In fact, Captain Lindemann insisted that his ship be referred to by its officers and ratings as 'he' rather than the traditional 'she', because no ship so formidable could possibly be thought of as feminine.
Below: Face-lift for Japan's battle fleet; *Fuso* in dry dock at Kure and *(bottom)* sister-ship *Yamashiro* on trials in 1934, showing the awesome 'pagoda' superstructure developed by Japanese designers between the world wars.

To THE PEACEMAKERS of 1919–20 there was little doubt that of all the weapons of modern warefare, the battleship and the submarine represented two of the greatest single dangers to an enduring world peace. The pre-1914 'battleship building race' had stoked the fires of world war; Germany's U-boat fleet, by introducing the barbarity of indiscriminate submarine warfare, had come close to winning the war outright in the first half of 1917. But as the victors of the First World War were unanimous that Germany should never again be allowed to build submarines after surrendering her wartime U-boat fleet, the submarine menace could no longer be considered pressing. Far more worrying was the obvious danger posed by the new generation of battleships, with ever more powerful weaponry, which was already taking shape around the world.

Only ten years before the High Seas Fleet's surrender, no navy had been able to produce a battleship with guns heavier than 12-inch; but the ensuing decade of escalation had seen battleship armament forging onward and upward through 13·5-inch, 14-inch, 15-inch and 16-inch to 18-inch.

There was, in 1920, scant encouragement in the fact that Britain was the only naval power to have produced an 18-inch gunned warship, and that the idea had immediately been abandoned as impracticable. The warship in question had been the light battle-cruiser *Furious* which, unlike her sister-ships *Glorious* and *Courageous* (each with four 15-inch), had been designed to carry a single 18-inch gun fore and aft. These light battle-cruisers had been intended to operate at high speed in shallow coastal waters, and were the first capital ships to pass the 30-knot barrier. But even in single mountings the deadweight of the 18-inch gun, and its shattering effects when fired, proved far too much for the modest 19,513-ton *Furious*. By the end of the war her 18-inch guns had been removed and she was being used as an experimental aircraft-carrier, with short flight-decks built on fore and aft. The experience thus gained was to have profound effects on the post-war battleship story. But although this bizarre experiment with the 18-inch gun had failed, it was clearly only a matter of time before the first 18-inch gunned battleships arrived on the scene.

The mainspring of the post-1918 building race was Japan's evident bid to become the dominant naval power in the Pacific by building the strongest possible battle fleet. The United States' obligation to match this challenge was also inevitable, and though there was no prospect of war between the United States and Britain there was also no prospect of the Royal Navy being allowed to fall behind the US Navy.

The Japanese had laid down the first 14-inch gunned ships, the four 'Kongos', in 1911–12, and the American reply had been swift: the four ships of the 'New York' and 'Nevada' classes, each with ten 14-inch guns in five twin mountings. The Japanese counter had been *Fuso* and *Yamashiro* (laid down in 1912 and 1913), with 12 14-inch guns, also in twin mountings. To which the Americans replied with *Pennsylvania* and *Arizona* (laid down 1913 and 1914). A much-improved, cleaner design, these ships adopted the triple gun mounting introduced by the European navies to sustain a main armament of 12 14-inch. These were followed at once by the three 'New Mexicos' (laid down January-October 1915), while Japan retained the six twin-

Profile pose for the benefit of Japan's naval rivals. *Front to rear: Nagato, Kirishima, Ise* and *Hyuga*.

turret formula for *Ise* and *Hyuga* (laid down May 1915). The American sequel was *California* and *Tennessee* (laid down 1916 and 1917) – but the Japanese abruptly broke the mould when they laid down *Nagato* and *Mutsu* in 1917 and 1918. For the 'Nagatos' were the first 16-inch gun battleships, with an arrangement of two superimposed twin turrets fore and aft. Less than three years after the first 15-inch gun battleships had entered service with the British 'Queen Elizabeths', the 16-inch gun battleship had arrived, to dominate the scene at the beginning of the 1920s.

The next projected Japanese and American capital ships confirmed that the prospects for 'no more war' were already imperilled by the replacement of the Anglo-German building race with a Japanese-American contest. In February and July 1920 Japan laid down two monstrous new battleships of 38,500 tons: *Tosa* and *Kaga*, with five twin 16-inch turrets. These were followed in December by the laying-down of *Akagi* and *Amagi*, the first of four battle-cruiser variants of the 'Tosas' with the same main armament but a speed of 30 knots. Willy-nilly, the United States replied by laying down no less than five 'South Dakotas' (43,200 tons), followed by a sixth in 1921. These were to have 12 16-inch guns, and *their* battle-cruiser equivalents were the six 'Lexingtons' laid down in 1920 and 1921. The 'Lexingtons' were to have ten 14-inch guns, mounted in a turret arrangement borrowed from the Italian 'Cavours': triple turret superimposed by twin turret fore and aft.

These awesome developments inevitably prompted a reluctant response from the British. The Admiralty had envisaged a peacetime 15-inch gunned battle fleet, slimmed down to the ten battleships of the 'Queen Elizabeth' and 'Revenge' classes. With the German opposition liquidated, the peacetime British battle-cruiser force would be limited to *Repulse*, *Renown*, *Glorious*, *Courageous* and *Hood*, the last British battle-cruiser launched in the war (August 1918). But in view of the 16-inch norm being pursued by Japan and the United States, the British laid down their first two 16-inch gunned capital ships in 1921. These were to be battle-cruisers, with the same turret arrangement as the 'Repulse' class (two turrets forward and one aft) but with triple gun mountings instead of the traditional British twin mounting.

To her eternal credit it was the United States which took the initiative in calling a halt to the new building race. The Washington Naval Conference called in November 1921 produced the most successful arms limitation treaty in modern history. The Washington Treaty was signed by the leading world naval powers – the United States, Britain, Japan, France, and Italy. They pledged themselves to honour a ten-year 'building holiday' in capital ships, and to keep within restricted guidelines which, it was hoped, would prevent battle fleets of giant 16-inch or 18-inch capital ships from ever taking shape. A formula was agreed upon which seemed most likely to restrict designers to 15-inch guns at most: 35,000 tons maximum displacement, with the ideal armament ceiling of 14-inch guns. These restrictions were to apply to all 16-inch gunned capital ships already under construction. Signatory powers who did not wish to scrap their new ships had the option of converting them to aircraft-carriers, as the British had already done with *Furious*. Encouragement of this new type, with its wholly unknown potential, was considered vastly preferable to further uncontrolled battleship or battle-cruiser construction. Any of the signatory powers could build two carriers of up to 33,000 tons from capital ship hulls already under construction; a ceiling of 27,000 tons was set for new carriers which would be 'built from the keel up'. Total 'carrier tonnage' was prescribed at 135,000 for Britain and the United States, 81,000 for Japan, and 60,000 for Italy and France.

The Washington Treaty halted the Japanese-American building race in its tracks. Between them the two navies only completed five 16-inch gunned battleships out of the 18 which had been taking shape before the Treaty's intervention. These were Japan's *Nagato* and *Mutsu* and the American *Colorado*, *Maryland* and *West Virginia*, of which only *Maryland* had been completed by the time of the Washington Conference. (The fourth of these 'Colorados', *Washington*, was left uncompleted in compliance with Treaty restrictions, and was expended as a gunnery and aircraft target in

Below : Repulse (six 15-inch guns), laid down in 1915. *Bottom : Hood*, laid down in September 1916, showing her main armour distribution (main belt 5/12-inch, turrets 11/15-inch). When completed in March 1920, *Hood* was the biggest, fastest, hardest-hitting capital ship in the world. So, 21 years later, was her destroyer *Bismarck*.

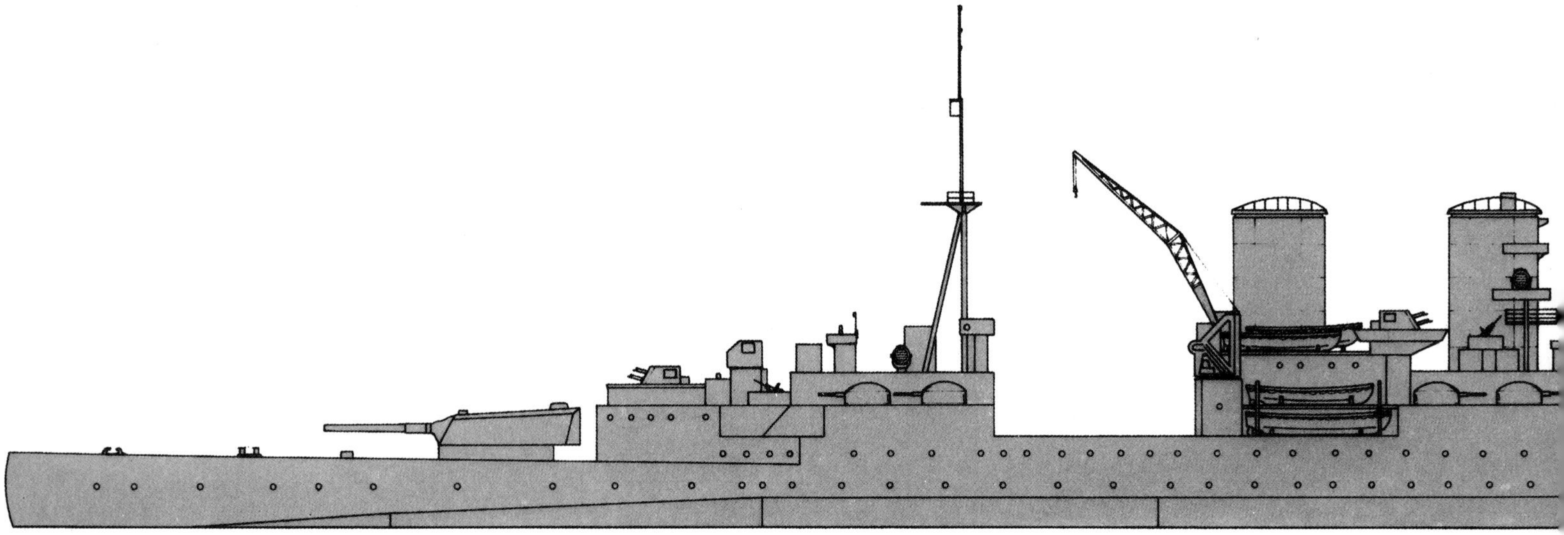

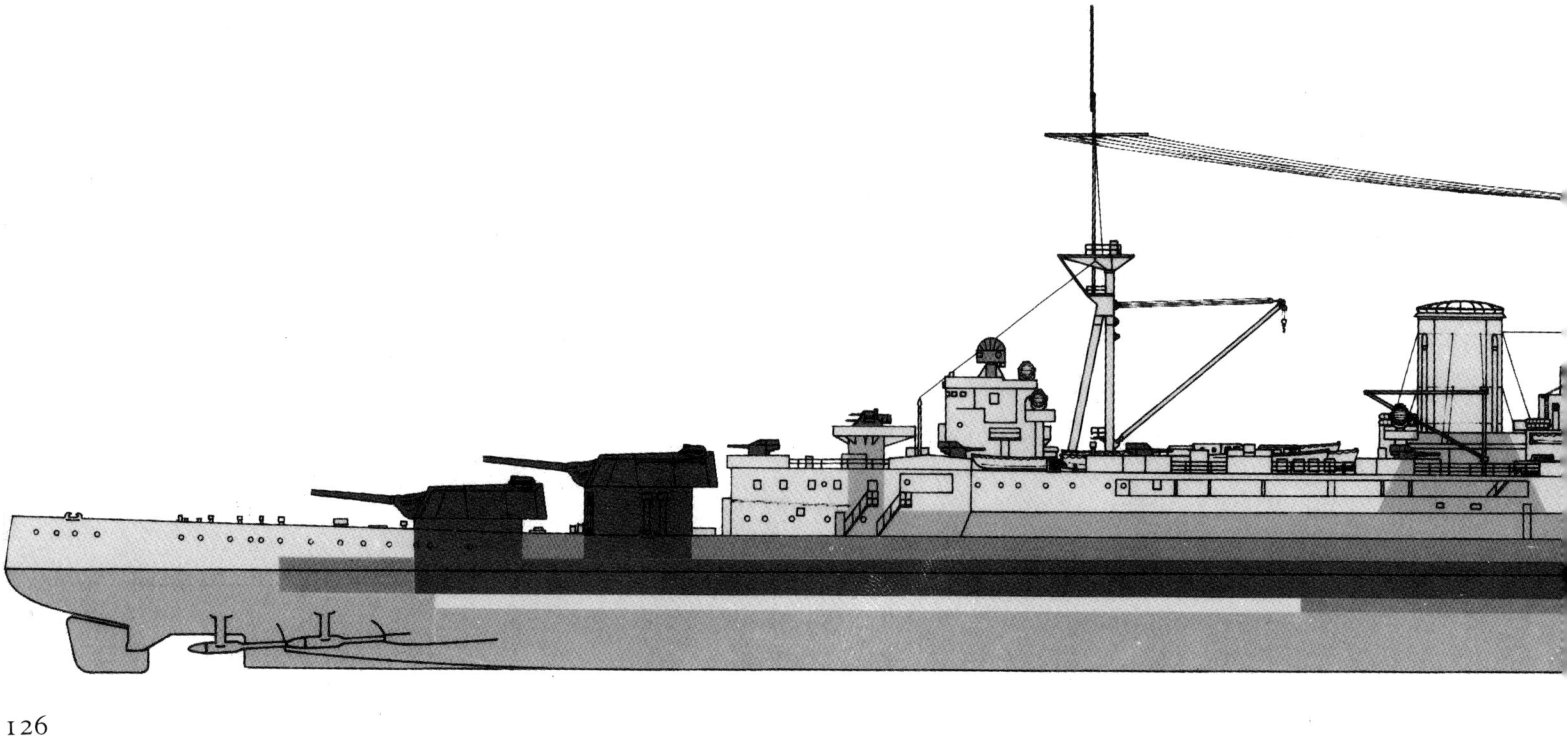

Hood on her trials. Few other capital ships ever matched her for elegance of line. *Hood*'s generous dimensions – 860½ ft overall length and 105¼ ft beam – gave her the stability of a battleship, but her low quarter-deck made her a 'wet ship' aft when at her top speed of 31 knots.

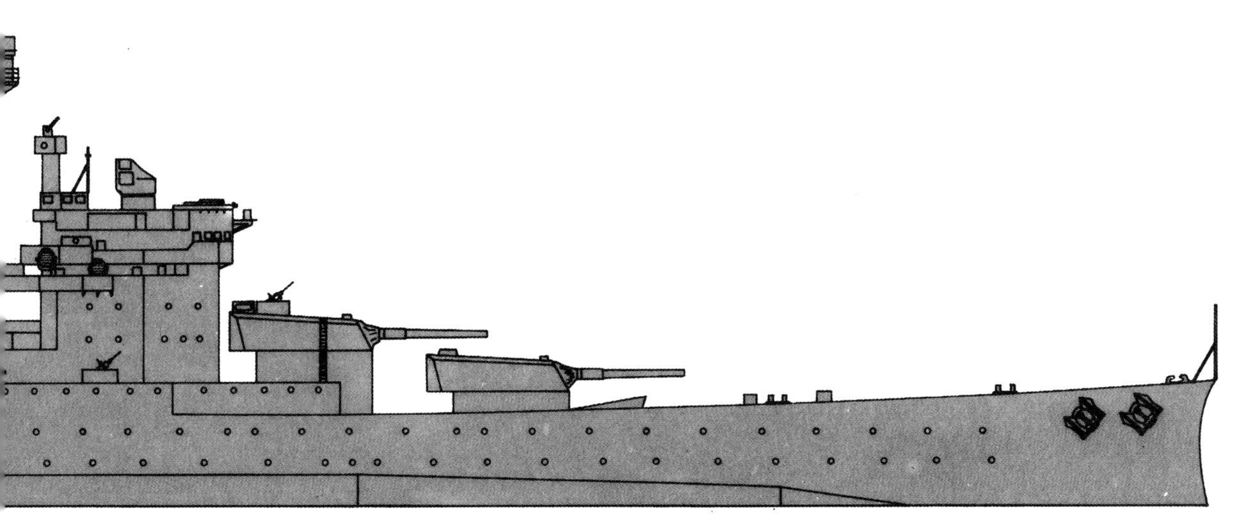

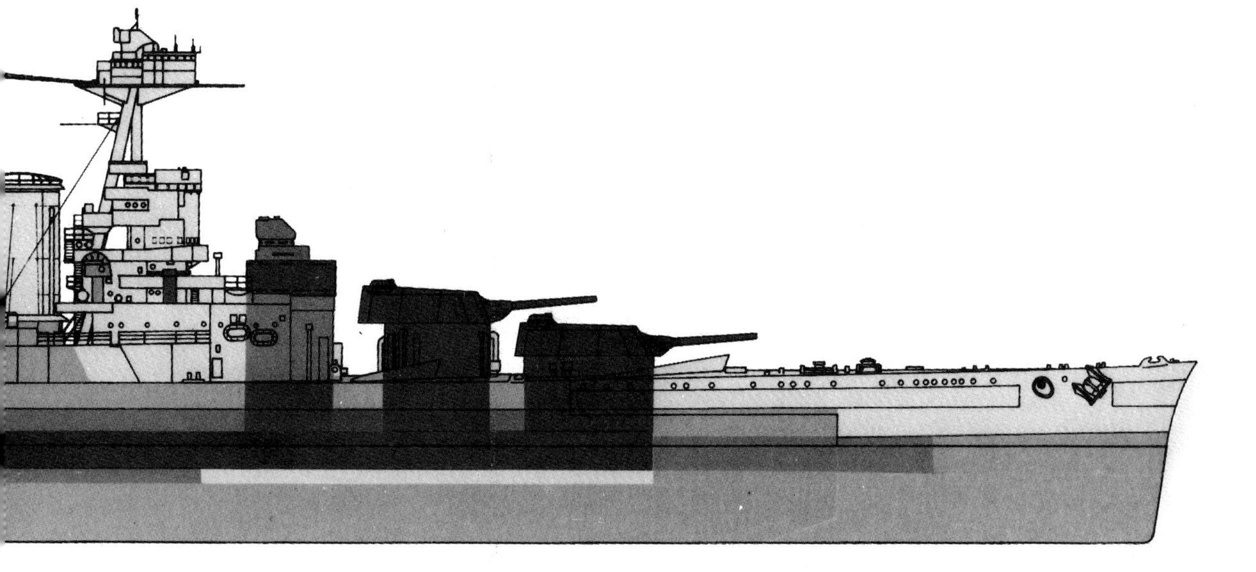

Ugly but much-loved hybrid: Britain's *Nelson*, showing her nine 16-inch guns and towering armoured citadel. Brutally truncated though it was by the Washington Naval Treaty, this design yielded much invaluable experience for the later 'King George V' class.

November 1924.) Though the 'Nagatos' and the 'Colorados' were identical in displacement (32,700 tons) and main armament (eight 16-inch guns), the 'Nagatos' had an impressive speed advantage over their American counterparts (26·75 knots, against the 21 knots of the 'Colorados').

Both Japan and the United States took up the 'carrier option' prescribed by the Washington Treaty for uncompleted capital ships. The original Japanese plan was for *Tosa* and *Kaga* to be abandoned, and for the projected battle-cruisers *Amagi* and *Akagi* to be completed as carriers. But when *Amagi*'s hull was badly damaged in the Great Tokyo Earthquake of 1 September 1923 it was decided to reprieve *Kaga* instead, with the result that *Kaga* and *Akagi* were together completed as the 1st Carrier Division of the Japanese Combined Fleet. The famous carrier partnership thus created was matched by the US Navy with the completion of *Lexington* and *Saratoga* as carriers in 1927.

Britain, however, did not follow the Japanese-American lead. In 1922 the Royal Navy already led the world in aircraft-carrier development with three conversions (*Furious*, *Argus* and *Eagle*) and one indigenous design (*Hermes*). The only other carriers were the American *Langley* (converted from the collier *Jupiter* in 1922) and the lightweight *Hosho*, an indigenous Japanese design completed in the same year. In view of this clear lead in carriers, the British therefore decided to complete two of their projected 16-inch gunned battle-cruisers as battleships, in strict observance of the Washington Treaty restrictions. To meet the all-important tonnage restriction, hull length and engine capacity were drastically reduced. All three triple 16-inch turrets were positioned forward of a heavily-armoured control tower, with the after hull trimmed short to an ugly stump. The result was the only pair of 16-inch gun battleships completed after the Treaty's signature and in observance of its terms: *Nelson* and *Rodney*, at 33,900 tons well within the Treaty tonnage limit of 35,000 tons, but with a maximum speed of only 23 knots.

To make up their permitted allowance in carrier construction, the British nevertheless decided to convert the light battle-cruisers *Courageous* and *Glorious*. The light battle-cruiser type had proved a snare and a delusion, the ultimate expression of Fisher's obsession with speed. At speeds over 30 knots it was impossible to fire accurate ranging salvos with only two 15-inch guns fore and aft; and though, by the end of the war, a hybrid role had been found for the pair with the light cruiser squadrons, the gunnery of the light cruisers they led actually proved more effective than that of *Courageous* and *Glorious* (known in the Fleet as 'Outrageous' and 'Uproarious'). With *Furious*, they were far more effective as carrier conversions, gleaning priceless experience for the indigenous British carrier

Hallmark of all American battleships from the 1890s to Pearl Harbor in 1941 was the tubular lattice-work 'cage' mast. This is USS *California* (12 14-inch guns), completed in June 1921.

fleet eventually ordered in the late 1930s.

In addition to halting the post-war drift into uncontrolled super-Dreadnought construction, the years 1920–25 also saw a wholesale clearance of obsolete battleships on an unprecedented scale. No less than 90 pre-Dreadnoughts – 29 British, 24 American, 12 French, 12 Japanese, nine Austrian and four Italian – were sold for scrap, expended as targets or decommissioned and disarmed for service as training ships or storage hulks. Hardly less spectacular was the scale of Dreadnought disposals by Britain, where only the last ten units of Fisher's mighty battle fleet were retained for modernisation and long-term service. By 1925, 15 British Dreadnoughts had been stricken from the active list: *Dreadnought, Bellerophon, Superb, Temeraire, Collingwood, St Vincent, Colossus, Hercules, Neptune, Conqueror, Monarch, Orion, Thunderer, Erin* and *Agincourt*, together with the 'first generation' battle-cruisers *Indomitable, Inflexible, New Zealand, Australia, Lion* and *Princess Royal*; the battleship *Canada* was returned to her original Chilean owners. Between 1925 and 1932 the British struck off another eight ships: *Ajax, King George V, Centurion, Iron Duke, Benbow, Emperor of India, Marlborough* and *Tiger*.

Other Dreadnought casualties in these years were the ex-Austrian *Tegetthof*, handed over to the Italians after the war and broken up by them in 1924–25; the 'Courbet' class *France*, lost by shipwreck in Quiberon Bay in August 1922; and the redundant American 'first generation' Dreadnoughts *Delaware, North Dakota, Florida* and *Utah* (the latter removed from active service but retained as a target ship until the Second World War).

Then there was Turkey's *Sultan Selim*, the former *Goeben*: a thorn in the Allies' flesh throughout the war as a one-ship 'fleet in being', yet the only Dreadnought capital ship to survive service with the defeated Central Powers. *Sultan Selim* had been badly damaged by mines and bombs during her last sortie in January 1918, and was ceded to Britain by the Treaty of Sèvres (August 1920) which dismembered the prostrate Turkish Empire. But the Treaty was repudiated by the nationalist hero Mustapha Kemal, first president of the Turkish Republic which ousted the sultanate in 1922. In the Treaty of Lausanne (July 1923) Turkey was allowed to keep *Sultan Selim*, renamed yet again as *Yavuz*. By 1930 *Yavuz* had completed an extensive reconstruction and modernisation, and served on to become the longest-lived 'first generation' battle-cruiser of the Dreadnought era.

No other nation suffered more from defeat in the First World War, Allied intervention and ensuing civil war than Russia; yet three Russian Dreadnoughts served on under the colours of the new Soviet Union. All four 'Ganguts' of the old Baltic Fleet survived the war to receive republican names: *Gangut* as *Oktyabrskaya Revolutsia*, *Petropavlovsk* as *Marat*, *Sevastopol* as *Parishkaya Kommuna*. *Poltava*, however, renamed *Mikhail Frunze*, was gutted by fire in 1920 and broken up in 1923. The 'Imperatritsa Marias' of the Black Sea Fleet had not been so lucky. *Imperatritsa Maria* had been sunk by internal explosion in October 1916; salvaged two years later, she was found to be beyond repair. *Imperatritsa Ekaterina II* was sunk on Trotsky's orders, off Novorossiisk, to prevent her capture by the Germans during their advance along the northern Black Sea coast in June 1918. *Imperator Aleksandr III* had the most poignant ending, as the last Russian Dreadnought to fly the colours of the Imperial Russian Navy. Completed after the Kerensky Revolution of March 1917, she was renamed *Volya* before passing under White Russian control as *General Alexiev*. After the defeat of the Whites in 1920 she became General Wrangel's flagship-in-exile, finally being interned by the French at Bizerta with the ancient *Georgi Pobiedonosets* as consort. Her Tsarist colours were hauled down for the last time on 29 October 1924 and between 1926 and 1937 she was dismantled.

Like a film of growth run backwards, the post-war years therefore saw the world's leading battleship navies undergo a spectacular shrinkage. The dying convulsions of the First World War, peacetime decom-

Above : Germany's first 'pocket-battleship' (*panzerschiff*) – *Deutschland*, showing her 11-inch main battery and pole mainmast.
Below : France's riposte – the battle-cruiser *Dunkerque*, with her 13-inch main armament grouped in two distinctive quadruple turrets, both before the superstructure.

missioning and the restrictions imposed by the Washington Treaty together created one of the most important turning-points in the history of the battleship. The peace-makers failed to ban a return to war, but they certainly succeeded in banning a return to the giant battle fleets of the Tirpitz/Fisher years. The next naval war would feature battle *groups* rather than battle *fleets*. These battle groups would still rely on the battleship's unchanged status as the ultimate vehicle for naval gunnery, but with battleships in ones and twos rather than tens and twenties. The true success of the Washington Treaty should be measured by comparing the odds at Jutland (37 British battleships and battle-cruisers against 27 German) with those at Surigao Strait, the last battleship action of the Second World War, 28 years later (six American battle-ships against two Japanese).

From the late 1920s the steady increase of worldwide international tension made it clear that the political and military treaties fencing in the peace were living on borrowed time. It had always been obvious that the Washington Treaty was nothing more than arms limitation by mutual consent. The only way of enforcing compliance was by going to war – the very calamity which the treaties were intended to avert. The 1930s were typified by the subtle arts of 'treaty-bending': paying lip-service to existing treaty provisions while working secretly to breach them. In heavy-gunned surface war-ships the process began in Germany and was imitated in short order by Japan, Italy, France and the United States. Thus Britain was left as the only signatory of the Wash-ington Treaty attempting to obey the spirit as well as the letter of treaty restrictions, while unwillingly facing up to the prospect of war with opponents who would be all the better armed because of their lack of similar scruples.

Down to the tenth anniversary of the Treaty of Versailles, Germany had been seen to be observing the strict limits on her peacetime fleet. She had launched four light cruisers, all well within treaty limits as regards tonnage and armament, and the time was approaching for the first 10,000-ton heavy cruiser permitted by the Treaty. When this 'cruiser' was launched in March

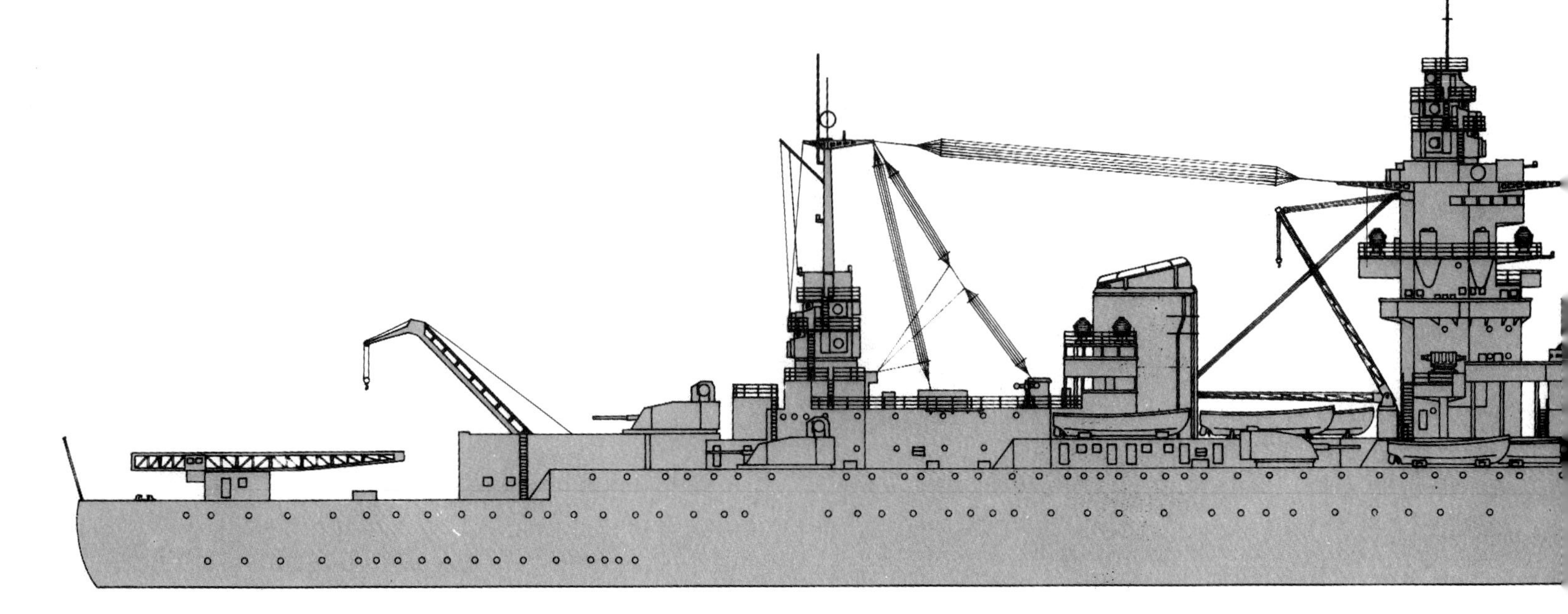

Admiral Scheer as completed. With the third 'pocket-battleship', *Graf Spee*, she was completed with a tapering armoured control tower, but this was replaced by a pole mast in 1940.

1931 it was a startling innovation: a heavy cruiser with battleship-sized main armament (six 11-inch guns in two triple turrets). *Deutschland*, the first of these 'pocket-battleships', as they were sneeringly dubbed by the British Press, could clearly out-gun any conventional cruiser and, with a top speed of 26 knots, could out-run any battleship in French or British service. This did not matter to the British, with their three 15-inch gunned battle-cruisers; but the French Navy had no such warships able to out-run as well as out-gun *Deutschland*.

This deficiency was speedily amended by France's *Strasbourg* and *Dunkerque*, laid down in 1932. They amounted to an entirely new breed of battle-cruiser, owing much of their design to the last two post-war battleships (Britain's *Nelson* and *Rodney*). *Strasbourg* and *Dunkerque* were armed with two *quadruple* 13-inch turrets, both positioned forward of an armoured citadel. The quadruple mounting was no novelty for the French: it had originally been designed for the 'Normandie' and 'Lyon' class super-Dreadnoughts which had been abandoned on the outbreak of war in 1914. As an additional anti-flash precaution, the guns of each turret were grouped in pairs, each pair served from a turret magazine vertically divided by an armoured partition. *Strasbourg* and *Dunkerque* had a clear 3-knot speed advantage over *Deutschland* and the two succeeding pocket-battleships, *Admiral Scheer* and *Admiral Graf Spee* (launched in 1933 and 1934). And with a main belt of $5\frac{3}{4}$–$9\frac{3}{4}$ inches, 5-inch deck armour and 13-inch turret armour, they were the best-protected battle-cruisers of their day. The point was that with their 26,500-ton displacement and 13-inch guns, *Strasbourg* and *Dunkerque* were well within treaty restrictions while the 'Deutschlands', though announced as 10,000 tons displacement, were actually 2,100 tons over.

The ominous precedent thus set by Germany was followed in short order by Japan, though the fact was not known at the time. In 1931–32 Japan had occupied Manchuria by brute force and in May 1933 had announced her withdrawal from the League of Nations (followed in October by Germany, where Adolf Hitler's Nazi Party

Above : Littorio's fine lines displayed to full advantage on trials
Right : Richelieu at Dakar in 1940, near completion.

had come to power in January). While still nominally bound by the Washington Treaty and its shaky renewal by the London Treaty of 1930, Japanese naval designers began in 1934 to plan the most powerful battleships of all time. These monsters were to have 18-inch main armament and a displacement of over 60,000 tons, the latter resulting from impenetrable armour and compartmentation. They were to be able to out-gun and sink whole squadrons of the most powerful battleships afloat – quality being called in to beat quantity. It was an awesome and daring concept, but it was not a new one: the original Dreadnought formula had been similarly intended. And it ignored two vital facts.

The first was that First World War combat experience had proved that human error, quite apart from conditions actually prevailing at sea, can nullify the best naval fire-power and technology which can be devised and built. And the second was that although it was certainly possible to devise a super-battleship which could *in theory* destroy all battleship opposition, the advent of the aircraft-carrier had brought a new uncertain element into naval warfare. Once detected by enemy carrier air reconnaissance, a super-battleship could be attacked by swarms of bomber and torpedo aircraft even when hundreds of miles away from the nearest enemy ship. Enough torpedo hits below the waterline would cripple the most powerful battleship – and though carrier strike aircraft had not been developed in time to draw blood in the First World War, their potential had certainly been revealed since. In a much-publicised demonstration by the American Colonel 'Billy' Mitchell in July 1921, the surrendered German Dread-

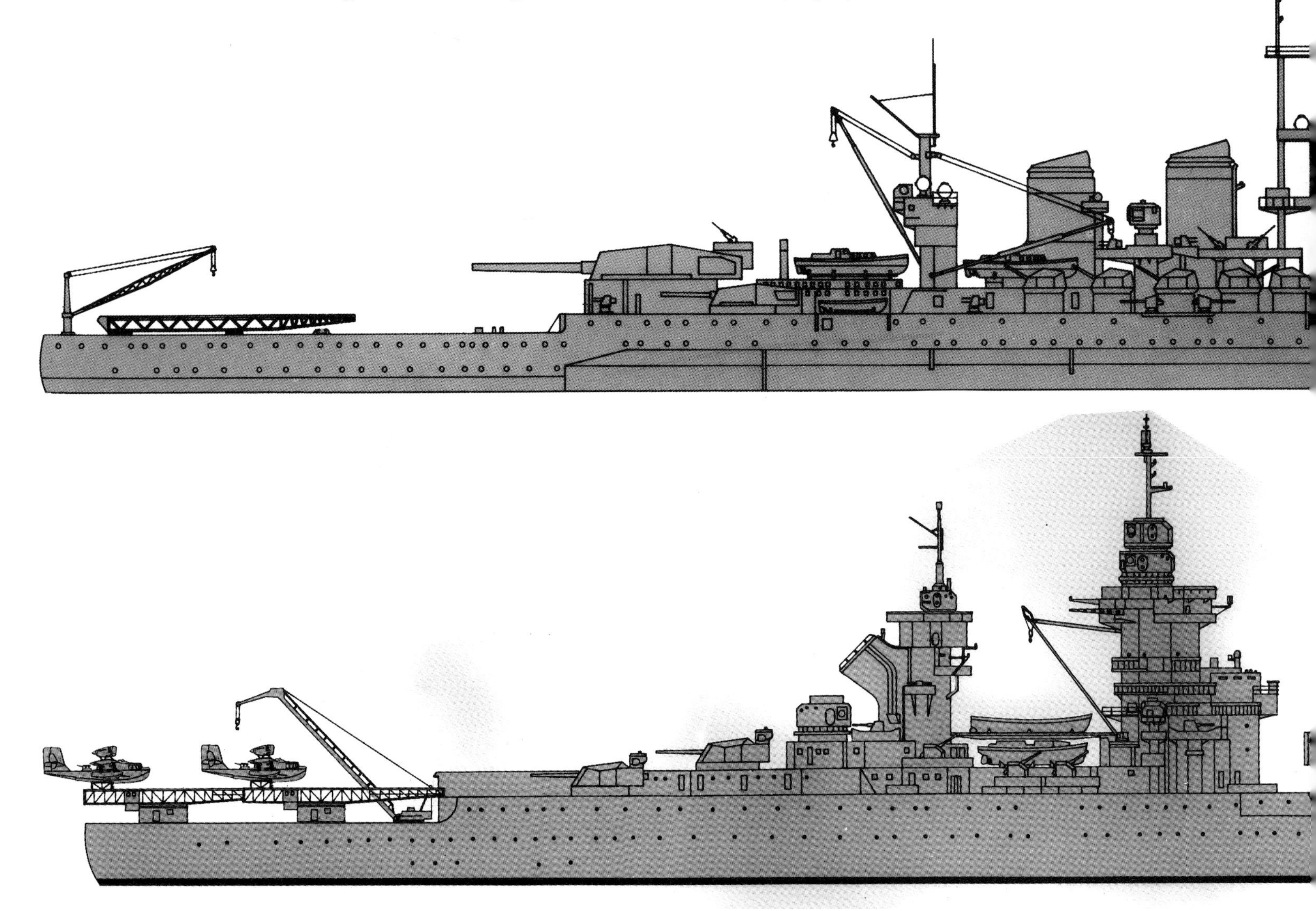

nought *Ostfriesland* had, after surviving 80 hits by smaller bombs, been sunk in ten minutes by six 1,000-kilo bombs. Thus, given persistent attacks by enemy carrier aircraft in sufficient strength, there could be no guarantee of immunity for a super-battleship.

It was ironic that Admiral Isoroku Yamamoto, Japan's C-in-C, Combined Fleet, pinned equal faith in battleship and carrier power. No man had greater confidence in the carrier's potential before the Second World War, and no navy built so many new carriers (seven in all) as did the Japanese in the 1930s. And it was a supreme irony that the only two battleships destined to be sunk exclusively by massed carrier air strikes were the super-battleships in which Yamamoto had reposed equal faith. It took three years and 23 planning stages before the plans for the 'Yamato' class super-battleship were finalised in 1937, and another three years before the first two, *Yamato* and *Musashi*, were launched. All that effort and all those resources would have been far better put into another half-dozen carriers. Yamamoto's greatest coup, the Pearl Harbor attack of December 1941, relied on carrier striking power to liquidate the traditional fire-power of the battle line – yet all his subsequent strategy was nostalgically aimed at a triumphant surface action to be won by his own battleships. It was as though some military genius of the Middle Ages had perfected the machine-gun, with the sole purpose of enabling his longbowmen to conquer unopposed.

As the Japanese began work on their super-battleship concept, the pace was quickening in European waters. In October 1933 Mussolini's Italy took the ageing

Italian and French super-Dreadnoughts of the late 1930s – *Littorio* (nine 15-inch guns) and *(bottom) Richelieu*, with eight 15-inch guns in two forward quadruple turrets.

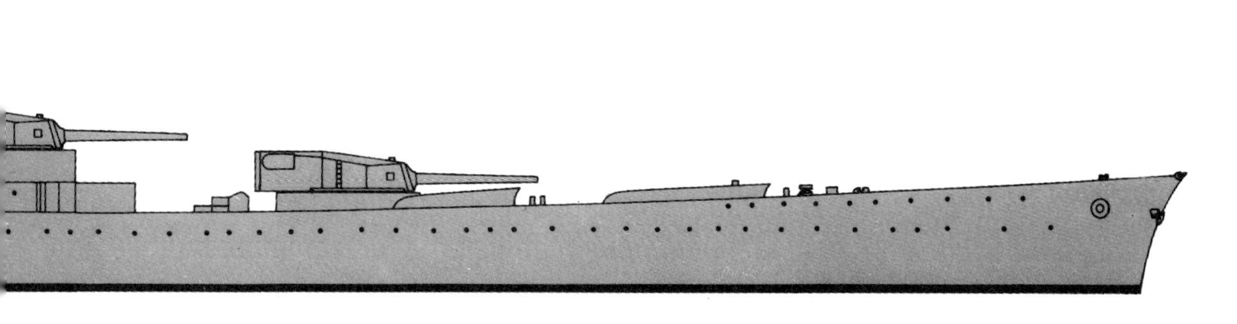

Conte di Cavour and *Giulio Cesare* in hand for an extensive, four-year reconstruction. In the following year (28 October 1934) two new Italian battleships were laid down, observing treaty limitations in their main armament but not in their stated displacement. By the time *Littorio* and *Vittorio Veneto* were launched in the summer of 1937 all remaining treaty restrictions had lapsed, and the new ships lay revealed at over 41,000 tons displacement, 28 knots and nine 15-inch guns in three triple turrets. *Vittorio Veneto* was completed in April 1940, *Littorio* in May, but neither was ready for service before August of that year.

The French reply to this new naval challenge in the Mediterranean was to lay down two 15-inch gunned battleships of their own, all the more quickly because of the experience gained with *Strasbourg* and *Dunkerque*. *Richelieu* and *Jean Bart* featured the same forward grouping of the main armament in two quadruple turrets, and were designed for a 2-knot speed advantage over their Italian rivals. The concentration of the main armament in quadruple turrets, avoiding the need for an after turret, enabled this speed advantage to be purchased without sacrificing armoured protection or exceeding 35,000 tons displacement.

The fast-reviving German fleet received two valuable additions in 1939, over a year before the 'Littorios' or 'Richelieus' were

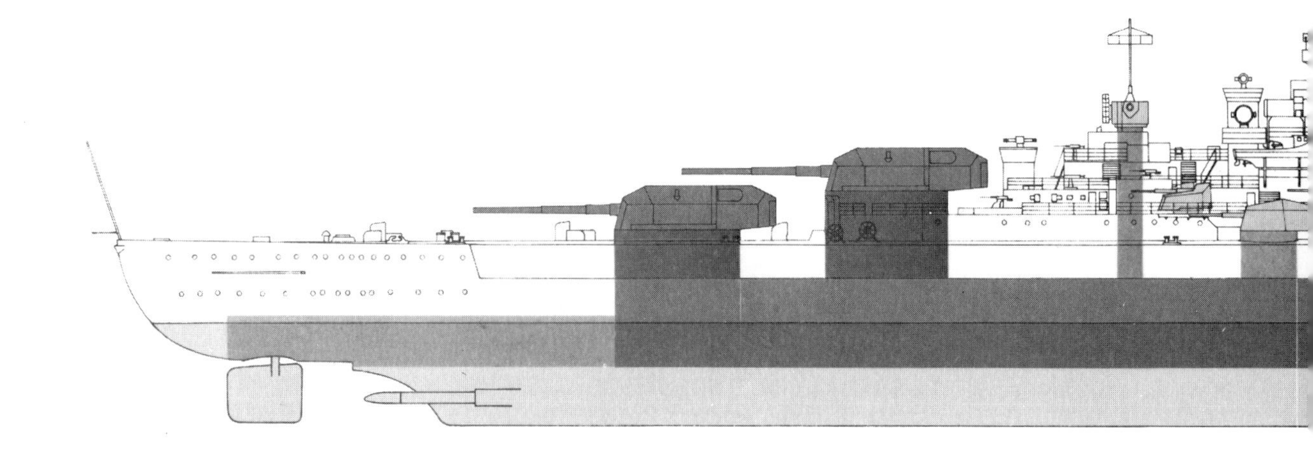

near completion. These were *Scharnhorst* and *Gneisenau*, laid down in 1935. Announced as battle-cruisers of 26,000 tons displacement, they were in reality small battleships of 32,000 tons, capable of $31\frac{1}{2}$ knots and, in relation to their size, two of the best protected capital ships ever built (main belt 12–13-inch, turrets 12-inch, decks 6-inch). This unique combination of speed and protection was purchased by choosing the lighter 11-inch gun. The rapidity of their construction was helped by taking the 'Deutschland' design and expanding it to incorporate a third triple 11-inch turret forward. They were formidable, handsome ships, and their good looks were enhanced still further after completion when their original straight stems were replaced with clipper bows.

Good looks and apparently impregnable armour were also features of the first full-sized German battleships built for the Third Reich: *Bismarck* and *Tirpitz*, laid down in the summer of 1936. Yet despite their 30-knot speed and eight 15-inch guns, *Bismarck* and *Tirpitz* actually reflected far less originality than had gone into *Scharnhorst* and *Gneisenau*. They were basically enlarged versions of the First World War 'Baden' class, and with one great weakness: communications from the main fire control position were not run safely below the upper deck armour. For all that, they represented an almighty threat to British

Scharnhorst, arguably the best battle-cruiser ever tested in combat, distinguished from *Gneisenau* by her tripod mast set aft.
Bottom : Main armour distribution plan of *Bismarck* – main belt $12\frac{1}{2}$-inch turrets 14-inch (compare with that of *Hood* on p. 126).

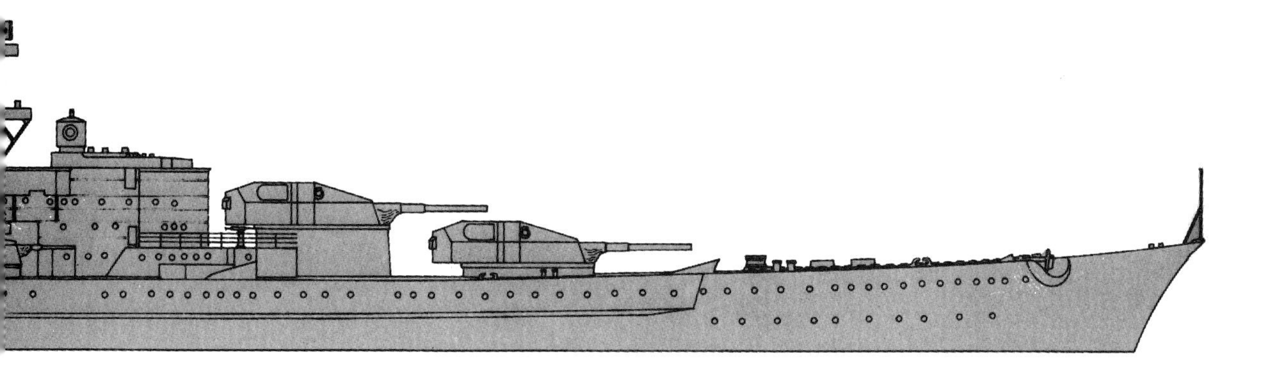

The biggest and most powerful battleship design of all time – Japan's *Yamato*, 71,659 tons at full load, seen making 27 knots with majestic ease in a heavy seaway.

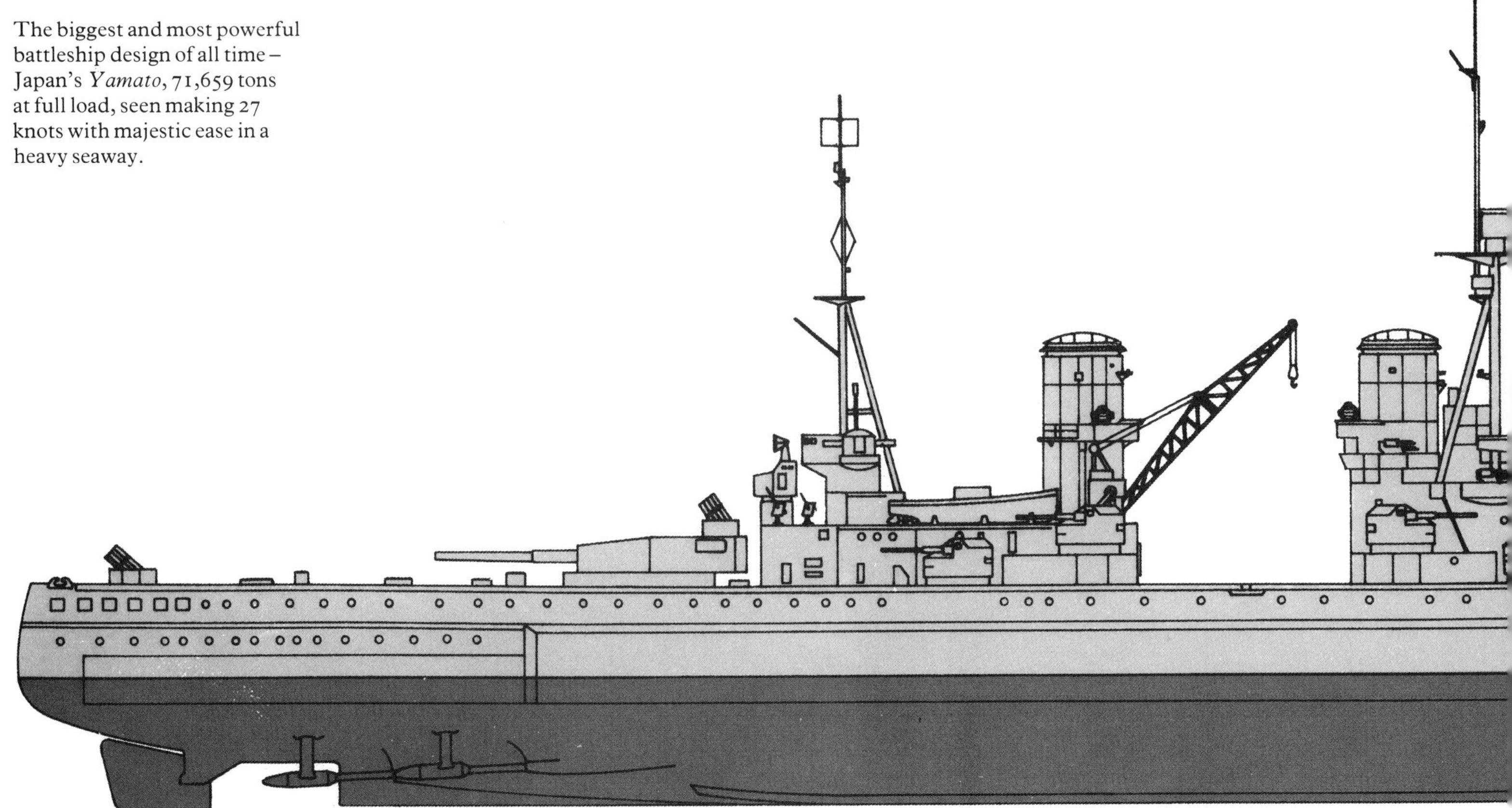

naval security; and though the British made merry over the fact that *Tirpitz* was launched on April Fool's Day (1 April 1939) they gave the Royal Navy precious little else to laugh about. Not even *Goeben* had done more to demonstrate the value of a one-ship 'fleet in being' than *Tirpitz* achieved in the Second World War. To the moment of her sinking in November 1944, the mere existence of *Tirpitz* affected the entire pattern of Allied naval dispositions in British home waters and the Atlantic.

The British reaction to these ominous new developments was hamstrung by the political insistence on adhering to the spirit of the Washington and London Treaties: the forsaken ideal of maximum 14-inch main armament and 35,000 tons displacement. When planning for the next generation of British battleships began in 1934, the decision was soon made to imitate the French and adopt the quadruple mounting. This would have yielded a broadside of 12 14-inch guns – but subsequent calculations revealed that the displacement target of 35,000 tons could only be achieved by sacrificing armoured protection. The solution adopted was to substitute a twin turret for the second quadruple turret, which yielded a saving of 675 tons' deadweight. But this re-design took time, and it was not before January 1937 that *King George V*, first of the new class, was laid down; she was not completed until October 1940. And of the other 'King George Vs' – *Prince of Wales*, *Duke of York*, *Anson*, and *Howe* – only *Prince of Wales* had been launched by the outbreak of war in September 1939. Apart from their well-distributed armour, the most interesting feature of the 'King George Vs' was the twin-gun 5·25-inch dual-purpose turret, eight per ship. The dual-purpose (DP) gun could either be fired against conventional surface targets, or swung vertically through 90° for use against aircraft.

It fell to the Americans to show the world, long after it had ceased to matter to anyone but the British, that the combination of 35,000 tons' displacement and 16-inch main armament was not, after all, impossible to achieve. In 1937 the first two American battleships since the 'Colorado' class were ordered: *North Carolina* and *Washington*, of 35,000 tons, 28 knots, and nine 16-inch guns in three triple turrets. They were the forerunners of the 'South Dakotas', laid down in 1938 – a broadly similar design, but with the hull shortened for greater manoeuvrability. In 1939 the first two 'Iowas' were laid down, with the same main and secondary armaments of nine 16-inch and 20 5-inch DP guns, but with greatly increased AA armament.

Defence against air attack, be it land-based or carrier-based, was in fact the biggest question-mark hanging over the battleships and battle-cruisers that went to war in September 1939. There was a dangerous assumption, particularly in Britain, that capital ship fire-power would be more than enough to beat off attacking aircraft – an assumption soon to be terribly disproved. In the coming war land armies were to learn that troops required to operate without the protection of supremacy in the air were exposed to inevitable defeat. The same held true for fleets.

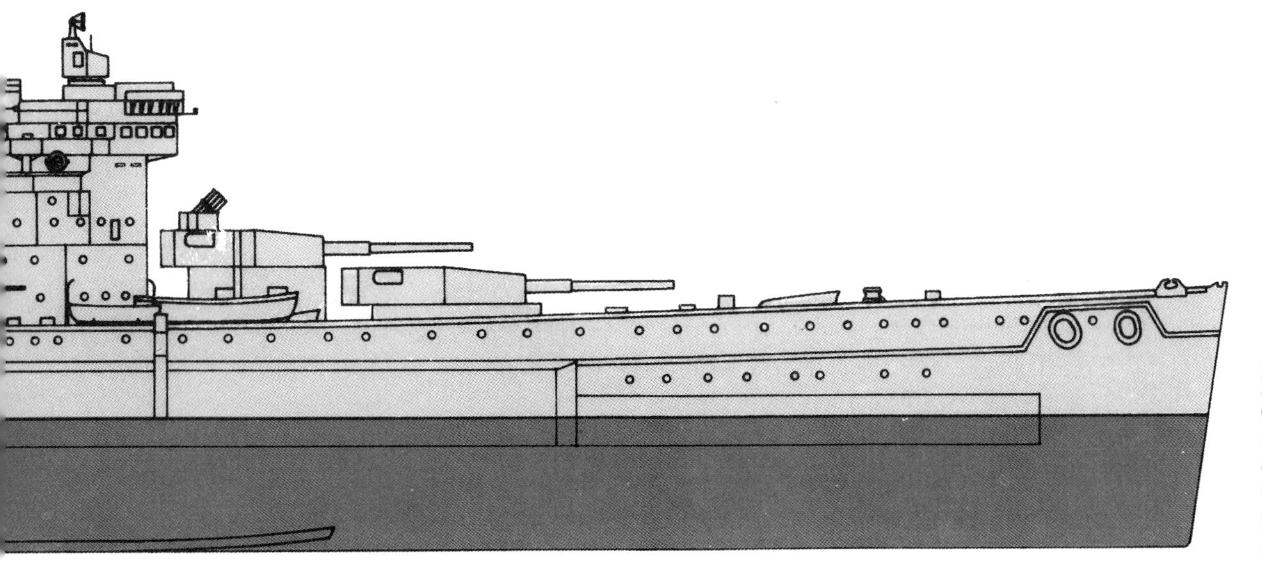

Duke of York, third of the British 'King George V' class. Originally designed for 12 14-inch guns, the 'KG V' design had its 'B' turret reduced to a two-gun mounting to permit a heavier allocation of armoured protection.

10. ATLANTIC AND MEDITERRANEAN, 1939–1945

IT IS UNUSUAL FOR NAVAL POWERS to hope that they will go to war against two enemies instead of one, but that was virtually the case of the French and British navies in 1939. Germany's naval prospects appeared so hopeless compared with those of 1914 that there seemed little chance of bringing the diminutive, unbalanced German fleet to action. War against Germany *and* Italy would enable the French and British to press their overwhelming naval advantage in the Mediterranean, at the expense of the Italians. Despite the German-Italian 'Pact of Steel' of May 1939, however, Mussolini surprised the Allies by opting for 'non-belligerence', hoping to enter the war at some propitious moment when the worst of Italy's chronic unreadiness for war had been put right.

Including ships already under construction, the French and British fleets numbered 13 aircraft-carriers (nine in service), 22 battleships (15 in service), and five battle-cruisers (all in service). The German Navy had two aircraft-carriers under construction, the battleships *Bismarck* and *Tirpitz* approaching completion, and only *Scharnhorst*, *Gneisenau* and the three pocket-battleships actually in service. France alone outnumbered Germany in submarines, and together the Allies had 129 submarines of all types to Germany's 57 (of which only 22 were ocean-going types). Grand-Admiral Erich Raeder, C-in-C of the German Navy, had had his 'Z-Plan' for a powerful, balanced fleet wrecked by the premature outbreak of war. But he had been Hipper's chief of staff in the First World War and was well aware that paper strengths and weaknesses are not the decisive factors at sea. While the reborn U-boat fleet was built up to undertake all-out commerce war on the Allies, Raeder planned to use every heavy surface warship he had – cruisers, pocket-battleships, battle-cruisers *and battleships* – as soon as *Bismarck* and *Tirpitz* entered service – as commerce-raiders in the Atlantic. This would compel the Allies to dissipate their naval supremacy in raider-hunting and convoy-protection operations, weakening the inevitable blockade which would otherwise strangle Germany's war industries. And Raeder planned to use mining and U-boat patrols to weaken the Allied fleets further by the inevitable attrition which these methods harvested in time.

Previous pages: Veteran of Jutland off the Normandy beaches – HMS *Warspite* bombarding German defences on D-Day, 6 June 1944. Over the following weeks battleship fire power played an often crucial role in the battle for Normandy. 'It was these broadsides from the warships, more than the defensive fighting of the enemy's troops, which halted our division's Panzer Regiment', lamented the Operations Staff Officer of one SS Panzergrenadier division.
Below: *Graf Spee* at large in the autumn of 1939 – on paper more than a match for the gallant British cruisers which brought her to action off the River Plate on 13 December.

Mercifully for the Allies, Hitler had been a soldier in the trenches in the First World War, not a sailor in the High Seas Fleet. As he himself admitted, he was a 'coward at sea', saddling his naval commanders with orders for caution at all costs whenever the big ships went out. To a limited degree this was sound, because a capital ship which remained safe and unsunk in harbour still tied down scores of enemy warships by virtue of its mere existence – the 'fleet in being' factor at work. But this was an inert substitute for the *offensive* naval strategy which Raeder wanted to inflict on the Allies. And the potential of this strategy was revealed between September and December 1939, when a total of 20 French and British warships – three battle-cruisers, three carriers and 14 cruisers – were formed into eight hunting groups to find the pocket-battleships *Deutschland* and *Graf Spee* in the Atlantic. In addition to these hunting groups, which were deployed from the Caribbean to Ceylon, the British committed the carrier *Furious*, battle-cruiser *Repulse*, battleships *Resolution*, *Revenge* and *Warspite* (plus two more cruisers for luck) to protecting North Atlantic convoys from Halifax to the United Kingdom. For good measure, the battleship *Malaya* and carrier *Glorious* were passed from the Mediterranean into the Indian Ocean via the Suez Canal. Even if the two pocket-battleships had not sunk a single Allied merchantman

The ship whose mere rumoured presence induced *Graf Spee*'s captain to scuttle his ship – the British battle-cruiser *Renown*.

(in fact they sank 11), this was an enormous dispersal of the Allies' naval advantage. And none of it prevented *Deutschland* from returning safely to Germany through the Allied blockade, or succeeded in finding *Graf Spee* before her eventual interception off the River Plate on 13 December 1939.

The River Plate battle should have been a test-case in miniature for the Japanese super-battleships taking shape on the other side of the world. With six 11-inch and eight 5·9-inch guns, Captain Langsdorff of *Graf Spee* held all the cards in long-range fire-power, not to mention armoured protection, over the three British cruisers opposed to him. It was a battle which *Graf Spee* should have won in theory – and nearly did in fact. When Langsdorff (his judgement not improved by having been stunned and slightly wounded in the head) broke off and ran for neutral Montevideo, the British heavy cruiser *Exeter* had been battered defenceless and half the guns of *Ajax* had been silenced. The actual naval *battle* of the Plate was, like Jutland, claimed as a technical victory by the Germans. But the *moral* victory had gone to the British Commodore Harwood, with his resolute attacks and successful splitting of *Graf Spee*'s fire. And the dramatic scuttling of *Graf Spee* off Montevideo came about because, in a brilliant piece of confidence trickery, the British managed to trick Langsdorff into believing that the carrier *Ark Royal* and battle-cruiser *Renown* were waiting to sink *Graf Spee* if he should dare to try a break-out. It was a classic example of how human misjudgement on one side, swayed by high courage and low cunning on the other, could together make nonsense of a clear-cut statistical advantage in big guns and armour plate.

While *Graf Spee* was still at large the German surface fleet had given two worrying demonstrations of its ability to escape from the North Sea with ease, using bad weather in the Norwegian Sea as a screen against British air reconnaissance. The German Admiralty was now making far more use of secure telephone and telex land-lines to bring its warships to readiness. As a result the British Admiralty never enjoyed the same flood of radio intercepts put to such good use by 'Room 40' in the First World War. Cracking the sophisticated new German codes also took time and improvised technology, which did not bear real fruit before 1943. For the first *four years* of the war, therefore, the interception of German capital ships depended far too much on lucky sightings, with the intelligence-gathering burden falling on air reconnaissance. The latter was naturally frustrated by the same adverse weather conditions which favoured sorties by German heavy units.

The first German sortie was made by *Gneisenau* with the light cruiser *Köln* and nine destroyers: a sweep up to the south coast of Norway between 8 and 10 October. The aim was to simulate a break-out into the Atlantic, hopefully luring heavy British forces within range of the German Air Force (*Luftwaffe*) and taking pressure off the pocket-battleships still at large in the Atlantic. This German sweep had much in

Above : HMS *Nelson* leads Home Fleet battleships in line-ahead.
Below : The ill-fated *Royal Oak* at speed, with 15-inch broadside trained to starboard.

common with similar ventures by the High Seas Fleet in the First World War, and despite the new air element the outcome was much the same. The important difference was that the German force was not sighted by the RAF until the early afternoon of the 8th, when it was already heading up the Norwegian coast. Shadowing British aircraft kept touch for four hours but had lost contact long before the Germans reversed course after nightfall. The British Home Fleet left Scapa Flow far too late to intercept, and by the time it had reached a blocking position between the Shetlands and Norway the German force was already two-thirds of the way home, returning to Kiel down the Kattegat.

The Home Fleet's problems were increased by its inability to use Scapa Flow as a main base, due to the total neglect of the Flow's defences (anti-aircraft as well as anti-submarine) over the past 20 years. This neglect stood revealed when *U-47* got into Scapa Flow and sank *Royal Oak* on the night of 13–14 October. She was the only capital ship in the Flow, as the rest of the Home Fleet had withdrawn to Loch Ewe on the west coast of Scotland. By the time of the next German sortie in the fourth week of November, the Home Fleet had been further weakened by the detachment of *Hood*, *Repulse*, and its only carrier, *Furious*. The new German foray was a high speed probe at the British naval patrols in the Iceland-Faeroes gap, followed by an extensive northerly detour before a return to Germany down the Norwegian coast. It was the debut of the operational partnership of *Scharnhorst* and *Gneisenau*, which sailed from Wilhelmshaven on the afternoon of 21 November.

Once again the British were left completely on the wrong foot. At 15.51 hours on the 23rd the armed merchant cruiser *Rawalpindi*, patrolling the Iceland-Faeroes gap, signalled that she was under attack by an enemy battle-cruiser approaching from the west – wrongly amended, a few minutes later, to an identification of the pocket-battleship *Deutschland*. In a gallant but wholly unavailing attempt at resistance, *Rawalpindi* was sunk by *Scharnhorst* in 14 minutes. Admiral Forbes, commanding the Home Fleet, was thus given no idea of the true composition of the German force; but even if he had been he could hardly have anticipated the brilliant evasive tactics of Admiral Marschall, the German commander. As they hunted for survivors from *Rawalpindi*, *Scharnhorst* and *Gneisenau* were briefly sighted by the cruiser *Newcastle*, but Marschall broke away under cover of a timely rain squall without his ships having been identified. Though the *Luftwaffe* had no coastal command as such, unusually good work by patrolling German flying-boats fed Marschall with accurate reports on the Home Fleet's attempts at interception over the next 48 hours. After a long detour east and north, Marschall timed his withdrawal to a nicety and re-entered the North Sea on the afternoon of the 26th, reaching Wilhelmshaven on the following day. Unbroken bad weather had deprived the British of a single sighting since *Newcastle* had lost contact on the evening of the 23rd.

This first war cruise by *Scharnhorst* and *Gneisenau* was only the curtain-raiser to their achievements during the battle for Norway which opened on 9 April 1940. The entire operational German surface fleet was used in an audacious *coup de main*, with simultaneous troop landings at Oslo, Kristiansand, Bergen and Narvik. *Scharnhorst* and *Gneisenau* had a special role: to lure British heavy forces away from the Norwegian coast while the troops went in. The most crucial German objective was Narvik, the furthest north; and it was 50 miles west of the Vestfjord approach to Narvik that *Scharnhorst* and *Gneisenau* were sighted by the British battle-cruiser *Renown*, at 03.37 hours on 9 April.

Vice-Admiral Whitworth in *Renown* had been given no idea that German forces were on the point of taking Narvik. In vile weather, with visibility repeatedly obscured by heavy snow squalls, he headed straight into the attack. During an intermittent running fight spanning the next 1½ hours *Renown* gallantly engaged both battle-cruisers. In exchange for only two hits which did no damage, *Renown* landed three 15-inch shells on *Gneisenau* which silenced the main control position and crippled the forward turret. By 05.00, however, the superior speed of the German ships had carried them out of sight to the north, with *Renown* labouring in vain pursuit. After another circuitous detour west and south, *Scharnhorst* and *Gneisenau* reached Wilhelmshaven on the afternoon of the 12th, their vital initial mission accomplished.

Gneisenau at anchor showing the beautiful flare of her clipper bow, which made the German battle-cruisers consistently fast ships in high seas.

After the troop landings on the 9th the *Luftwaffe* took over the task of covering the invasion forces. The fleet had suffered heavily, with three cruisers sunk, plus the heavy cruiser *Hipper* and pocket-battleship *Lützow* (as *Deutschland* had been renamed after her Atlantic cruise) damaged. The ten German destroyers which had carried the Narvik landings had two of their number sunk and another five damaged by a spirited British destroyer attack at dawn on 10 April. The surviving eight were destroyed like rats in a trap when the British battleship *Warspite*, escorted by nine destroyers, steamed majestically up Narvik fjord on the afternoon of the 13th. *Warspite*'s attack left the German troops in Narvik completely isolated, but these fleeting British successes were not repeated at Trondheim, where Allied forces re-embarked under heavy bombing (1 May) after failing to eject the Germans from central Norway. Narvik

The surface menace to Britain's convoy routes which demanded battleship escort from 1940: *Hipper* (*top centre*) with *Admiral Scheer* off the Norwegian coast, and (*above*) secure behind her torpedo-nets in a Norwegian fjord.

finally fell to an Allied expeditionary force on 28 May; but by then the campaign in the West, opened by the Germans on 10 May, was already in its third disastrous week. With Holland and Belgium overrun and France on the verge of defeat there was nothing for it but to evacuate Narvik (2–7 June). And it was during these final evacuations that *Scharnhorst* and *Gneisenau*, with the latter fully operational again after two months of repairs, struck with deadly effect.

Marschall had taken the battle-cruisers to harry the transports withdrawing from Narvik when, at 16.00 hours on 8 June, they surprised the aircraft-carrier *Glorious* with only the destroyers *Ardent* and *Acasta* in company. The flight-deck of *Glorious* was cluttered with RAF Hurricanes which had landed-on from their improvised airfield in the Narvik area, which was probably why she had no reconnaissance aircraft up. Caught with no hope of escape, *Glorious* was set ablaze and sunk by 11-inch gunfire from *Scharnhorst* and *Gneisenau*, despite the destroyers' gallant attempts to lay smoke and counter-attack with torpedoes. Both were sunk as well, but a torpedo from *Acasta*'s last salvo scored a damaging hit on *Scharnhorst* abreast her after turret. (This was the first of only two occasions when battleships succeeded in surprising carriers and engaging with gunfire, each time with deadly results.) Twelve days later, however, while covering *Scharnhorst*'s limping retreat to Germany, *Gneisenau* also suffered heavy damage from a torpedo fired by the submarine *Clyde*. Both *Scharnhorst* and *Gneisenau* remained *hors de combat* for the rest of the year.

On 22 June France accepted Germany's humiliating surrender terms, leaving Britain to fight on alone – but determined not to let the French fleet pass under German control. *Courbet* and *Paris* had escaped to Britain before the Germans took their home ports, but the rest of the French battleships were in Mediterranean or West African ports. The new *Jean Bart*, which had still not received her guns, made an epic escape from St Nazaire to reach Casablanca, while *Richelieu*, on the verge of completion, lay at Dakar. This left *Strasbourg*, *Dunkerque*, *Bretagne* and *Provence* at Mers-el-Kebir in Algeria, and *Lorraine* serving with the British Mediterranean Fleet at Alexandria.

Six days after the French surrender, Admiral Somerville took over the new 'Force H', specially formed at Gibraltar to contain and if need be attack the French battle fleet in Mers-el-Kebir. To accomplish this, Somerville had *Hood*, *Valiant*, *Resolution* and the carrier *Ark Royal*. On 3 July, when the French Admiral Gensoul rejected Somerville's ultimatum – to join the British, or scuttle his ships, or face attack – Force H inflicted a crushing half-hour bombardment on Gensoul's ships. *Bretagne* blew up, *Provence* ran aground, *Dunkerque* was crippled – but *Strasbourg* escaped to the open sea and reached Toulon, despite an unavailing attack by Swordfish aircraft from *Ark Royal*. Happily, at Alexandria the British Admiral Cunningham persuaded his French colleague to accept voluntary disarmament and internment for the smaller French squadron there, avoiding a second tragedy. No action was taken against *Jean Bart* at Casablanca, but on 7–8 July the carrier *Hermes* attacked *Richelieu* at Dakar. Though she remained able to use her guns to help repel the abortive British and Free French attempt on Dakar in September, *Richelieu* needed a full year before she became operational.

After this brutal neutralisation of the French Fleet in the western Mediterranean, Force H and the British Mediterranean Fleet turned their attention to the problems of keeping Malta supplied. Contrary to all expectations, Italy's entry into the war on 10 June did not result in the immediate invasion and conquest of the island. What remained to be seen was whether Force H and the Mediterranean Fleet could reinforce and supply Malta from opposite ends of the Mediterranean. Convoys to Malta would have to be protected with such battleship/carrier/cruiser forces as could be spared from other waters. Nothing could be done to change the overwhelming strategic advantage of Italy: her dominance of Malta and the central Mediterranean by land-based air power, and her ability to concentrate the Italian fleet against the numerically weaker British forces operating from Gibraltar and Alexandria. The Italian fleet, however, had no carriers and liaison with the air force (*Regia Aeronautica*) was bad. The British advantage lay in vastly superior fighting spirit, better gunnery and the unique benefits of carrier support.

For the first two months the tactical balance, battleship for battleship, lay in the favour of the British. Although *Conte di Cavour*, *Giulio Cesare*, *Andrea Doria* and *Caio Duilio* were all faster than their British counterparts, the latter two ships were still completing their reconstruction, and the 12·6 guns of all four were outranged by the British 15-inch. Thus on 9 July 1940 *Conte di Cavour* and *Giulio Cesare*, returning after escorting an Italian convoy to Libya, clashed with *Warspite*, *Malaya* and *Royal Sovereign* with the carrier *Eagle* in support, off the Calabrian 'toe' of Italy. Within minutes of her first salvo *Warspite* landed a damaging hit on *Cesare* and the Italian Admiral Campioni turned and ran for home, vainly pursued by *Eagle*'s aircraft.

In August 1940 the balance nevertheless swung heavily in Italy's favour when not only *Andrea Doria* and *Caio Duilio* but the new *Littorio* and *Vittorio Veneto* joined the Italian fleet. Even when Cunningham at Alexandria was reinforced by *Valiant* and the new fleet carrier *Illustrious* in early September, followed by *Barham* in early November, the British Mediterranean Fleet was still outnumbered by six to five in battleships. Cunningham was undaunted. He had only been waiting for the arrival of a modern carrier to take a leaf out of Togo's book at Port Arthur in 1904, and launch a night torpedo attack on the massed Italian fleet in its base at Taranto.

The famous raid finally took place on the night of 11–12 November 1940: 21 Swordfish torpedo-bombers, launched from *Illustrious*, of which only two were lost to copious but inaccurate anti-aircraft fire. At Taranto the tremendous potential of the carrier stood revealed at last, when a single carrier achieved the sinking of half a battle fleet from 170 miles away. *Conte di Cavour* was damaged beyond repair, and though *Littorio* and *Duilio* were raised they remained out of action for the next six months – the winter of 1940–41, in which the arrival of German air and land forces changed the whole course of the Mediterranean war.

In March 1941, during the ill-fated British attempt to reinforce Greece against the German invasion which finally broke in April, a sea battle was fought which introduced an entirely new element to naval surface combat: radar. Land-based air-warning radar had been instrumental in winning the Battle of Britain in August-September 1940, and the value of the new device to naval operations had always been obvious. The addition of air-warning, surface search and finally gunnery control radar systems to the existing directors and fire-control tables completed the battleship's transformation into a complete wea-

Below: The tragedy of Mers-el-Kebir – France's Mediterranean battle fleet under bombardment by the British Force 'H', 3 July 1940. *Bottom:* New menace in the Mediterranean – *Littorio* joins the Italian battle fleet in Taranto.

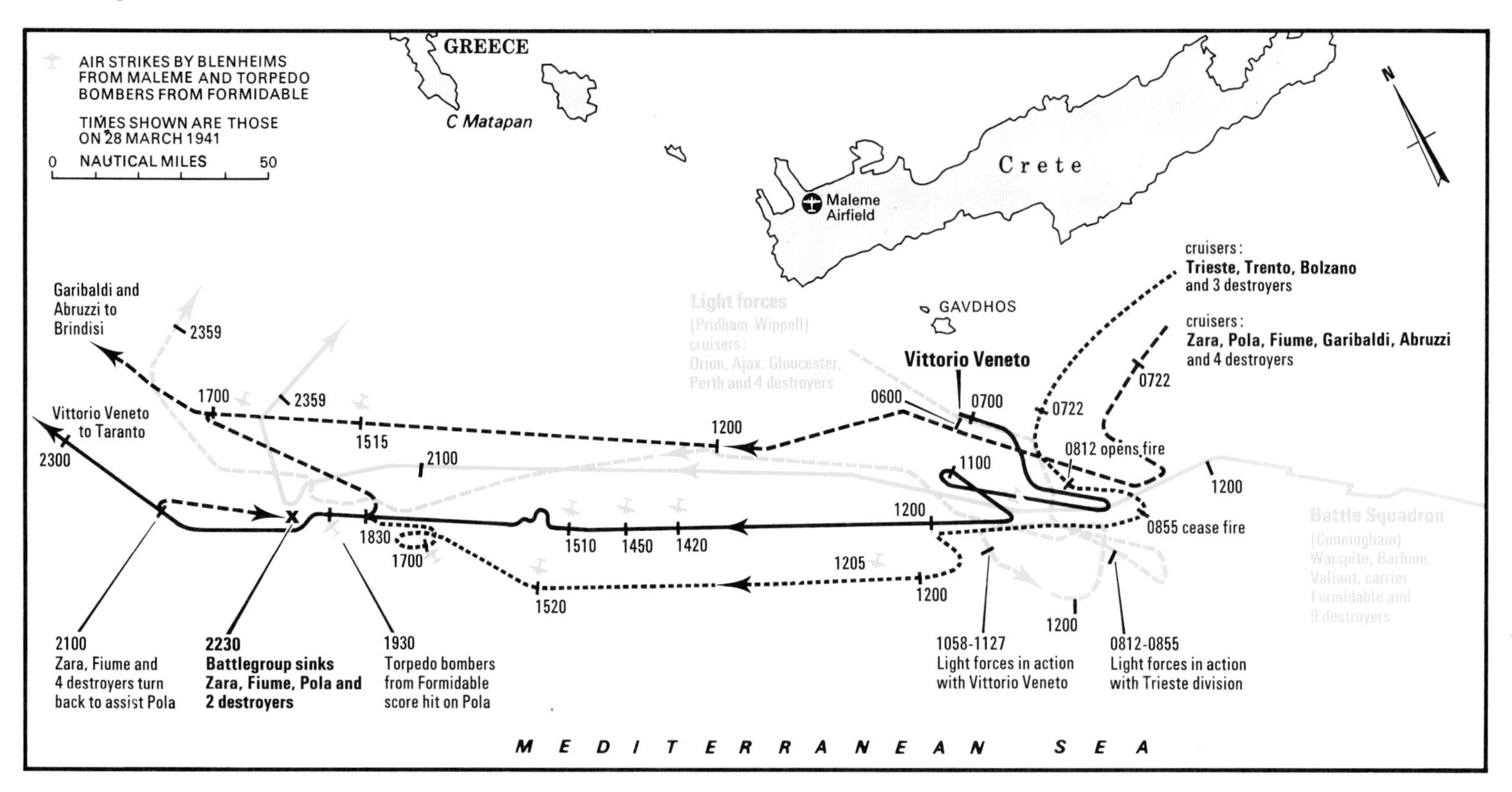

pons system, able to function by day and night regardless of 'eyeball' visibility. By late 1940 even the old battleships doled out so sparingly to the Mediterranean theatre were being fitted with shipborne radar; and in the Battle of Cape Matapan (28–29 March 1941) the new device first proved its inestimable work in a fleet action.

Matapan could well be called 'the first modern sea battle'. No previous naval action had featured, indeed been dominated by long-range air reconnaissance, carrier and land-based air strikes, and finally a brilliantly successful night gunnery action made possible only by radar. The battle was brought about because the Italian fleet, after much German pressure to adopt a more aggressive strategy, sortied for a strike at the British convoy-routes from Egypt to Greece. Admiral Iachino's striking force consisted of *Vittorio Veneto* and a powerful cruiser/destroyer force (eight cruisers in all); Cunningham's fleet of *Valiant*, *Barham*, *Warspite*, the new fleet carrier *Formidable*, plus four cruisers. The British fleet sailed at dusk on the 27th after three of Iachino's cruisers had been sighted 320 miles west of Crete by long-range air reconnaissance. Air searches from *Formidable* on the morning of the 28th soon found the leading Italian cruisers, which were then sighted by the British cruiser force – then *Vittorio* was sighted. Contact was lost as the British cruisers fell back on Cunningham's battleships, but a first air strike from *Formidable* attacked *Vittorio* around noon. No hits were scored but the knowledge that a carrier was in the offing was enough to make Iachino turn and run for base.

It was now up to *Formidable* to try and cripple *Vittorio* before the Italian battleship's superior speed could take her out of danger. At 15.10 hours a second carrier strike scored a single torpedo hit on *Vittorio* which briefly dropped her speed to 8 knots; but prompt repair-work soon enabled her to work up to first 17, then 19 knots, with Cunningham still some 87 miles away. A third carrier strike went in at dusk, to be greeted by the massed AA fire of the cruisers which Iachino had gathered closely round *Vittorio*. The battleship suffered no further hits but the cruiser *Pola* was crippled in the confused attacks. Iachino, believing himself safe from pursuit under cover of darkness, sent back the cruisers *Zara* and *Fiume* to assist *Pola*; and it was this luckless trio which fell victim to Cunningham, who was determined to force a night action if at all possible.

Visibility that night was about 2½ miles at worst, but at 22.00 *Valiant*'s radar detected *Pola* at 8 miles range. Homing in on radar, Cunningham's battleships closed to point-blank range, illuminated *Zara*, *Pola* and *Fiume* with their searchlights, and shattered all three ships with a ten-minute 15-inch bombardment. The two Italian destroyers in company were sunk soon after by destroyers. Thanks to naval aviation and radar, the veteran British battleships (all of them veterans of Jutland) had accounted for three heavy cruisers and two destroyers for the loss of only one carrier aircraft (the one which hit *Vittorio* during *Formidable*'s second strike). In addition to the three carrier strikes, no less than six attacks (bomber and torpedo) were made during the action by land-based aircraft operating from airfields in southern Greece and Crete. Though these scored no hits, the Italian fleet was unable to reply without a carrier of its own in company and they certainly added to Iachino's sense of vulnerability.

The victory of Matapan occurred when Atlantic commerce-raiding by heavy German surface units was still going from success to success. In 1940 seven German disguised merchant raiders had broken out into the Atlantic and Pacific (one of them via the North-East Passage and Bering Strait, by courtesy of the Nazi-Soviet Non-Aggression Pact). In late October 1940 the pocket-battleship *Admiral Scheer* began a five-month cruise in the Atlantic and Indian Oceans, ending with her triumphant return to Germany (April 1941) having sunk 16 merchant ships (99,059 tons). As in the case of *Graf Spee*, *Scheer*'s tally of victims was surpassed in importance by the disruption it inflicted on the cycle of British convoy sailings, demanding the allocation of battleships to convoy-escort duties wherever possible. But *Scheer*'s cruise was only the prelude to the splendid Atlantic war cruise of *Scharnhorst* and *Gneisenau* (23 January–22 March 1941), which accounted for 22 merchant ships (115,622 tons).

The German battle-cruisers were most competently handled by the new Fleet Commander, Admiral Lütjens, who had replaced Marschall. He twice refuelled in mid-Atlantic from tankers sent out from Germany; used his ships' high speed to avoid all convoys which were found to be escorted by battleships; and was quick to alter course and position whenever sighted by British search aircraft (which happened twice). The movements of *Scharnhorst* and *Gneisenau* during the cruise were directed in harmony with those of *Scheer*, and the battle-cruisers were finally ordered to return not to Germany, but to Brest. There they were to prepare for another Atlantic cruise, this time in harmony with *Bismarck*, due to make her first sortie with the new heavy cruiser *Prinz Eugen* in April.

Had this plan matured in full there seems little doubt that the four ships could have halted Atlantic convoy sailings by the early summer of 1941. They would have been able to slaughter any convoy, with or without battleship protection. But it was soon found that *Scharnhorst* needed a lengthy engine overhaul, and on 6 April *Gneisenau* was badly damaged at Brest by an RAF torpedo attack. Nevertheless, confident that they would be able at the very least to match the recent achievements of *Scharnhorst* and *Gneisenau*, Raeder sent *Bismarck* and *Prinz Eugen* into action on their own. They sailed from Gdynia in the Baltic on 18 May, with Lütjens in command.

The British, however, were coming to grips with the problem of intercepting Atlantic surface raiders. Well aware that *Bismarck*'s debut was imminent, they had stepped up their air and sea patrols from the Norwegian coast to Greenland. Air reconnaissance spotted the German ships in Norway's Grimstad fjord on the 21st, and by the evening of the 22nd Admiral Tovey, commanding the British Home Fleet, was poised for his first intercepting move. But it would take time for *Rodney* to join *King George V* and the new fleet carrier *Victorious*, and so Tovey sent *Hood* and *Prince of Wales* – the latter so new that her main armament was still not fully operational – to block the westernmost exit from the Atlantic: the Greenland Strait between Greenland and Iceland. Alerted by the cruisers *Norfolk* and *Suffolk*, which shadowed the Germans on radar as they entered Denmark Strait on

Below: The awesome power of *Bismarck*'s guns in action against *Hood* and *Prince of Wales* (24 May 1941), as seen from *Prinz Eugen*.
Overleaf: The climax at Matapan; pinned in the searchlight beams after being relentlessly tracked down by radar the three hapless Italian cruisers are destroyed by a deluge of 15-inch shells from Cunningham's battleships.

the evening of the 23rd, *Hood* and *Prince of Wales* steered to intercept; and battle was joined at 05.52 hours on the 24th.

Hood's tragedy was that there had never been time, since the outbreak of war, to complete the lengthy reconstruction which would have converted her from a battle-cruiser to a fast battleship. *Bismarck*'s third salvo straddled *Hood*, causing an ammunition fire on the upper deck which was still burning when *Bismarck*'s fifth salvo hit. The subsequent Board of Enquiry concluded that at least one 15-inch shell detonated first a 4-inch, then a 15-inch magazine, breaking her back and sinking her in less than a minute. *Bismarck* and *Prinz Eugen* then concentrated their fire on *Prince of Wales*, forcing her to withdraw after taking a hit on the control tower which killed every man on the bridge except the Captain and a signalman.

Bismarck, however, had taken two damaging hits from British heavy shells which flooded the forecastle with 2,000 tons of seawater and pierced several fuel tanks. This persuaded Lütjens to abandon the planned Atlantic cruise, detaching *Prinz Eugen* for independent operations and taking *Bismarck* into Brest for repairs. The ensuing epic chase ranks as the most dramatic single naval event of the Second World War. At 22.00 on the 24th, *Victorious* launched her first-ever air strike (nine Swordfish) which landed a hit on *Bismarck*'s main armour belt. This hit caused no crucial damage in itself, but the ship's evasive manoeuvres certainly caused further flooding. With the skill he had shown throughout the *Scharnhorst*/*Gneisenau* cruise, Lütjens evaded the cruiser *Suffolk* which was shadowing *Bismarck* on radar. By the time *Bismarck* was located again, by a Catalina flying-boat at 10.36 on 26 May, she was only 690 miles from Brest. The only chance now lay with *Ark Royal* and *Renown* of Force H, pounding north from Gibraltar. (In view of what had happened to the much stronger *Hood*, *Renown* was ordered not to engage even if she got the chance.) And it was *Ark Royal*'s Swordfish which, operating in appalling conditions, scored the vital hit aft at 21.15 on the 26th, jamming *Bismarck*'s rudders at 12°. Her speed cut to a crawl, *Bismarck* was finally intercepted by Tovey with *King George V* and *Rodney* at 08.00 on the 27th, after a last exhausting night fighting off repeated destroyer attacks.

The British battleships were running dangerously low on fuel, but *Bismarck*'s inability to manoeuvre or steam at full speed

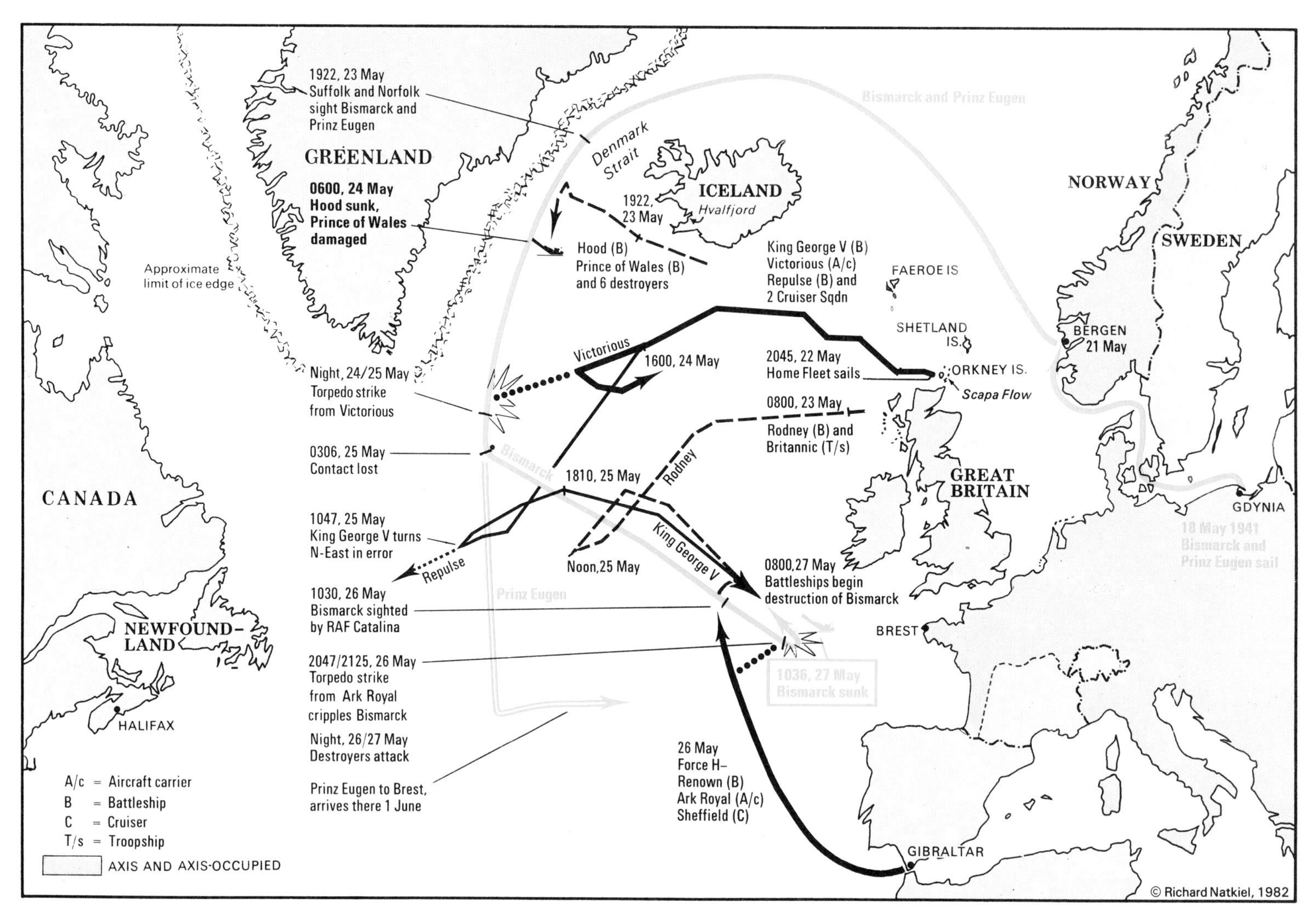

The chase of *Bismarck*, the most extensive air/sea pursuit of a single battleship in all naval history. By 26 May, before the Fleet Air Arm attack by *Ark Royal*, it seemed certain that *Bismarck* would reach the shelter of the *Luftwaffe*'s French-based air umbrella before the Home Fleet's battleships could engage.

made the ensuing execution mercifully brief. The last battle began at 08.47 and after half an hour *Bismarck*'s main armament, deprived of central control, was already petering out; the last German 15-inch salvo was fired at 09.31. By 10.15 *Bismarck*'s upperworks had been totally wrecked but her surviving crewmen fought their ship to the last with every weapon still able to fire. Helped on her way by scuttling charges, *Bismarck* finally rolled over to port and sank at 10.39. Only 110 survivors were rescued out of *Bismarck*'s complement of over 2,200 – but *Hood* had had only three survivors out of 1,419.

The loss of *Bismarck* abruptly halted the run of Atlantic commerce raids by heavy German warships. Within months, however, the still-formidable German battle fleet – *Lützow*, *Scheer*, *Scharnhorst*, *Gneisenau*, and *Tirpitz* approaching completion – was offered a far more promising zone of operations than the Atlantic. On 22 June 1941 the German invasion of Russia began, and three months later, in response to desperate Soviet appeals, the British sailed the first supply convoy to North Russia: PQ.1. This new development, assisted by British commando raids on the Norwegian coast throughout 1941, persuaded Hitler that the heavy surface units should be redeployed to Arctic Norway. There they could defend the Norwegian coastline and strike at the North Russian convoy route, all under the umbrella of the *Luftwaffe*. Before this could be done, however, *Scharnhorst* and *Gneisenau* must be extricated from Brest, where they had been joined by *Prinz Eugen* on 10 June.

From the moment of their arrival in Brest, the German warships had become the main target for RAF Bomber Command. During their Atlantic foray they had disrupted the entire Atlantic convoy cycle; immobile in Brest, they did the same for the British attempt to sustain a strategic bombing offensive against Germany. Three-quarters of the total tonnage of bombs dropped by Bomber Command in 1941 were aimed at the Brest squadron. It was a miracle that none of the ships sustained more than superficial damage, but this good luck, Hitler argued against the protests of his admirals, could not be expected to endure. The Brest squadron must return to Germany by the quickest route: straight up the Channel, covered by the *Luftwaffe*. Given good luck, bad weather and the ships' high speed the British, Hitler insisted, would never be able to react in time to stop them.

The resultant 'Channel Dash' of 11–12

February 1942 saw Hitler triumphantly vindicated, but it was the end of the line for the *Scharnhorst*/*Gneisenau* partnership. Both suffered mine damage, and while *Gneisenau* was still in dock (26 February) she suffered two grievous hits from heavy bombs. *Gneisenau* was taken out of commission in July 1942 and repairs were finally abandoned six months later. *Tirpitz*, however, had safely completed her transfer to Trondheim. By the end of February 1942 no less than 11 PQ convoys had reached Murmansk virtually unscathed; and in *Tirpitz* Admiral Ciliax, who had commanded during the 'Channel Dash', was determined that PQ.12 should not escape. Tovey's Home Fleet was, however, in the offing with *Victorious* in company and on 9 March *Tirpitz* was attacked by 12 Albacore torpedo aircraft. Brilliantly handled at full speed, *Tirpitz* evaded all torpedoes dropped at her, but she had clearly been lucky to escape *Bismarck*'s fate on her first operational sortie.

As the Arctic summer lengthened, convoys PQ.13–16 were fought through to Russia with ever-increasing losses from German air, destroyer and U-boat attacks. Tovey pleaded for the suspension of the convoys until autumn, but this was overruled on political grounds. Russia's plight was geninely desperate – the Stalingrad offensive opened on 28 June – and she needed all the war materials that could be sent. Knowing that the British would never dare risk the Home Fleet within *Luftwaffe* range, Raeder concentrated *Tirpitz* and *Hipper* in Trondheim, ready to strike at the next convoy: PQ.17.

The destruction of PQ.17 duly took place – but not under the guns of *Tirpitz*. When RAF reconnaissance found her berth at Trondheim empty – she was in fact moving north with *Hipper* to join *Lützow* in Altenfjord – the Admiralty concluded that she was already in the Barents Sea. PQ.17 was therefore peremptorily ordered to scatter at

Above: The last German photograph of *Bismarck* (from *Prinz Eugen*), down by the bows with the damage incurred in her fight with *Hood*.
Below: Fine shot of *Scharnhorst* heading up Channel in the race home to Germany from Brest – the 'Channel Dash', 12 February 1942.

Norman Wilkinson's painting of the gallant but vain Swordfish attack on the German battle-cruisers as they headed out of the Dover Narrows into the North Sea during the 'Channel Dash'.

Another sea crashes over *Scharnhorst*'s ice-crusted bows after her transfer to Norwegian waters in March 1943.

21.36 hours on 4 July, leaving its individual merchant ships to be picked off by the U-boats and German bombers ranging the Barents Sea. Sunk with the 23 ships (out of 33) were 430 tanks, 210 aircraft and 3,350 vehicles – enough to have fitted out an army. It was a military as well as a naval disaster, and it caused the suspension of the PQ convoys for the rest of the Arctic summer. Never has the mere threat of attack by a single batteship, truly the shadow without the substance, had such deadly results. Though the carrier had already been accepted as the new arbiter of fleet actions by the summer of 1942, the PQ.17 tragedy emphatically proved that the battleship's redundancy still lay far in the future.

Yet the Germans never fully understood the real reason for their success with PQ.17. They believed that it had come about solely through the prowess of the U-boats and *Luftwaffe*, not because of the threat posed by *Tirpitz*. When the British sailed PQ.18 in September with a strong destroyer escort and one of the new escort carriers, *Tirpitz* had been brought down to Trondheim for a long refit. Despite days of vicious fighting and unprecedentedly heavy *Luftwaffe* attacks, the convoy battled through; it had lost 13 out of 40 ships, but four U-boats and 41 German aircraft had been destroyed in exchange. In December the British started sailing Russian convoys in two halves, each easier to protect than a single big convoy. When *Lützow* and *Hipper* carried out a perfect pincer interception on one of these sub-convoys (JW.51B) on 31 December 1942, they were out-faced and driven off by the high courage of the British cruiser/destroyer escort.

In one of his more famous rages, Hitler ordered the entire battle fleet to be scrapped, driving Raeder to resign in protest. His successor Dönitz persuaded Hitler to give the fleet another chance, however, concentrating *Tirpitz*, *Scharnhorst* and *Lützow* in Altenfjord by the end of March 1943. In the face of this overwhelmingly strong concentration the British had no choice but to suspend all Russian convoys for the entire summer of 1943 – yet another success for the battleship, and for the inert pull of the 'fleet in being'.

One reason for the British Home Fleet's weakness in the spring and summer of 1943 was the sequence of tremendous events under way in the Mediterranean, which had seemed unthinkable only a year before. After Matapan the Mediterranean Fleet had suffered slow but steady attrition, while the strength of the Italian battle fleet revived with the return to service of *Littorio* and *Duilio*. On 13 November 1941 *Ark Royal* was torpedoed and sunk by *U-81*, leaving Force H without carrier cover. Twelve days later *U-331* sank *Barham* off the Egyptian coast, while on the night of 18 December three Italian human torpedoes sank *Valiant* and *Queen Elizabeth* in Alexandria. Their decks remained above water, causing Italian Intelligence to believe that they were still operational; but these losses left Cunningham with no battle fleet to support Malta convoys as the German-Italian bombardment of Malta rose to its height.

By the spring of 1942 German air supremacy in the central Mediterranean was unchallenged; and if the Italian battle fleet had pulled its weight the British would never have been able to force through just enough supplies to keep Malta going. In March and June 1942, half-hearted sorties by *Littorio* with strong cruiser/destroyer support recoiled in the face of spirited counter-action by outnumbered British forces. The supreme effort was the 'Pedes-

tal' convoy to Malta (11–13 August 1942), in which the fast tanker *Ohio* and 13 freighters were escorted within German-Italian air range by *Nelson*, *Rodney* and the carriers *Eagle*, *Victorious* and *Indomitable*. The covering force then withdrew to Gibraltar. After 48 hours of constant bombing and U-boat attacks only *Ohio* and three battered freighters survived to struggle into Malta. But this sufficed to keep Malta-based strike aircraft sinking the Italian tankers carrying fuel to Rommel's *Panzerarmee* in Egypt, thus ensuring his eventual defeat at Alamein in October-November 1942.

The next major operation after 'Pedestal' was a momentous reversal of the fortunes of the Mediterranean war: the Anglo-American 'Torch' landings in French North Africa (8 November 1942). Battleship cover for the triple thrust at Casablanca, Oran and Algiers included three American battleships: *Texas*, *New York* and the new 'South Dakota', *Massachusetts*, whose 16-inch battery effectively silenced the fire of *Jean Bart* at Casablanca. British battleship/carrier cover for the landings inside the Mediterranean was provided by *Rodney* and *Furious* at Oran and by *Duke of York*, *Renown*, *Formidable* and *Victorious* at Algiers.

From 'Torch' to the end of the war, battleship fire support was regarded as essential for every major amphibious landing in the European theatre – radar-controlled main armament for bombarding shore targets, air-warning radar and massed AA guns to increase the fleet's security from aerial attack. A constant increase in AA fire-power, particularly light quick-firing guns, was a feature common to all battleship navies as the war progressed. To take just one example, *King George V* joined the fleet in late 1940 with an AA battery of four eight-barrelled 2-pdr pom-poms and four experimental AA rocket launchers. By July 1943, when she supported the invasion of Sicily, her AA battery had been increased to five eight-barrelled pom-poms, one four-barrelled pom-pom, and 38 single 20 mm Oerlikons. Two years later, at the end of the Pacific War, it consisted of eight eight-barrelled pom-poms, 24 single 20 mm Oerlikons, six twin 20 mm Oerlikons, two quadruple 40 mms and two single 40 mms.

Within a year of 'Torch', Allied naval supremacy in the Mediterranean was total. Germany's invasion of Vichy France and attempted grab at the French fleet in Toulon (27 November 1942) prompted Admiral Laborde to scuttle his fleet – a sad end for *Strasbourg*, *Dunkerque* and *Provence*. After the Allied capture of Sicily and the fall of Mussolini (25 July 1943) the Italian Government sued for peace. To prevent the Italian battle fleet being seized by the German forces in mainland Italy, its formal capitulation was demanded by the Allies and made on 9 September 1943. The surrendered Italian battleships were *Vittorio Veneto*, *Littorio* (renamed *Italia* at the end of July), *Giulio Cesare* and two raised and repaired victims of Taranto, *Andrea Doria* and *Caio Duilio*. The third 'Littorio', *Roma* (completed in August 1942) was not so lucky. As she headed south to surrender the *Luftwaffe* attacked and sank her with a new weapon, the air-to-surface rocket missile – the first warship victim of the dawning missile era. *Roma*'s fate underlines the immense importance attached to the Italian battle fleet by virtue of its mere existence, lacklustre though its operational performance had been for the past three years. It accepted surrender almost exactly 25 years after the Imperial German High Seas Fleet – a unique moment for *Warspite* and the

Heavy cruiser *Hipper* at sea during Operation *Regenbogen* ('Rainbow'), the abortive pounce on Convoy JW.51B on 31 December 1942. The swastika marking is to prevent German aircraft from bombing their own fleet; until British escort-carriers could be spared for the Russian convoy route, every bomber in the Arctic skies was German.

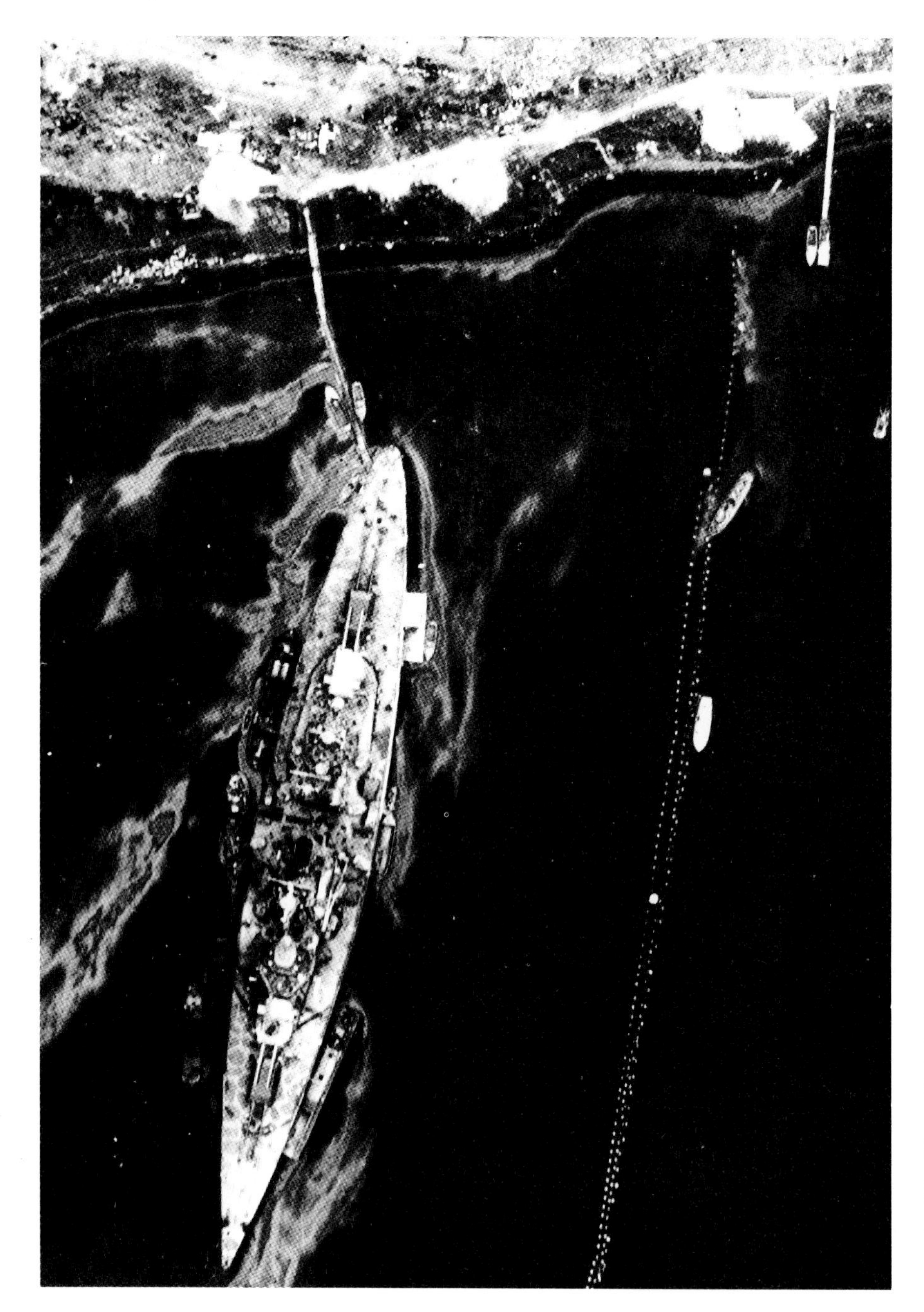

RAF reconnaissance check on *Tirpitz* at her heavily protected anchorage in Kaafjord, having virtually completed repairs to the damage suffered in the Fleet Air Arm attack of 3 April 1944.

repaired *Valiant*, the only British battleships present at both surrenders.

Though the Italian fleet's surrender relegated the battleship's role in the Mediterranean to coastal bombardment for the rest of the war, there was still plenty of action in the Arctic. On the previous day (8 September 1943) *Tirpitz*, *Scharnhorst* and ten destroyers sailed from Altenfjord to destroy Allied shore installations on Spitzbergen. Safely achieved against no naval opposition, this mission was the only 'battle honour' which *Tirpitz* ever achieved. On 22 September she was badly damaged in Altenfjord in a daring attack by British midget submarines (X-craft), which had been specially developed for the purpose. This left *Scharnhorst*, after *Lützow*'s withdrawal to Germany at the end of the month, as the only operational German capital ship in the Arctic theatre – but when the British resumed their 'JW' convoys to Russia in November, Dönitz was determined that she should justify the fleet's existence in Hitler's eyes by attacking a convoy at the first favourable opportunity.

The result was the Battle of the North Cape (26 December 1943), the last battleship action in European waters. It was an encounter for which the British commander, Admiral Fraser, was minutely prepared after weeks of studying the problem. *Scharnhorst*'s assets were formidable: superior speed and protection, the British lack of carrier cover, and the prevailing darkness and foul weather of the Arctic winter. British assets were superior heavy-calibre fire-power, radar expertise, and the determination to force an action.

This was indeed an 'all-radar' battle. It was radar which found *Scharnhorst* as she searched for convoy JW.55B; radar which tracked her as she withdrew after two clashes with the cruiser squadron covering the convoy; and radar – or rather the German lack of it – which caused her to steam right into the arms of Fraser's battle group coming up from the south-west. When Fraser's only battleship *Duke of York* opened fire at 16.46 hours *Scharnhorst* was totally surprised, caught in the glare of the British starshells with her guns still fore and aft. Even so, *Scharnhorst* stood up well to the ensuing gunnery duel and was within minutes of running clean out of range when, at 18.20, a 14-inch shell damaged one of her boiler rooms. Power was restored, but not before Fraser's destroyers had closed and hit *Scharnhorst* with four torpedoes. Like *Bismarck*, *Scharnhorst* was fought to the last, only sinking at 19.45 after having taken at least 13 direct hits and 11 torpedoes from the cruisers and destroyers which finished her off.

By the spring of 1944, however, *Tirpitz* was nearly ready for sea again, available for any operation which the Germans might try to disrupt the Allied build-up for the Normandy invasion. This was averted by a Home Fleet carrier strike at *Tirpitz* in Altenfjord (3 April 1944) which caused extensive damage to her upperworks and kept her safely *hors de combat* until June. It was during the battle for Normandy that radar-controlled gunfire, ranging over 20 miles inland, played its most spectacular role, repeatedly breaking up concentrations of German tanks. But as long as *Tirpitz* remained in the far north, able to float and fire her guns, the British Admiralty dared not undertake large-scale transfers of carriers and battleships to join the Americans in the Pacific. Only after *Tirpitz* was over-

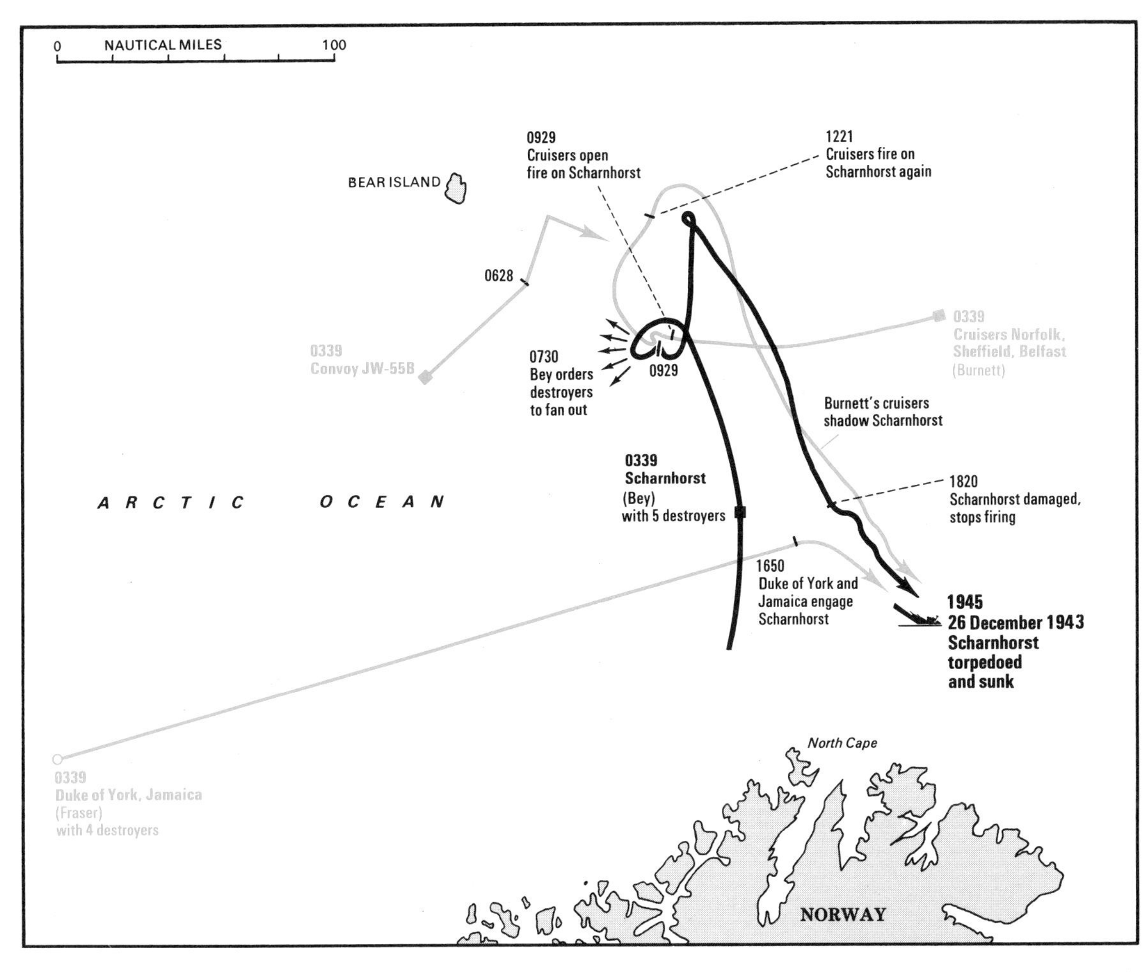

Left: The interception of *Scharnhorst* by the British Home Fleet, 26 December 1943.
Below: *Warspite*'s 15-inch guns bombarding the Italian coast.

whelmed and capsized by 6-ton streamlined 'Tallboy' bombs dropped by RAF Lancasters (12 November 1944) was the long-standing menace of the 'Lone Queen of the North' dispelled at last.

Though the German U-boat arm was preparing for a renewed submarine offensive in spring 1945, the German surface fleet was finished. *Gneisenau*'s hulk was sunk as a blockship at Gdynia in March 1945, and in April *Scheer* and *Lützow* were knocked out by bombs at Kiel and Swinemunde. It had therefore taken the British *five and a half years* to destroy the German battle fleet which had been so hopelessly outnumbered in September 1939, and yet which had played such a disruptive and dramatic role throughout the war.

11. THE PACIFIC, 1941–1945

Previous pages: American battleships in line-ahead during the latter months of the Pacific War. The fire-power of the American battle line was an integral feature of every major landing operation, but the US Pacific Fleet's battleships only engaged their opposite numbers three times: twice off Guadalcanal in November 1942, and finally in Surigao Strait in October 1944.
Below: The holocaust of Pearl Harbor, 7 December 1941: *West Virginia* (*left*) and *Tennessee*, with rescue craft trying to dodge the blazing fuel oil on the water. Note early radar array on *West Virginia*'s foremast, at left. Both ships were raised and repaired, to serve with the battle line in the decisive campaigns of 1944–45.

THE BATTLESHIP WAR in the Pacific could not have been in greater contrast to that of the Atlantic and Mediterranean theatres. Apart from the obvious fact that the war against Japan lasted two years less than that against Germany, there were only five occasions in the entire Pacific War when battleships took part in fleet actions, and only three – twice at Guadalcanal (1942) and once at Leyte Gulf, two years later – when Japanese and American battleships actually fired at each other. Nor, at any stage in the Pacific War, did unescorted capital ships take part in commerce raiding or protracted convoy escort duties; and no single Japanese or American battleship ever played the same 'fleet in being' role achieved so successfully by Germany's *Tirpitz*.

For all that, battleships played an integral and often vital part in naval operations throughout the Pacific War, and it was fitting in every sense that the final surrender of Japan should have been signed on the deck of the American battleship *Missouri* in Tokyo Bay. It was also in the Pacific that the battle-cruiser took its last form, that the battleship reached the penultimate stage of its development, and that the last battleship action of all time was fought.

Of the battleship's calamitous debut in the Pacific War, on the receiving end at Pearl Harbor on 7 December 1941, little more need be said. Though the British strike at Taranto 13 months before had shown what could be achieved by carrier strike aircraft against a battle fleet surprised in harbour, the US Pacific Fleet was not on a war footing and was preparing for normal peacetime Sunday routine when the Japanese struck; the flagship *Pennsylvania* was actually in dry dock. Of the eight American battleships sunk and crippled at Pearl Harbor, six – *Nevada*, *Pennsylvania*, *Tennessee*, *California*, *Maryland*, and *West Virginia* – were subsequently repaired for extensive service in the Pacific War, and five of them took part in the last battleship action off Leyte in October 1944. The Japanese also mistook the non-operational target ship *Utah* for a 'front-line' unit of the Pacific Fleet, and their successful efforts to sink her took some pressure off the others. But there was no disguising the magnitude of the disaster. The carnage of Pearl Harbor left only two capital ships, from Ceylon to the American West coast, to face the intact

might of the Japanese Combined Fleet.

These were the British 'King George V' *Prince of Wales*, veteran of the *Bismarck* action seven months earlier, and the battle-cruiser *Repulse*. When the Japanese hit Pearl Harbor both were at Singapore, on their way to Australia to form the core of an intended British Pacific Fleet and hopefully act as a deterrent on Japanese ambitions in the Pacific. *Repulse* and *Prince of Wales* had never been intended to operate without air cover, though this misapprehension still prevails. They were to have been joined by the new fleet carrier *Indomitable*, but this was prevented by *Indomitable*'s suffering damage by grounding in the West Indies. Even after this setback the ships were only envisaged as operating under Australian land-based air cover; and there was fighter cover available (a squadron of obsolete Brewster Buffaloes) for inshore operations off the Malayan coast.

The decisive factor, however, was that the British Admiral Phillips clung to the belief that aircraft were no match for capital ships – and it should be remembered that in December 1941 it could still be argued that not one battleship, fully alerted and at sea, had ever been sunk by air attack. Phillips therefore felt fully justified in sailing from Singapore on 8 December, believing that he had an excellent chance to destroy the Japanese invasion fleet which had been reported off the northern Malayan coast. When sighted at sea by Japanese air reconnaissance on the afternoon of the 9th, Phillips had already been told that fighter protection could not be provided in the area of his planned attack. Heading back to Singapore, he closed the beaches of Kuantan to investigate a false report of Japanese landings there – only to be caught, on the morning of the 10th, by a force of 30 Japanese level bombers and 50 torpedo aircraft which had taken off from Saigon that morning.

The one-sided battle which followed featured two concentrations of Japanese attacks separated by a 20-minute lull (12.00–12.20 hours). Against these attacks the sparse, heavy-calibre AA armament of *Repulse*, and *Prince of Wales*' woeful lack of strength in rapid-fire 20 mm and 40 mm guns, proved entirely inadequate. It is certain that the Japanese attacked with a speed and precision unbelievable to their victims – but the Japanese aircraft had no fighter escorts. It is also certain that the RAF had a Buffalo fighter squadron at Sembawang, an hour's flight from the action off Kuantan, ready to give the fleet cover if asked. But Phillips' obsession with keeping radio silence deprived his ships of fighter cover during the most intense attacks (12.20–12.45) which sealed their fate. Phillips never did call on the RAF; the fighters only took off, far too late, in response to an attack report by *Repulse*. They only arrived on the scene after both ships had sunk, *Repulse* at 12.33 and *Prince of Wales* at 13.20. Japanese losses were only three aircraft shot down and one crashed on returning to base.

In its full implications, the sinking of *Repulse* and *Prince of Wales* was a far more shattering event in naval history than any of Nelson's classic victories – stemming, as these also did, from a novel application of existing resources. So far as the story of the battleship is concerned, the disaster off Kuantan reduces even Jutland to insignificance. Given enemy air supremacy, the long-standing faith in the battleship's *deterrent* value (for that is what *Repulse* and *Prince of Wales* had been sent east to wield) stood revealed as precisely nil – even if one of the battleships concerned happened to be one of the world's newest and apparently most powerful. Nor has the loss of an impressive battle squadron ever had a more dramatic political result. If the myth of the battleship was thus revealed, so was the myth of British, and hence European, imperial supremacy in the Far East. This certainly did not mean that every colonial native subject in the path of the Japanese advance hailed the Japanese as liberators, but the resultant demoralisation undoubtedly helped the initial landslide of Japanese victories between December 1941 and May 1942. Crowned as it was ten weeks later by the greatest military humiliation in modern British history, the fall of Singapore, the sinking of *Repulse* and *Prince of*

HMS *Prince of Wales* arrives at Singapore in December 1941, showing obvious signs of the long voyage out round Africa. Contrary to Churchill's hopes the presence of British capital ships in Singapore acted as a magnet rather than a deterrent to Japanese air attacks.

Wales put the first irreparable crack through the foundations of the British Empire.

It was in every sense the end of an era, for no more Allied battleships or battle-cruisers were lost after *Repulse* and *Prince of Wales*. Carriers excepted, they were the last of the 20 British capital ships lost in the two World Wars (15 in the First, five in the Second). *Repulse* and *Prince of Wales* were the only ships of their type to be sunk outright by aircraft at sea. Of the previous 18 British casualties only four – *Indefatigable*, *Queen Mary*, *Invincible* and *Hood*, all battle-cruisers – had been sunk by enemy gunfire. Twelve had been sunk by stealth: seven by U-boats, four by mines, and one (*Goliath*, at Gallipoli) by night surface torpedo attack. The other two – *Bulwark* (1914) and *Vanguard* (1917) had perished by spontaneous ammunition explosion.

Even if the Japanese attacks of 7 and 10 December 1941 had failed to sink a single Allied battleship instead of eliminating the lot, the pooled British, Dutch, Australian and American naval resources would still have been scattered between Singapore, the Dutch East Indies, Australia and Pearl Harbor. With the Allied battleships liquidated in the first four days of the war, only cruisers and destroyers remained to be thrown in the path of the Japanese drive south. These were duly crushed in the Battle of the Java Sea (27 February 1942) in a vain attempt to delay the fall of Java. Nothing was left but the two American carriers which had escaped the Japanese blow at Pearl Harbor (*Lexington* and *Enterprise*), and whatever force the British could spare to defend the Indian Ocean.

Japan's battle fleet at sea: *Mutsu*, with her forward 16-inch turret trained to port, followed by *Ise* and *Fuso*.

At the end of March 1942 Admiral Somerville took over the British Eastern Fleet, based on Ceylon. He had five old, slow battleships (*Warspite*, *Revenge*, *Ramillies*, *Resolution* and *Royal Sovereign*), the equally ancient light carrier *Hermes* and the untried fleet carriers *Formidable* and *Indomitable*. Grimly aware that he only had 57 strike aircraft and 36 fighters in all three carriers, Somerville fell back on a 'fleet in being' strategy. When the Japanese carrier fleet broke into the Bay of Bengal in April, Somerville withdrew from Ceylon, prepared to retreat to the African coast if necessary. This left the five Japanese carriers free to bombard Ceylon and the Indian coast, sinking *Hermes* and two cruisers before they withdrew east (9 April). Though Somerville had preserved a British naval presence in the Indian Ocean, there was little to indicate that the Japanese run of success was already nearing its end.

While the Japanese carriers continued their rampage westward to Ceylon, the American carriers began a series of nuisance raids in February and March against the easternmost Japanese-held outposts in the central Pacific. These culminated (18 April) in the famed 'Doolittle Raid' on Tokyo, using US Army B-25 bombers flown off the new carrier *Hornet*. The actual damage inflicted by this tiny force was negligible, but it spurred Admiral Yamamoto to make the elimination of the American carriers his next objective. He planned an all-out attack on a target which the US Pacific Fleet would have no choice but to defend: the US Marine base at Midway, westernmost point of the Hawaiian Island chain.

As a preliminary to Midway, Australia was to be isolated by the seaborne conquest of Port Moresby in New Guinea and the establishment of a Japanese base at Tulagi in the Solomon Islands. But the latter move was frustrated by the first carrier-versus-carrier engagement in the Coral Sea (4–8 May). The American carrier *Lexington* was lost and *Yorktown* damaged, but their presence had caused the withdrawal of the Moresby invasion force. Hardly less important was the over-confident Japanese belief that *two* American carriers had been lost in the Coral Sea, leaving only two to contest the supreme blow at Midway. Another fatal Japanese error was assuming that US Naval Intelligence had no inkling of the Midway plan, whereas Admiral Chester Nimitz had been provided with all salient details by his radio decoders at Pearl Harbor.

Nimitz never even troubled to bring up

the three old battleships (*New Mexico*, *Idaho* and *Mississippi*) which had been transferred to the American Pacific coast from the Atlantic since Pearl Harbor's ordeal in December. All he was hoping for was that his last three front-line carriers (*Hornet*, *Enterprise* and the hastily-repaired *Yorktown*) could, by a surprise attack, cause the Japanese to reprieve Midway as the Coral Sea fight had reprieved Moresby. What he got was beyond his wildest dreams: the sinking of all four Japanese fleet carriers involved in the Midway attack, in exchange for only *Yorktown* (4 June 1942). The only way in which the Japanese could have won through after this disaster would have been a fatal night pursuit by the American Admiral Spruance, blundering within range of the battleships *Hiei* and *Kongo* together with 21 Japanese cruisers and destroyers. When Spruance prudently declined to take such a risk, holding his carriers in readiness for further action on the 5th if need be, Yamamoto had no option but to call off the Midway attack and withdraw.

After Midway, the American pre-emptive invasion of Guadalcanal in the Solomons (7 August 1942) began a unique phase in the war at sea: six months of furious Japanese attempts, by air, land, and sea, to make it impossible for the Americans to hold Guadalcanal. The resultant campaign of attrition, with both sides throwing in all they had in response to the shifting pressure of the battle, saw the combat debut of the new American battleships *North Carolina*, *Washington* and *South Dakota*. The first requirement of the American battleships was to provide AA fire support for the carrier task groups in daylight carrier actions – an entirely novel role for battleships, but for which the Americans were particularly well equipped. Supporting the carriers *Enterprise* and *Saratoga* off the Eastern Solomons (24 August 1942), *North Carolina* contributed the unprecedented AA fire-power of ten twin 5-inch DPs, four quadruple 1·1-inch guns and 40 rapid-fire 20 mms. This undoubtedly helped save *Enterprise* (though the carrier suffered three bomb hits) and savaged the main Japanese carrier strike, with less than ten out of 80 Japanese aircraft returning to their carriers. *North Carolina*, however, was damaged by a torpedo from the Japanese submarine *I-15* on 15 September, a disastrous day on which the carrier *Wasp* was sunk by the submarine *I-19*. *North Carolina* was replaced by *South Dakota* and *Washington*, but the American carrier strength was thus reduced to *Hornet* and *Enterprise*.

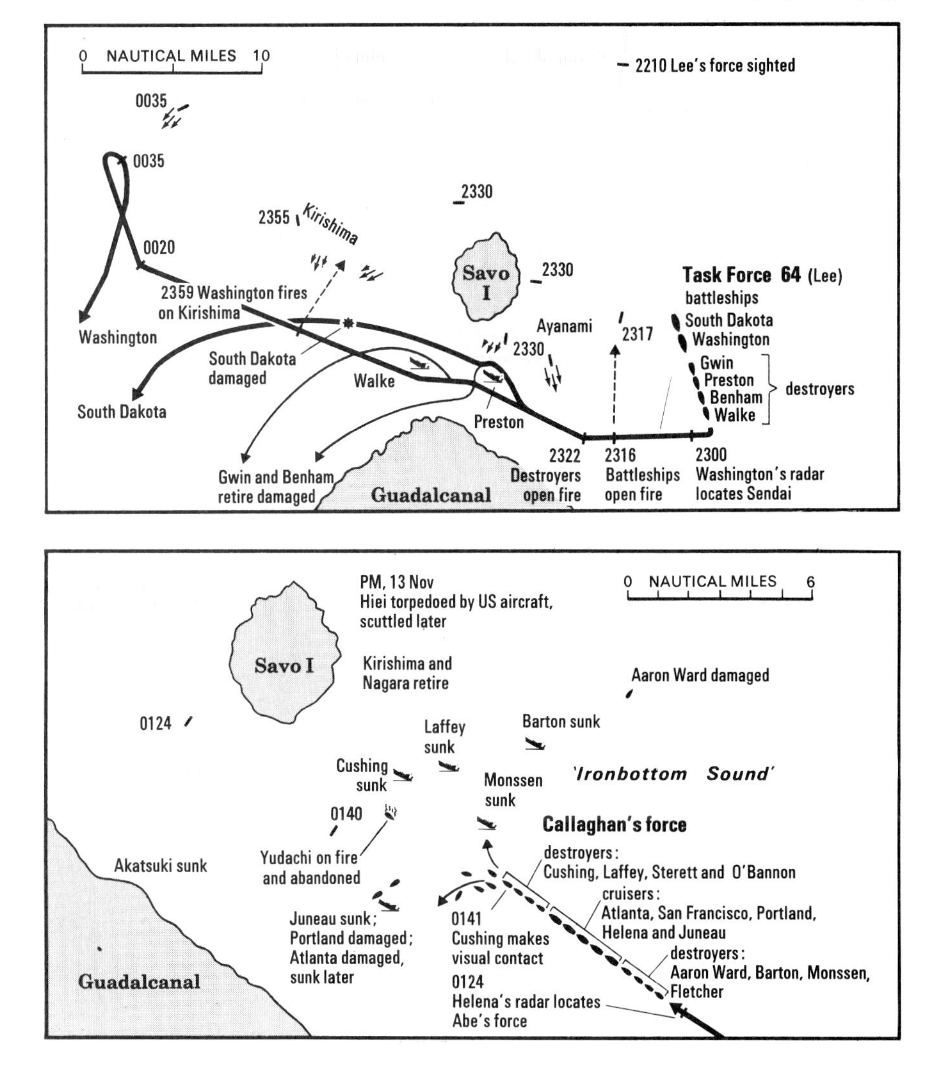

The battleship actions off Guadalcanal in November 1942. *Hiei* was the first Japanese battleship lost, in 'First Guadalcanal' (*top*), followed two nights later by *Kirishima*. All told, the Guadalcanal ordeal cost Japan the equivalent of an entire peacetime fleet: two battleships, one carrier, five cruisers and 12 destroyers.

In the first week of October the Japanese were the first to add battleship fire-power to the furious night actions off Guadalcanal. The crux of the campaign was the American ability to keep operating aircraft from Henderson Field, the island's only airstrip. On the night of 13–14 October the battleships *Kongo* and *Haruna* pounded Henderson Field for 90 minutes with a hail of 14-inch shells, with subsequent night bombardments continued by cruisers. Admiral Halsey, directing the attempts to keep the Marines on Guadalcanal supplied and supported, refused to risk his battleships in among the islands where superior Japanese night-fighting tactics had so far proved superior. *South Dakota* gallantly supported *Enterprise* during the last carrier action of the Guadalcanal campaign: the Battle of the Santa Cruz Islands (26 October 1942). In addition to her increased rapid-fire AA battery (eight twin 5-inch DPs and 56 40 mms), *South Dakota* located incoming Japanese attacks on her air-warning radar, while her 18-inch armour saved her from a bomb hit on the forward turret. Once again, though *Hornet* was sunk and *Enterprise* damaged, victory was measured in Japanese carrier air strength remaining after the action: only 100 of all types, enough to

operate only two out of their four carriers.

After the Santa Cruz carrier clash the sea battle for Guadalcanal reverted to intense night actions fought close inshore. On the night of 12–13 November the Japanese committed the battleships *Hiei* and *Kirishima* to their latest cruiser/destroyer attack. Not for the first time, the Americans were surprised despite the advantage of being equipped with search radar, but hit back valiantly with 8-inch and 6-inch gunfire at point-blank range. Though the cruisers *San Francisco* and *Atlanta* were fearfully damaged, the Japanese battleships were firing bombardment shell, the Americans armour-piercing. Though a total wreck above the waterline, *San Francisco*'s armoured hull was not penetrated. *Hiei*, on the other hand, limped out of the battle with severe damage to her upperworks. With the coming of daylight on the 13th *Hiei* was caught by US Marine Corps bombers from Henderson Field, battered to a halt, abandoned and scuttled: the first Japanese battleship lost in the Second World War.

Though *Kirishima* escaped unscathed from the chaos of 'First Guadalcanal', she returned 48 hours later to resume the bombardment of Henderson Field with two heavy cruisers and a light cruiser/destroyer screen. This time, however, Halsey had also decided to commit his battleships:

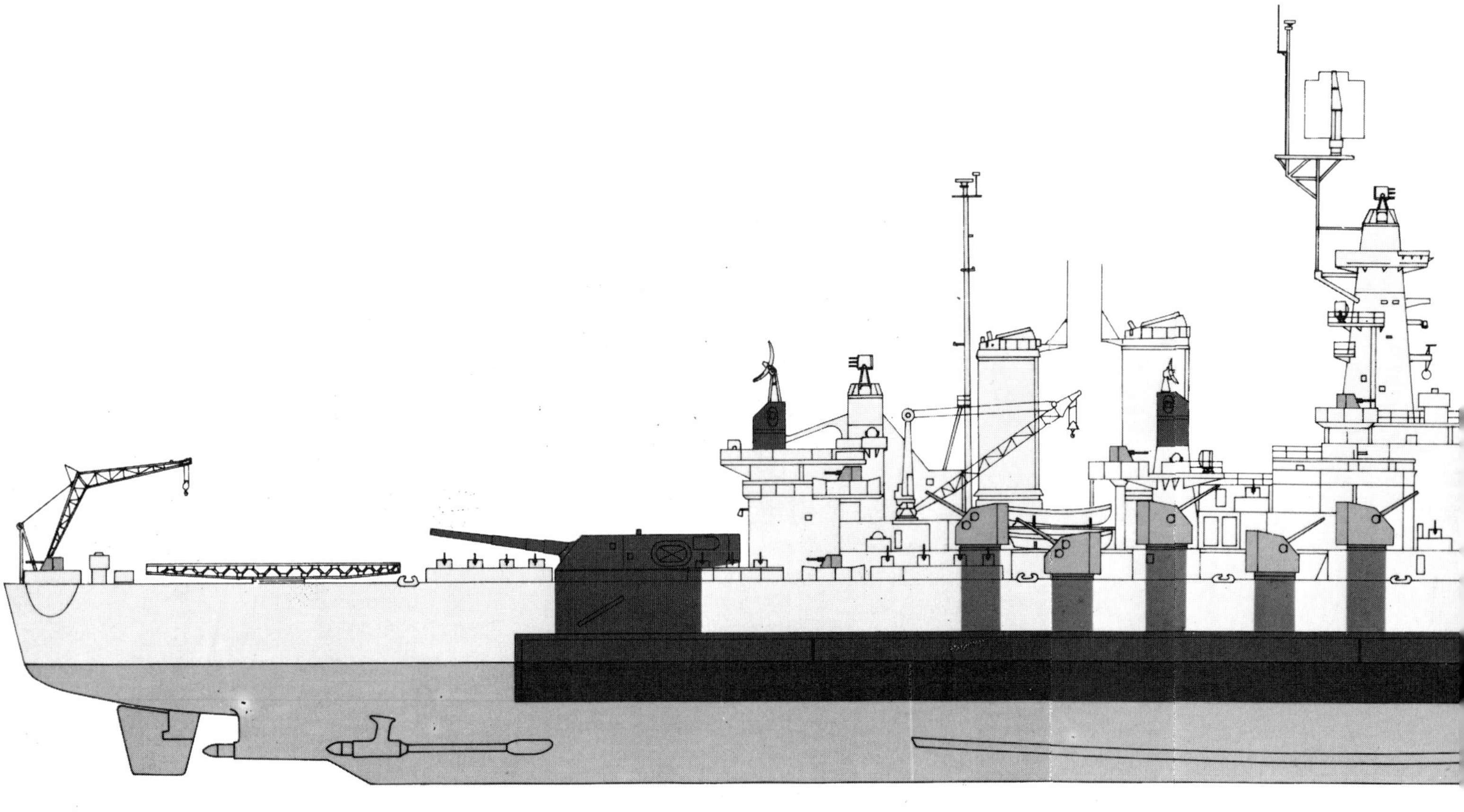

Above left: South Dakota (nine 16-inch guns). The centre gun of the after turret has been depressed, probably for cleaning.
Below left: Lost at 'Second Guadalcanal': the 'Kongo' class *Kirishima*.

South Dakota and *Washington*. The result was another extraordinary night battle, revealing the dangers as well as the benefits of total reliance on radar gunnery control. After a few salvos with *Washington* which repelled *Kirishima*'s advance screen *South Dakota*'s electric power failed, blinding her radars and silencing her guns. *South Dakota* lost touch with *Washington* and came under punishing fire from the Japanese heavy ships – the same crisis which had ruined *Hiei* two nights earlier. It fell to *Washington* to retrieve the situation and show what battleships of the latest type could achieve, even under the most unfavourable circumstances. Firing by radar, *Washington* landed nine 16-inch and about 40 5-inch shells on *Kirishima* in seven minutes, reducing her to a total wreck which the Japanese evacuated and scuttled. The remainder of the Japanese force withdrew.

The intervention of the American battleships in 'Second Guadalcanal' marked the turning-point of the Solomons campaign. The loss of two Japanese battleships in 48 hours caused Yamamoto to abandon his efforts to neutralise Henderson Field by gunfire. Though the Japanese scored a final tactical victory in another cruiser/destroyer night action off Tassafaronga Point (30 November–1 December), this only postponed until 4 January the Japanese decision to abandon Guadalcanal and evacuate the remnants of the Japanese army. Few of the 12,000 Japanese troops successfully taken off in the first week of February 1943 were fit for further service, and on 21 February the American advance up the Solomon Islands chain began with the seizure of the Russell Islands.

The 1943 Solomons campaign culminated in the American capture of Bougainville (November 1943–January 1944) and the isolation of the former Japanese fleet base at Rabaul in New Britain (December 1943–March 1944). Though neither battleships nor carriers took part in the actual fighting, 1943 was nevertheless a decisive year in the balance of the rival battleship/carrier fleets. After Midway, with the disastrous loss of carrier supremacy, the Japanese had reduced their battle fleet from 12 to ten by taking *Ise* and *Hyuga* in hand for conversion as battleship-carriers. Their two after turrets were removed and the deck raised by two levels topped by a short flight-deck, creating hangar accommodation for 22 seaplanes. This clumsy attempt to give the battle fleet additional air-reconnaissance 'vision' was no substitute for Japan's failure to keep pace with the United States in carrier construction. In 1943 the US Pacific Fleet, after the ordeals of the previous year, gained overwhelming carrier superiority with the arrival of the 'Essex', 'Independence' and 'Sangamon' class carriers.

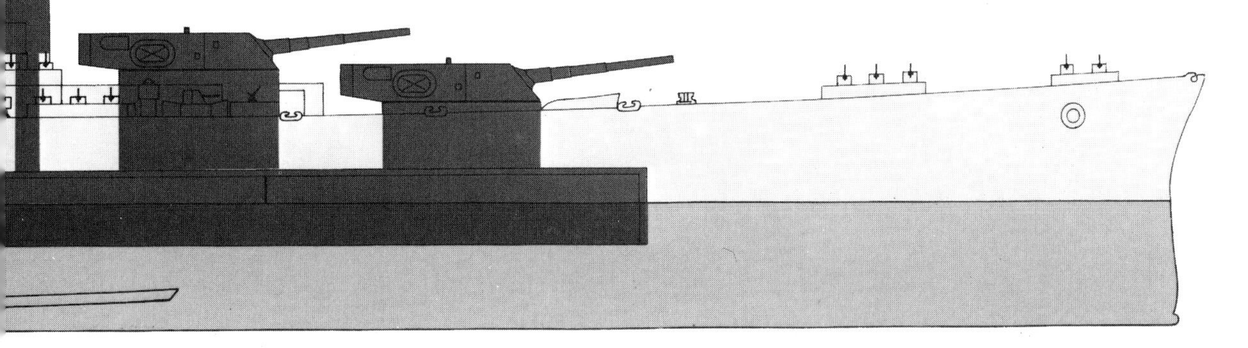

The 'North Carolina' class *Washington*, showing main armour distribution: main belt 16-inch, turrets 18-inch.

Japan's *Ise* as reconstructed in 1936, and converted to a battleship-carrier after Midway (*right*). An aircraft (probably a Zero floatplane) can be seen on the flight-deck, and a Type 21 radar array on the 'pagoda' mast.

The Americans also gained battleship superiority with the return to service of six of the eight ships bottomed at Pearl Harbor in December 1941, all with vastly increased 40 mm AA batteries. The four American 'Iowas' (*Iowa*, *New Jersey*, *Missouri* and *Wisconsin*), all with 80 40 mms, joined the fleet in 1944.

After the loss of *Hiei* and *Kirishima* off Guadalcanal in November 1942 the Japanese battle fleet was further reduced, from eight to seven, on 8 June 1943. *Mutsu*, *Nagato*'s sister-ship, was destroyed by the fate which had met seven capital ships in the First World War: spontaneous ammunition explosion. This was less than two months after Admiral Yamamoto had been shot down and killed over Bougainville (18 April 1943) by long-range American fighters operating from Guadalcanal. Yamamoto's successors in command of the Combined Fleet, Admirals Koga and Toyoda, were both determined that the fleet must be husbanded until a decisive blow could be struck. This was to be delayed until the Americans tried to take an objective which was essential to the security of the Japanese home islands. The Combined Fleet did not therefore contest the American capture of the Gilbert and Marshall Islands (November 1943–February 1944), which opened the battle for the central Pacific. Instead the Japanese gathered themselves for all-out efforts to hold the Marianas and Philippines.

The Americans used their new-found warship superiority well. In 1943 the US Pacific Fleet passed under alternating command, designated '5th Fleet' when com-

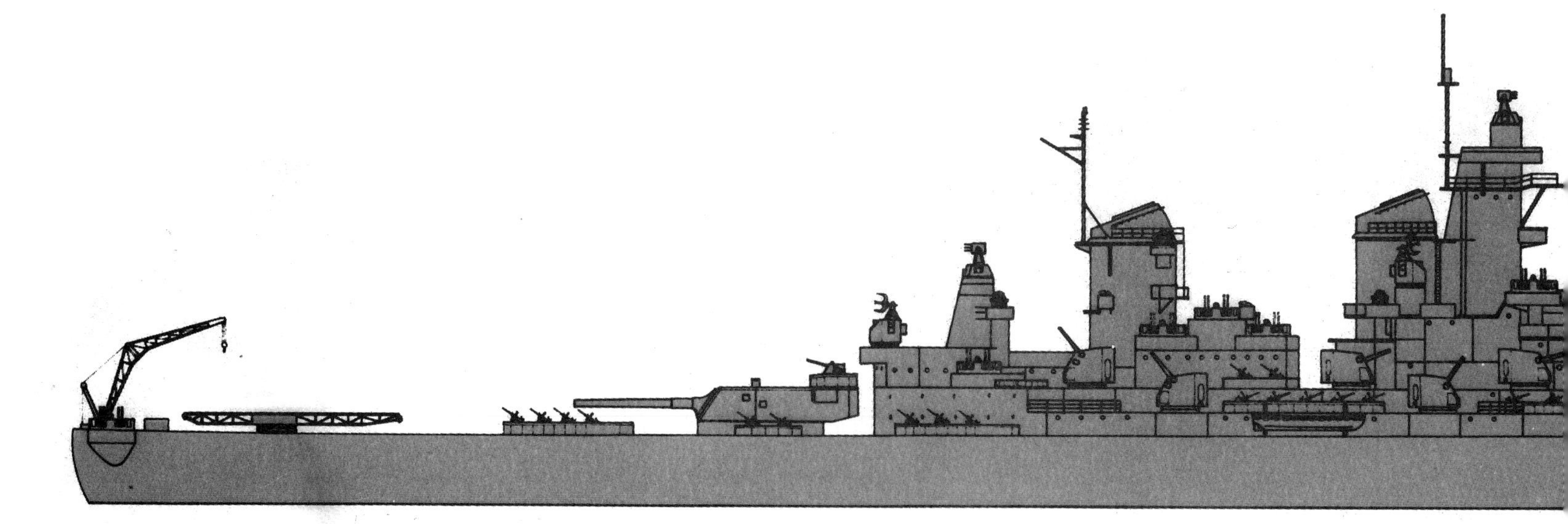

manded by Admiral Spruance, '3rd Fleet' when commanded by Admiral Halsey. Traditional fleet structure was stood on its head to meet the unique demands of the Pacific War. Instead of the traditional format of a battle fleet screened by cruisers and destroyers and supported by carriers, it was now the battleships which supported the carriers. The fleet's main punch was wielded by the huge Task Force (TF) 58/38, consisting of four carrier task groups (TG), with about four carriers per group. Each task group was given cruiser and later battleship AA fire support, and cruised within a ring of picket destroyers. A separate task group was the 'battle line' (usually six to eight battleships), with a cruiser/destroyer screen.

In the 18 months after the 'island-hopping' advance on Japan began in 1943, the American fleet evolved entirely new methods of waging naval war. The immense distances involved meant perfecting ship-to-ship refuelling and replenishment at sea, with much attention to shipboard amenities to lessen discomfort and sustain morale. Apart from the obvious security they provided for all other units of the fleet, battleships were best suited for prolonged operations of this kind, featuring as they did particularly good 'habitability'.

To increase task force protection still further, the Americans took the battle-cruiser format to its ultimate stage of development with the launching (August and November 1943) of *Alaska* and *Guam*. These fine battle-cruisers took over where *Scharnhorst* and *Gneisenau* left off, with AA

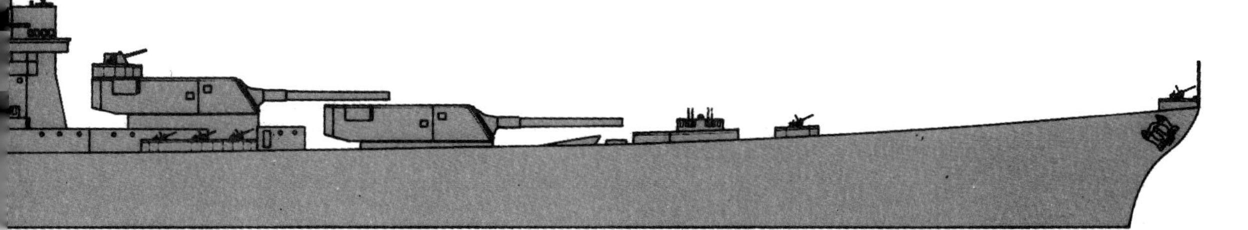

America's 'last generation' battleship design: *Iowa*, the biggest battleship type built for the US Navy. She displaced 45,000 tons and measured 887¼ ft overall, with a beam of 108¼ ft.

Night bombardment of Tarawa (Gilbert Islands) at the beginning of the 'Atoll War' in November 1943, by *Maryland*. She carried her eight 16-inch guns in four twin turrets.

fire-power being added to high speed and excellent protection. Displacing 27,500 tons, *Alaska* and *Guam* were armed with nine 12-inch guns in three triple turrets, six twin 5-inch turrets, and 56 40 mm AA guns. Though particularly well suited for task force operations in the Pacific, with a top speed of 33 knots, their completion was delayed by the need to concentrate on more vital warship types, with carriers and escorts to the fore, and they first saw action in the Okinawa campaign in early 1945.

The penultimate fleet action of the Pacific War, the Battle of the Philippine Sea, took place on 19–20 June 1944 after the Americans landed on Saipan in the Marianas.

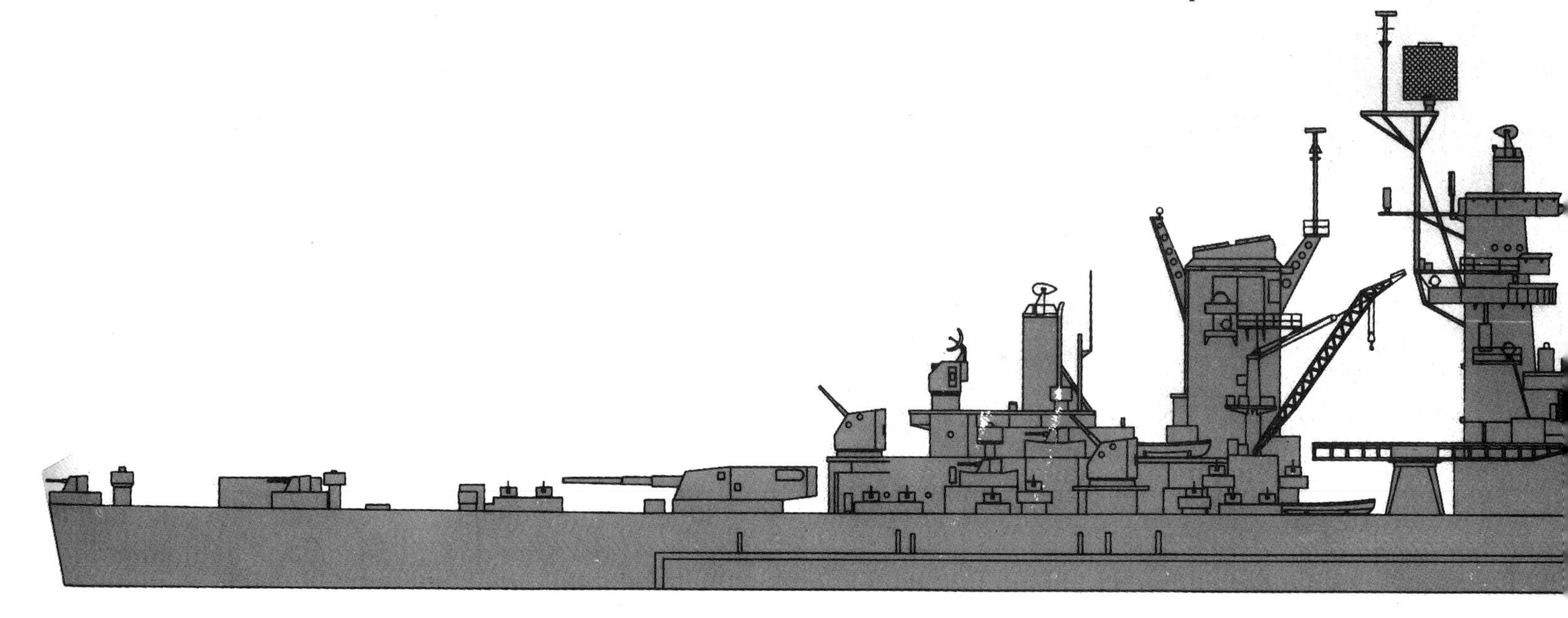

After fulfilling its now-familiar role of pre-landing bombardment, Admiral Lee's battle line (TG 58.7) moved west to intercept the expected counter-move by the Japanese fleet. But the hoped-for surface action never took place. Instead the battle was decided in the air, with the slaughter of the Japanese carrier air crews – the 'Great Marianas Turkey Shoot'. As the Japanese airmen tried desperately to get through and attack the American carrier task groups a Japanese torpedo aircraft crashed into *Indiana* on the waterline, but without the torpedo exploding. Even without the loss of two of his four irreplaceable fleet carriers (*Taiho* and *Shokaku*), the annihilation of his air strike potential spelled defeat for Admiral Ozawa. The last massed American air strike on the 20th sank the light carrier *Hiyo* and damaged the 'Kongo' class battleship *Haruna*, along with the carriers *Zuikaku* and *Chiyoda* and cruiser *Maya*. As after Midway, Admiral Spruance was content to let the Japanese retreat. The overriding American objective, securing the Saipan invasion, had been achieved.

The 'Great Marianas Turkey Shoot' was the beginning of the end for what was left of the Japanese Combined Fleet. Having lost some 65 per cent of its aircraft, the rump of the Japanese carrier force was left without any striking potential and the onus reverted, willy-nilly, to the battle fleet: *Yamato*, *Musashi*, *Nagato*, *Kongo*, *Haruna*, *Yamashiro* and *Fuso*. Admiral Toyoda's SHO-1 plan for the defence of the Philippines envisaged one mighty combined operation by every surviving heavy warship still able to put to sea. The objective was to achieve what Phillips had intended to do when he had sailed from Singapore in December 1941: get in among the invasion fleet and murder it with heavy-calibre gunfire. To make this possible, the empty Japanese carriers were to act as decoys, luring away the American carrier armada while the battleships approached and closed the invasion beaches.

SHO-1 suffered from the same flaw as had Phillips' intended attack off Malaya in December 1941. It was impossible for the battleships to get to the scene while the enemy invasion fleet was at its most vulnerable: lying close in with the troops actually going ashore. SHO-1 also woefully over-estimated the help which Japanese land-based aircraft in the Philippines would be able to give the fleet. For all that, aided by grave mistakes on the American side, the SHO-1 battleships came perilously close to handing the US Navy the biggest defeat it had suffered since Pearl Harbor.

The American softening-up attacks for the invasion of the Philippines lasted over a week and ranged from the northern island of Luzon to Formosa. Not until American destroyer transports and minesweepers moved into Leyte Gulf on the 17th could the Japanese deduce that Leyte Island was the intended lodgement point. Toyoda ordered SHO-1 to commence on the morning of the 18th. Dispersed in two main concentrations, the fleet was to arrive in Leyte Gulf for a combined attack on the invasion fleet early on the 25th. Vice-Admiral Kurita was to advance from Singapore via Borneo with *Yamato*, *Musashi*, *Nagato*, *Kongo*, *Haruna*, 12 cruisers and 15 destroyers, enter the western Philippines via the Sibuyan Sea and debouch into Leyte Gulf via San Bernardino Strait. Meanwhile Vice-Admiral Nishimura, with *Yamashiro*,

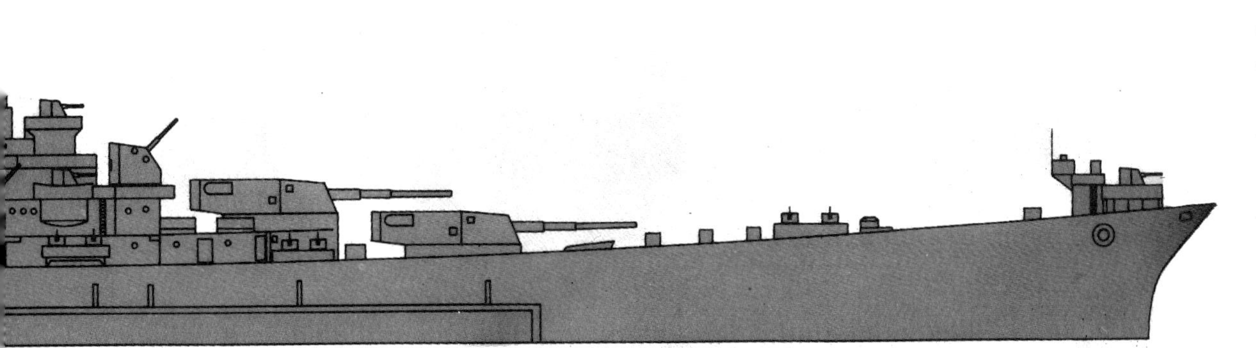

The ultimate battle-cruiser design: USS *Alaska*, with nine 12-inch guns, 9-inch belt armour and an excellent AA battery of 12 DP 5-inch and 56 40 mm guns. At 33 knots *Alaska* and sister-ship *Guam* provided invaluable AA fire support for the fast carrier task groups from the Okinawa campaign to the end of the Pacific War five months later.

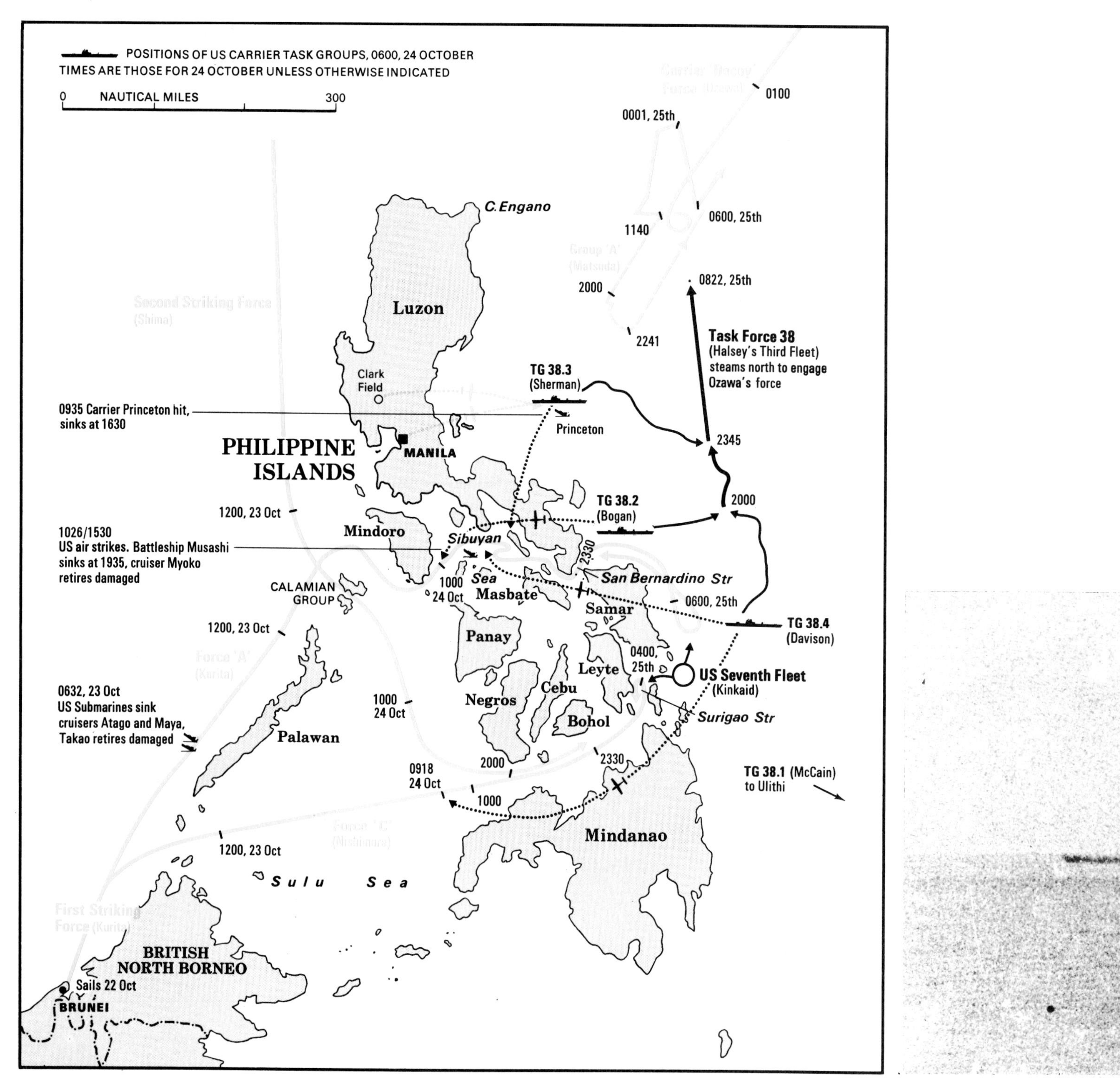

Above: The epic of Leyte Gulf (23–25 October 1944), the greatest sea battle of all time.
Right: Musashi, sinking by the bows but still on an even keel after hours of excellent damage control by her crew.
Below right: Pennsylvania leads the American battle line. Halsey's withdrawal of Task Force 34's battleships to pursue Ozawa's empty carriers left San Bernardino Strait wide open and precipitated the crisis of the Leyte Gulf battle off Samar.

Fuso, the cruiser *Mogami* and four destroyers, would cross the more southerly Sulu Sea, pass the Surigao Strait while Kurita was negotiating San Bernardino Strait, and enter Leyte Gulf from the south. Nishimura would be reinforced by Vice-Admiral Shima's three cruisers and four destroyers, heading south from Japan. All this would be made possible by Ozawa, with the carriers *Zuikaku*, *Chitose*, *Chiyoda*, and *Zuiho*, plus the battleship-carriers *Ise* and *Hyuga*, luring the carrier task groups of Halsey's 3rd Fleet away to the north.

For this invasion, however, the Americans were committing *two* fleets, each with carriers backed by a battleship task group. Vice-Admiral Kinkaid's 7th Fleet gave close cover to the landing force with six lightweight escort-carrier task groups (18 carriers in all) and Rear-Admiral Oldendorf's Fire Support and Bombardment Group. After its pre-landing bombardment programme the latter moved south to block Surigao Strait with the repaired 'Pearl Harbor' battleships *Maryland*, *West Virginia*, *Mississippi*, *Tennessee*, *California* and *Pennsylvania*, eight cruisers and 28 destroyers. Halsey's 3rd Fleet consisted of four carrier task groups (16 carriers in all). Two of these, TG 38.2 and TG 38.3, enjoyed the battleship fire support of *Iowa*, *New Jersey*, *Massachusetts* and *South Dakota*. Vice-Admiral Lee, victor of 'Second Guadalcanal', commanded an attenuated battle line (*Alabama* and *Washington*). The 3rd Fleet's job was to secure the invasion fleet in Leyte

Gulf, and the vulnerable escort carriers of 7th Fleet, from any seaborne attacks from the north via San Bernardino Strait. So the stage was set for the greatest naval action in history: the Battle of Leyte Gulf (23–25 October 1944).

From the morning of the 23rd to the small hours of the 25th, everything went the Americans' way. Attacked by submarines as it headed north-east of Borneo, Kurita's force lost three cruisers (including Kurita's flagship *Atago*), forcing a hasty shift of flag to *Yamato*. Early on the 24th, Kurita's and Nishimura's battleships were all sighted heading east through the Sibuyan and Mindanao Seas. Heavy American carrier strikes ensued, concentrating on Kurita's force and the monsters which no American carrier airman had yet seen: *Yamato* and *Musashi*. These attacks are remembered as the 'Battle of the Sibuyan Sea', first act of the Leyte Gulf drama after the prologue on the 23rd, and they had two important results.

The first and most dramatic was the prolonged series of attacks concentrated on *Musashi*, marked by one torpedo and one bomb hit in the first strike. Her gallant resistance ended in the evening of the 24th when she capsized and sank, having taken more punishment than any other battleship: no less than 19 torpedoes and about ten bombs. *Musashi*'s magnificent construction and gallant counter-flooding by her crew kept her on an even keel, settling steadily by the bows, until the water was lapping her massive forward 18-inch gun turrets. She went down at 19.35 hours on 24 October, never once having sighted an enemy warship

Below: The Battle of Surigao Strait, the last battleship-versus-battleship action in history.

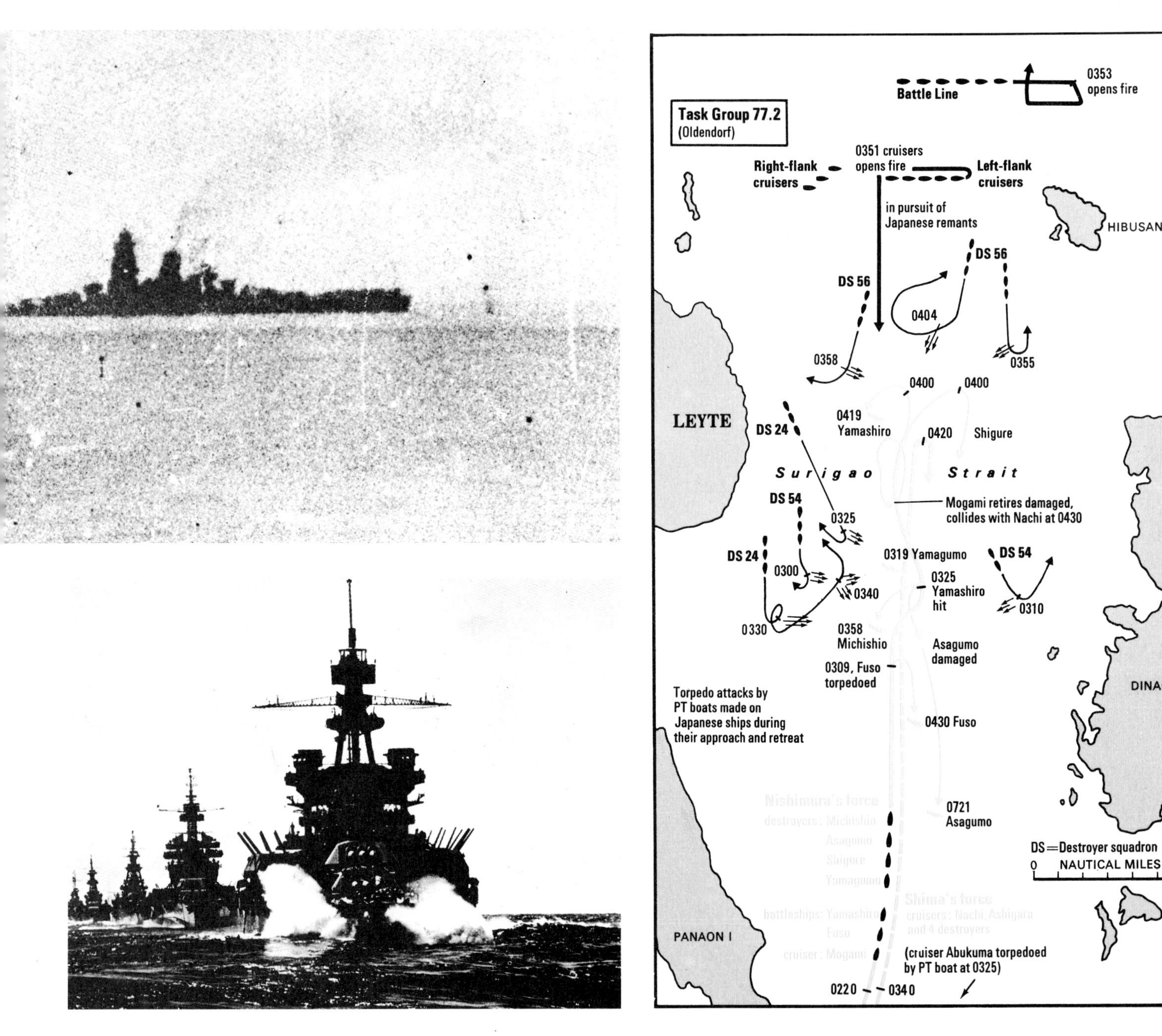

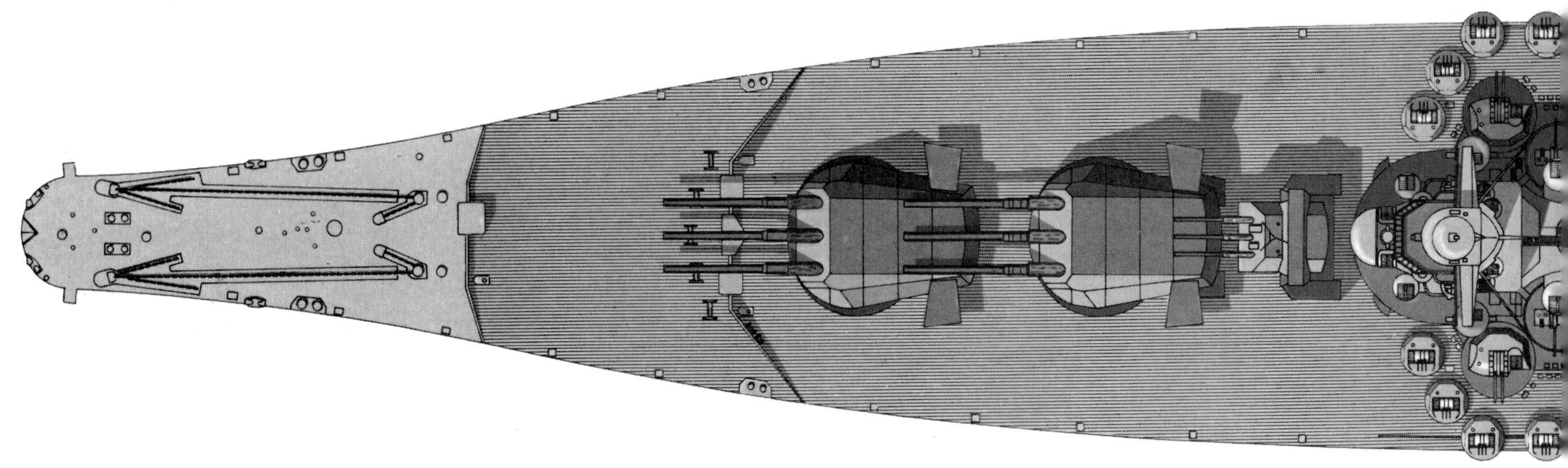

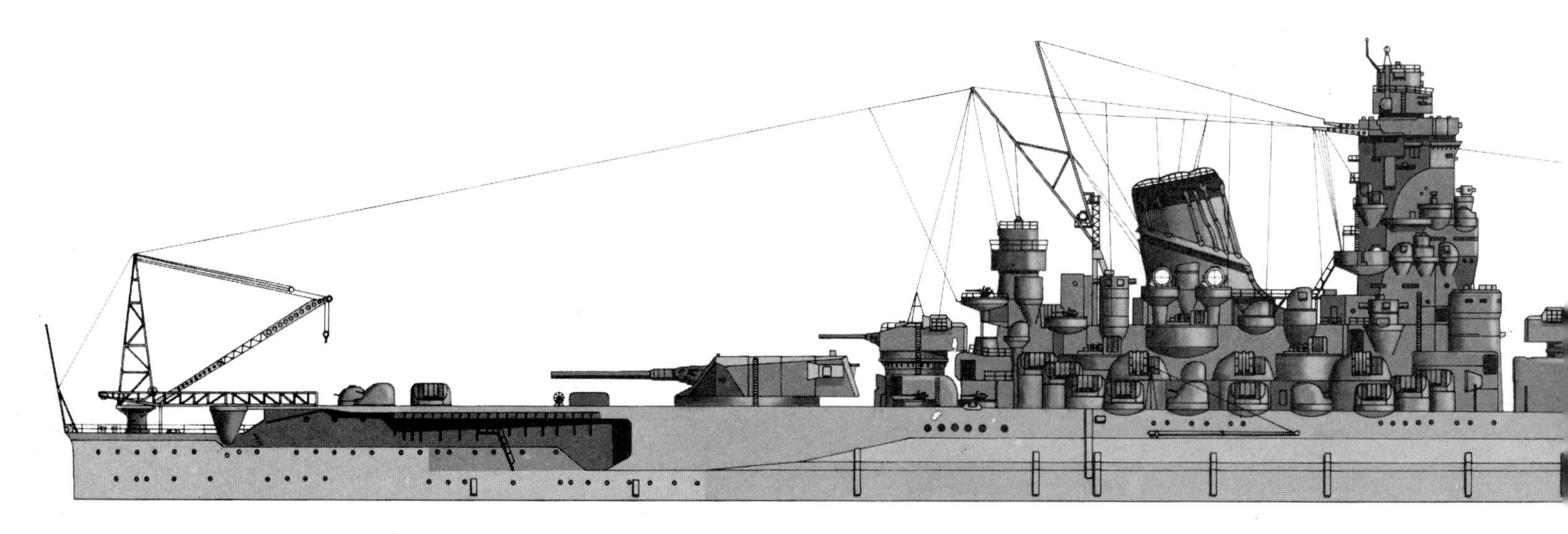

Left: Smoke and dust erupts from the coast of Saipan, under bombardment (14 June 1944) on the eve of the American landings in the Marianas.

from start to finish of her operational career.

The second important result of the Sibuyan Sea attacks was to throw the SHO-1 timetable badly off balance. Lacking any of the land-based air cover which he had been told would be forthcoming, Kurita left *Musashi* to her fate and headed back to the west for four hours (15.00–19.00). Though he finally decided to resume the advance on Leyte Gulf, there was now no chance that his arrival would coincide with that of Nishimura from the south. For his part Nishimura knew perfectly well what was waiting for him; one of his scout planes had sighted Oldendorf's battleships at noon on the 24th. Nevertheless, upheld by outdated memories of the early Japanese achievements against superior forces off Guadalcanal two years before, Nishimura pressed on with his part of SHO-1 and stood on into Surigao Strait.

Though the 'Battle of Surigao Strait' was the last battleship-versus-battleship action in history, the lion's share of the annihilation of Nishimura's force was accomplished by torpedo-boats and destroyers between

The greatest battleships ever built were Japan's *Yamato* (*left*) and sister-ship *Musashi*. A third ship of the same class, *Shinano*, was converted to a 'super-carrier' after Midway but was torpedoed and sunk by the American submarine *Archerfish* in November 1944.

'Yamato' class specifications: *Displacement:* 64,170 tons standard; 71,659 tons full load. *Length overall:* 863 ft. *Beam:* $127\frac{3}{4}$ ft. *Draught:* $35\frac{1}{2}$ ft. *Maximum speed:* $27\frac{1}{2}$ knots. *Armour:* Main belt 16-inch, deck $7\frac{3}{4}$-inch, turrets 20/$25\frac{1}{2}$-inch. *Armament:* Nine 18-inch; 12 6·1-inch; 12 5-inch AA; 24 25 mm AA; four 13 mm, six aircraft. *Complement:* 2,500.

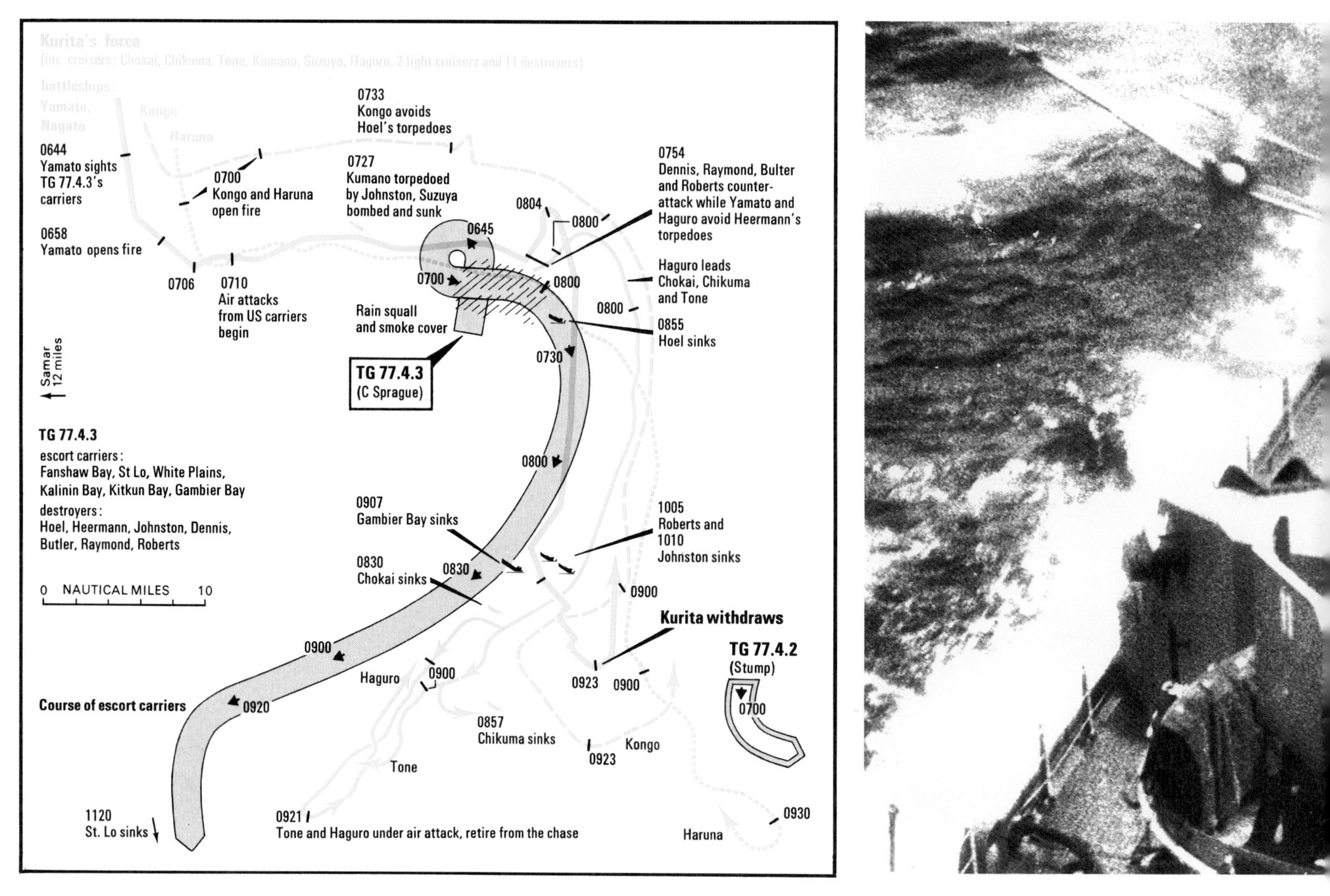

22.50 on the 24th and 03.51 on the 25th. No battle fleet commander ever had an easier job of it than Oldendorf, who had all the time he needed to lay his battleships and cruisers across the line of the Japanese advance. By the time they opened fire at 03.51 *Fuso* had broken in half after a torpedo hit (03.09) and three of the four destroyers leading *Yamashiro* and *Mogami* were sunk or sinking. Oldendorf's devastating 18-minute bombardment (03.51–04.09) is a reminder of how far battleship gunnery had come in the past 20 years; it should be compared with negligible results achieved in gun actions of similar duration at Jutland. *Yamashiro* and *Mogami* were overwhelmed, with *Yamashiro* being finished off (04.19) by a final destroyer torpedo attack. *Mogami* struggled back down the Strait, ablaze from stem to stern, and met her end at daybreak. Meanwhile Shima, arriving with his cruiser/destroyer force, sighted the wrecks of Nishimura's far more powerful squadron and prudently withdrew.

The Surigao Strait triumph was, however, followed by the climax of the Leyte Gulf actions: the 'Battle off Samar', in which Kurita's battleships came within an ace of reversing earlier setbacks. The fault was Halsey's. He had reacted to Kurita's dogged approach on the 24th by concentrating the 3rd Fleet's battleships as a new task force, TF 34. A fatal coincidence, however, was the sighting of Kurita's change of course to the west, followed 40 minutes later by the sighting of the southernmost of Ozawa's decoy carrier force. Halsey reacted by setting off in pursuit, taking the newly-formed TF 34 with the 3rd Fleet's carrier task groups – *and omitting to tell Kinkaid that the 3rd Fleet's battleships were no longer covering 7th Fleet from the north.* Practically the first warning of the peril facing the 7th Fleet's escort carriers came at 06.59 when the first shells from Kurita's battleships landed astern of *White Plains* and *Fanshaw Bay*.

Caught completely by surprise, the six escort carriers of Rear-Admiral Sprague's 'Taffy 3' had no choice but to run for it, working up to full speed and trusting to their seven escorting destroyers for whatever respite might be won. Fortunately for the appalled Americans, Kurita made a crucial error in signalling a general chase. His four battleships and eight cruisers set off in independent pursuit, with several ships consequently masking the fire of others. Supremely gallant American destroyer attacks added to the confusion of the Japanese battleships, with *Yamato* swinging clear out of the fight to avoid torpedoes; but

Centre: The last menace: *kamikaze* attack. This is a bomb-laden Zero, trying to immolate itself on *Missouri* during the Okinawa campaign (April–June 1945). In fact the Japanese pilot, having miscalculated his death dive, crashed in the sea alongside.

nothing could prevent Kurita's cruisers from steadily overtaking the fleeing carriers to port. By 08.30 the rearmost carrier, *Gambier Bay*, was under point-blank fire from the cruisers and within half an hour she was a burning, abandoned wreck. Though air attacks from the other 7th Fleet carriers were now coming in, it seemed that nothing could avert the destruction of 'Taffy 3'.

'We were saved', Sprague commented later, 'by the definite partiality of Almighty God'. At 09.25 the harried Americans watched in disbelief as their pursuers turned in their tracks and withdrew north. Though he already had in his grasp the crushing surface victory for which the Japanese battle fleet had yearned since the outbreak of the Pacific War, Kurita believed that he was being drawn within range of Halsey's carriers. This impression was reinforced by the sighting of the escort-carriers of 'Taffy 4' to the south. Bearing in mind the tribulations through which his fleet had passed during the previous 48 hours, and the certainty that it would now be exposed to ever-increasing air attacks, Kurita's decision to withdraw is easier to understand.

The last act at Leyte Gulf was the slaughter of Ozawa's decoy force off Cape Engano from 08.30 on the 25th. For Halsey this was a supreme frustration: TF 34's battleships were deprived of a resounding victory by the crisis off Samar, which prompted a direct intervention from Admiral Nimitz in Pearl Harbor: 'WHERE IS TASK FORCE 34?' Though he headed back towards Samar with TF 34, Halsey was too late to intercept Kurita. Because of Halsey's tardiness in accepting the peril to 7th Fleet which his dispositions had caused, TF 34's role at Leyte Gulf was restricted to steaming between two major actions without being able to take part in either.

Leyte Gulf is justly remembered as 'the greatest sea battle in history' (though Jellicoe and Scheer had commanded 254 ships at Jutland to the 244 at Leyte). The Americans lost a light fleet carrier (to land-based air attack), two escort-carriers (one to surface gunnery off Samar, one to land-based air attack), and three destroyers (sunk off Samar by Kurita's force). But the last great foray by the Japanese battle fleet had been an unqualified failure. The Japanese lost three battleships (*Musashi*, *Fuso* and *Yamashiro*), four carriers, no less than ten cruisers, and nine destroyers.

For the last ten months of the Pacific War the Japanese pinned their faith in *kamikaze* suicide attacks on the American fleet, reinforced as this was, from March 1945, by the spearhead of the British Pacific Fleet. The brunt of these attacks fell on the carriers and battleships and it was the latter, with their 'hosepipe' AA fire-power and armoured protection, which were best equipped to survive. *New Mexico*, *Nevada* and *Maryland* were all damaged by *kamikaze* attacks in 1945 but none succumbed – and as often as not only minutes intervened before the ship was back in action again.

Bent on avenging Pearl Harbor with no help from friends, the Americans churlishly kept the British Pacific Fleet stationed where it could not attack the last surviving warships of the Japanese Fleet. By April 1945, as the battle for Okinawa approached its climax, only one Japanese battleship was still able to sail: *Yamato*, recklessly expended in an attempted one-way voyage to the Okinawa beaches. She never even sighted the island. Instead, caught by intense 5th Fleet carrier strikes in the East China Sea, *Yamato* sank at 14.23 on 7 April 1945 after taking ten torpedo hits and at least six bombs. The last of the super-battleships had gone, victim of the Japanese failure to accept the alterations to the battleship's role wrought by the rise of naval aviation.

12. END OF AN ERA, 1945-1960

Previous pages : Fine shot of *Jean Bart* (French 'Richelieu' class) in November 1955. *Below :* Sister-ship *Richelieu* in January 1955.

If the battleship had proved to have one oustanding virtue by the end of the Second World War, that virtue was versatility. The startling rise to supremacy of the aircraft-carrier had made the traditional fleet gunnery action a rarity, yet by no stretch of the imagination could battleships be dismissed as redundant luxuries. The battleship's supreme value as a platform for anti-aircraft fire had been demonstrated time and again in the Pacific War. It was surpassed only by the battleship's range and accuracy in 'taking out' pinpoint shore targets by radar-guided gunnery. These were enduring virtues, and it is not merely nostalgic to lament the battleship's worldwide demise after 1945.

Under the new distorting glare of nuclear weaponry another proven virtue of the battleship was easy to overlook: longevity. No other warship type could be kept in service so long, subjected to such extensive reconstruction, sustain such radical changes in weaponry. For nearly 40 years the myth has endured that heavy surface warships, 'which can be sunk by a single missile', are clearly hopelessly redundant – yet, as the Japanese super-battleships proved in 1944–45, no other type of warship is harder to sink than the battleship.

The contradictory attitudes towards the battleship's post-1945 role were perhaps summed up in the British *Vanguard*, commissioned in the spring of 1946. At 42,500 tons, *Vanguard* was the heaviest British battleship ever built. Though completed to the most modern standards, incorporating features adopted as standard by the US Navy in the Pacific War, *Vanguard* was in fact designed around four twin 15-inch turret mountings which had been in store for the past 20-odd years. These were the guns and turrets of the light battle-cruisers *Glorious* and *Courageous*, removed for those ships' conversion as aircraft-carriers after the Washington Treaty. The rest of her armament drew heavily on experience gleaned from the 'King George Vs' and the experience of the later war years: eight twin 5·25-inch DP mountings, and no less than 71 40 mm guns – the heaviest anti-aircraft battery ever carried by a British warship. Remote power control was used throughout *Vanguard*'s gun mountings and fire-control system, in which radar guidance was an integral element. Her electric power – enough to supply a fair-sized town – was regulated by a centralised control system, damage being automatically isolated to prevent other shipboard services from being impaired.

Yet *Vanguard*, unlike her older American

Above : Warspite, wrecked in Mounts Bay in April 1947 while on tow to the breaker's yard. She was broken up where she lay after 30 years of famous service, not to mention excellent value for taxpayers' money.
Right : Yavuz (ex-*Sultan Selim*, ex-*Goeben*) at Constantinople.

Mighty silhouettes against the sunset: *Iowa* and *Wisconsin*, mothballed in the US Atlantic Reserve Fleet.

counterparts, never fired a shot in anger in support of the troops in Korea. Within 12 years of her first commission, her final consignment to the scrapyard was already in sight. The stalwarts of First World War vintage had been weeded out en masse between 1946 and 1950: *Valiant*, *Malaya*, *Queen Elizabeth*, *Warspite*; *Ramillies*, *Resolution*, *Revenge*, *Royal Sovereign*; the battle-cruiser *Renown*; *Nelson* and *Rodney*. The fate of the 'King George Vs' was little longer delayed. Within five years of the surrender of Japan all four had been reduced to reserve, and all were scrapped in 1957–58. The bland decision that assaulting British forces would never again need battleship fire support was disproved at Suez in 1956 and again, in 1982, in the Falklands War. With just one battleship available for rapid re-commissioning in the style perfected by the post-war US Navy, the Port Stanley airstrip (used by the Argentines throughout the war) could have been quickly and cheaply rendered unusable by a single bombardment.

American practice was in total contrast to the British: a strange combination of ruthlessness, kindliness and prudence. The ruthlessness was represented by the expenditure of *Arkansas*, *New York*, *Nevada*, and *Pennsylvania* in the atom-bomb tests at Bikini in 1946; the kindliness by the preservation of *Texas*, and later of *North Carolina* (1961) and *Alabama* (1964) by the states whose names they bore. As in the Royal Navy, American practice concentrated on disposing of the oldest ships first – yet *Tennessee*, *California*, *Colorado* and *Maryland* were not scrapped until 1959, while *West Virginia* was given two further years' reprieve, finally going to the breakers in January 1961. *Washington*, *South Dakota*, *Indiana* and *Massachusetts* had followed by 1963.

The full measure of American prudence with regard to battleship disposal, however, was displayed with the four 'Iowas', twice returned to service off the beaches of Korea and Vietnam – and a third time in the 1980s, modified yet again to serve in the age of the intercontinental nuclear missile.

13. AMERICAN RESURRECTION, 1960–1983

Previous pages: New Jersey's 16-inch broadside roars out again after her recommissioning for service off Vietnam in 1968.
Below: New Jersey sails again from Pearl Harbor, September 1968.
Opposite: New Jersey on broadside firing tests in the Atlantic, May 1968.
Opposite, top left: Iowa being moved in preparation for reactivation, April 1982.
Opposite, top right: Recommissioning ceremony for *New Jersey*, 28 December 1982.
Opposite, below left: New Jersey in dry dock before her 1968 recommission.

THE BATTLESHIP STORY is studded with paradoxes. In the 1920s the battleship had been proscribed as the world's costliest instrument of destruction, but 40 years later, after a decade and a half of eclipse by aircraft-carriers, the battleship returned to service because it was one of the most *economical* naval weapons, ideally suited to modern 'triphibious' (land/sea/air) operations. Yet, even after this had been most convincingly demonstrated off Vietnam in 1968, the resuscitation of the world's last battleship squadron was stubbornly resisted by the navy that owned it. Intense lobbying was needed to bring about the battleship's eventual return, and the success of that lobbying was due not to the nostalgia of ex-battleship men but to former airmen.

Though all four of the American 'Iowas' had served off Korea, only *New Jersey* was taken out of the seals and cocoons which had protected her, since her last decommission in August 1957, for service off Vietnam. The reason as announced by the US Navy Department (1 August 1967) was 'to provide an extended range and increased destructive power' to the fleet's fire support force off Vietnam. This was, of course, a belated resumption of the heavy shore-bombardment role which had been one of the battleship's main functions in the latter years of the Second World War. But there was more to it than that. *New Jersey*'s recommission was not merely to give heavy-calibre fire support to the American and South Vietnamese *land* forces. It was, rather, to attack targets which were proving increasingly costly for the tactical air forces. The pressure for *New Jersey*'s recommissioning came less from the Navy than from the Army and Marine Corps airmen, who were facing escalating losses in attacks on well-protected North Vietnamese strongpoints. By 1967, in fact, air strikes on targets such as bridges (always difficult for fast-moving aircraft to hit) had become a far tougher proposition than in the Second World War.

New Jersey's 16-inch broadside was therefore re-enlisted to take the mounting strain off the airmen, by taking out pinpoint targets with the accuracy of radar-guided gunnery. Before the Vietnam War shifted deep inland into Laos and Cambodia, operations were largely confined to the long coastal strip. Some 80 per cent of the targets previously earmarked for tactical air strikes (over a thousand such targets in all) were therefore within range of *New Jersey*'s guns. To answer the inevitable criticism of the $21 million required for *New Jersey*'s refit

USS NEW JERSEY

and recommission (modern radars were an obvious necessity), it could be argued that this sum was equivalent to about six shot-down F4 Phantom aircraft, to say nothing of the cost of training lost crews.

During her six-month tour off Vietnam *New Jersey* achieved a new battleship record: the greatest number of heavy shells ever fired by a single battleship in one commission. Between 1943 and 1945 *New Jersey*'s total expenditure of 16-inch shell had been 771 rounds. Off Vietnam in 1968–69, nearly a quarter of a century later, she fired 5,688 rounds. The measure of the veteran battleship's success was not to be found merely in targets destroyed, but in the wide areas within range of her guns which were estimated to have been completely evacuated by the Vietcong and their supporters.

Despite the undoubted success of the experiment with *New Jersey*, it was neither repeated not extended to the other three 'Iowas', and *New Jersey* was again decommissioned and cocooned in 1969. This was partly because the US Army and Air Force Commands thereafter fell into the trap of abandoning the tactical scalpel for the strategic sledge-hammer, resorting to massed bombing raids on North Vietnam and Cambodia. Both in the United States and North Vietnam, the psychological effects of the bombing were far-reaching and could certainly have been anticipated. In America it led to growing revulsion and protest against the war, aided by virtually unanimous international condemnation. But in North Vietnam, as had happened in Germany and Japan during the Second World War, civilian morale was inflamed and hardened rather than undermined. Nothing could be done to alert villagers 20 miles inland to the dreadful destruction of a 16-inch salvo out of the blue. But incoming bombers could be detected on radar, air-raid warnings sounded, and an easy hate-and-defiance propaganda campaign waged against the murderers in the sky. *New Jersey*'s return to mothballs in 1969 epitomised the relinquishment of selective striking power for indiscriminate bombing which helped lose America the Vietnam War.

But there was another reason for the battleship's return to storage in 1969: sheer embarrassment, in the year which saw the first American Moon landing, at the proven efficiency of a weapon-system and technology popularly regarded as extinct. Whenever the official history of the twentieth century's technological revolution comes to be written, it will be impossible to record the deep-rooted influence on that revolution of the ancient urge to 'save face'. This took the form of a feverish pursuit of the most 'up to date' military technology, one of the earliest manifestations of which had indeed been the international battleship mania of the pre-1914 years. One of NATO's basic morale-sustaining lifebelts in the confrontation with the Soviet bloc has always been insistence on the so-called supremacy of Western technology. This has led to a dangerous Western obsession with technology for its own sake, especially in politicians with their constant eye on the opinion polls and tomorrow's flashy headline; and unfortunately for the West it is the politician who decides defence priorities.

Technology-mania leads directly to a state of mind which arrogantly rejects the lessons of even recent history as hopelessly out-dated. In 1937 the British Admiralty, announcing the perfection of the asdic (sonar) submarine-detecting device, proclaimed that the U-boat menace could never confront Britain again – a false prophecy terribly exposed between 1940 and 1943. In 1966 Denis Healey, Defence Minister of the Wilson Labour Government, similarly proclaimed the obsolescence of the aircraft-carrier as surplus to Britain's naval defence requirements, with the assurance that British forces would never again be operating beyond range of land-based air cover. This was also disproved, again at wicked cost, in the Falklands War of April–June 1982. It was in precisely similar vein that American President Jimmy Carter, in the spring of 1980, turned down the proposal to restore the 'Iowas' to service. It was 'inefficient', Carter maintained, 'to apply hundreds of millions of dollars to resurrect 1940s' technologies'.

Opposition to the resurrection of the 'Iowas' was by no means restricted to ignorant politicians and public commentators. The US Navy itself fought a stubborn rearguard action to the scheme, arguing that public funds would be better spent on more carriers, nuclear submarines and advanced electronics. *New Jersey*'s recommission was only announced in 1967 after the retirement of Admiral McDonald, who while Chief of Naval Operations had blocked the scheme all along the line. Intense lobbying was needed to break down this resistance, and it was significant that this lobbying was conducted not by ex-battleship men but by ex-airmen, veterans of Korea and Vietnam.

Right : New Jersey in action again, firing by radar against an inland target, Vietnam, April 1969.
Below : Iowa makes a stately turn to port during the Korean War in October 1952.

Chief protagonist was Charles Myers, Jr, ex-Korean War fighter pilot, test pilot, and from 1973 to 1978 a tactical air-warfare specialist at the Pentagon.

Myers began with the blessing of an open mind and a readiness to learn from naval history. His researches showed him that the 'Iowas', despite having been launched in 1942–44, had only served a total of 13 of their allotted 30 years of operational life. The cost of reactivating just one of them matched that of a single brand-new frigate, or of a dozen aircraft. After leaving the Pentagon in 1978 Myers doggedly tracked down all former combat fliers with influence in political life, and 'sold' his ideas to them with enthusiasm and success. Breakthrough point came when Myers converted John Lehman, chairman of the Republican Party's defence committee – and Secretary of the Navy to Ronald Reagan, who replaced Carter as President in 1980.

The proposal of Myers which hooked Lehman (and, when first put to him in December 1980, the President-elect) cast the battleship in an entirely new role. The 'Iowas' would indeed retain their 16-inch guns, for use in conventional conflicts when required – but they would also be modified to carry the new Tomahawk cruise missile, able to deliver a thermonuclear warhead 1,500 miles. The missile's range would be boosted by the battleships' own range of 15,000 miles at 17 knots (5,000 at 30 knots), making the ships the most potent conventional/strategic units in the US Navy – unlike the ballistic-missile firing giant submarines, which are designed to take no part in conventional operations. Though it remains to be seen what effect the awesome concussion of 16-inch guns will have on the electronics and circuity of the missile era, no other warship type has ever been earmarked for such a total transformation.

The initial vote of funds to reactivate *New Jersey* passed through Congress in spring 1981, but in November of that year there was heated opposition to the request of funds for *Iowa*. This, however, was overborne by some forceful talking – notably Senator Denton of Alabama, who pointed out that if *New Jersey*'s guns had been available to take out the Thanh Hoa bridge in 1965, he would not have been shot down while attacking the bridge. Nor would he have spent the next 7½ years as a prisoner in the notorious 'Hanoi Hilton'. 'There is a reason for those ships', affirmed Denton, 'and thank God the Navy is coming forward asking for them again'.

Below : High-angle 16-inch trials in *New Jersey*, October 1982.
Below left : New Jersey in dry dock (February 1982), showing one of her four massive screws.
Right : Ordnance team in *New Jersey* prepares for the first 16-inch firing, 28 September 1982.

INDEX

Numbers in italic denote reference to illustrations.

PRINTED IN BELGIUM BY proost INTERNATIONAL BOOK PRODUCTION